The Effective Teaching of English

THE EFFECTIVE TEACHER SERIES

General editor: Elizabeth Perrott

THE EFFECTIVE TEACHER SERIES

The Effective Teaching of English

Robert Protherough,
Judith Atkinson,
John Fawcett

LONGMAN
London and New York

Longman Group Limited,
Longman House, Burnt Mill, Harlow,
Essex CM20 2JE, England
and Associated Companies throughout the world.

Published in the United States of America
by Longman Inc., New York

First published 1989
Fourth impression 1994

British Library Cataloguing in Publication Data
Protherough, Robert
    The effective teaching of English. – (The
    effective teacher series).
    1. Education. Curriculum subjects: English
    Language. Teaching.
    I. Title. II. Atkinson, Judith. III. Fawcett,
    John. IV. Series.
    420'.7
    ISBN 0-582-29720-6

Library of Congress Cataloging in Publication Data
Protherough, Robert.
    The effective teaching of English / Robert Protherough,
    Judith Atkinson, John Fawcett.
        p. cm. — (The effective teacher series)
    Bibliography. p.
    Includes index.
    ISBN 0-582-29720-6
    1. English philology — Study and teaching. I. Atkinson,
    Judith. II. Fawcett, John. III. Title.   IV. Series.
    PE1065.P76   1989
    428'.007 — dc 19

Set in Linotron 202 10/11 pt Times

Produced through Longman Malaysia, VP

C O N T E N T S

EDITOR'S PREFACE

This new series was inspired by my book on the practice of teaching (*Effective Teaching: a practical guide to improving your teaching*, Longman, 1982) written for teacher training students as well as for in-service teachers wishing to improve their teaching skills. The books in this series have been written with the same readership in mind. However, busy classroom teachers will also find that the books serve their needs as changes in the nature and pattern of education make the re-training of experienced teachers more essential than in the past.

The rationale behind the series is that professional courses for teachers require the coverage of a wide variety of subjects in a relatively short time. So the aim of the series is the production of 'easy to read', practical guides to provide the necessary subject background, supported by references to encourage and guide further reading together with questions and/or exercises devised to assist application and evaluation.

As specialists in their selected fields, the authors have been chosen for their ability to relate their subjects closely to the needs of teachers and to stimulate discussion of contemporary issues in education.

The series covers subjects ranging from *The Theory of Education* to *The Teaching of Mathematics* and from *The Psychology of Learning* to *Health Education*. It will look at aspects of education as diverse as *Education and Cultural Diversity* and *Assessment in Education; The Teaching of English* and *The History of Education*. Although some titles such as *The Administration of Education* are specific to England and Wales, the majority of titles, such as *Comparative Education, The Teaching of Modern Languages, The Use of Computers in Teaching* and *Pupil Welfare and Counselling* will be international in scope.

In a period when education is a subject of general debate and is operating against a background of major change, there is little doubt that the books, although of primary interest to teachers, will also find a wider readership.

Elizabeth Perrott

ACKNOWLEDGEMENTS

The authors are particularly indebted to those teachers, most of them early in their careers or returning to them, whose lengthy written submissions and interviews have helped to shape this book, as well as providing some of its subject matter. So that these teachers would be able to describe their experiences openly and candidly, they were assured that they and their schools would not be identified in print. However, the fact that we are unable to mention them by name does not diminish our appreciation of their help, and we hope that awareness of being involved in this guide for others may be some reward.

In a wider sense we are grateful to the many colleagues, pupils and authors who have influenced our thinking during what amounts – in sum – to seventy years of teaching in fifteen different educational establishments. The most conscious debts are acknowledged in the references.

Finally, we have appreciated the guidance offered to us by the editor of this series, Professor Elizabeth Perrott.

CHAPTER 1

Introduction: becoming effective

How long does it take to train a teacher of English? The statutory answer seems to be four years (a degree plus a PGCE or an honours B.Ed.) followed by an ill-defined 'probation', after which one is 'qualified'. However, if you ask English teachers at what stage they began to think of themselves as fully effective, few of them will say that it took less than five years in school. Some will tell you that it was only as Head of Department that they really began to understand the processes in which they had previously been involved. It takes years to discover, for example, how best to organize groups for topic work, which stories to recommend to individuals and why, when to intervene and when to leave children alone. Even after years of experience you never know it all: every new group has fresh needs and presents fresh problems. In some respects it is not unlike learning to drive: you pass a test and are allowed out on your own, but you go on learning to drive in different situations and conditions for as long as you continue driving. Effectiveness is the mark of not being 'stuck', not giving the same lessons in the same way year after year.

Little attention has been given to that developmental process by which English teachers come to see themselves as becoming effective or professional. This book seeks to remedy that by considering formal training in the light of what follows. It is grounded in a series of detailed interviews and written commentaries by some thirty young or returning English teachers, most of them in the first five years of their careers. That seems to be the crucial period: it includes four of the six 'critical phases' that have been identified within the lifetime careers of teachers.[1] The aim has been to discover what kinds of learning go on after as well as during formal training, and what conditions seem to aid that process. The book is organized sequentially to deal with issues in the order that they become important for these young teachers. It considers first the preparation for work in a new and unfamiliar school, then the teaching and learning processes in an English classroom, and finally the teacher's wider responsibilities within the department and beyond.

It is necessary to be clear why initial training, however good,

can only be a beginning. The pattern in universities and colleges
has not been designed according to any firm principles. It has
evolved in response to pressures (often conflicting ones) from
demographic factors, from economic events, from social, political
and educational considerations, and from wider changes in the
whole structure of education. Successive governments have
declined to increase the one year of post-graduate training to
two, or to make the induction year a reality by releasing probationers from their schools for substantial continuing education.
They have, of course, increased the demands on those involved
in professional training (by requiring that institutions be
'accredited', by extending the working year by six weeks, and by
regulations about entry requirements and course content) but
without providing adequate resources to raise standards. Officially the myth continues that once teachers are 'qualified', little
more remains to be done. They are ready to go on running for
forty years, with some topping up of oil and water and an
occasional service. Everybody involved in the process knows that
it is inadequate. The policy of the NAS/UWT is for an eight-year
period of training, the last three of which should be spent in
school. A teacher's authority rests not just on the capacity to
teach a lesson and the possession of subject knowledge and skills,
but also on being the kind of person who can form good relationships with pupils and who has become what colleagues will call
'a professional'. Learning to teach is only part of the much more
complex process of *becoming an effective English teacher*, which
includes learning to survive and being socialized into a particular
professional group: '. . . the process by which people selectively
acquire the values and attitudes, the interests, skills and knowledge – in short the culture – current in groups to which they are,
or seek to become, a member'.[2] Such a process extends before
and after any training period. Student-teachers are bracketed
between selective memories of their own time in school and
imaginative anticipations of themselves as teachers. The memories are potent. One account of recent research in teacher
education pointed to considerable evidence of 'the extent to
which trained teachers' *own school experience* is more significant
in their professional performance than the curriculum of any
training course'.[3] Indeed, Herbert Kohl has said that many
student-teachers he has known 'are becoming teachers to negate
the wounds they received in school'.[4] Twenty years ago, a survey
of 2000 intending teachers found that about a third of them
believed decidedly that their own teachers had exerted 'a
powerful influence for good' on their own development (and
about a tenth believed that at least one of their teachers had
exerted a distinctly *bad* influence).[5] Such influences can be inten-

sified by friends and relations. It is surely significant that nearly 40 per cent of the PGCE students in Bernbaum's national survey had close relatives who worked in education.[6]

Looking forward and predicting how to become an effective English teacher is harder than it sounds. For one thing, nobody has satisfactorily defined that effectiveness, let alone established how it can be conveyed to others, and still less the means by which it can be developed in practice. Only recently has a book appeared that tries to look systematically at the ways in which English teachers are prepared for their work, and at the alternative methods that might be practised.[7] There are elements of technical expertise, of course, that can be formally transmitted, acquired and tested. These include not only mechanical skills (like writing legibly on the blackboard, using recorders and projectors efficiently) but also more advanced abilities such as framing questions appropriately, or using role-play approaches to texts. Particularly in English, however, there are other – equally important – elements of professional expertise that cannot be directly conveyed in this way. Sometimes called *indeterminate* capabilities, these are inseparable from the personality of a particular competent professional. They cannot be isolated or generalized, because they appear differently in the strategies of different teachers, and because in many cases they depend on instinctive rather than considered reactions to particular situations. When people say that teachers are born, not made, or that there are an infinite number of good ways of teaching English, they are thinking particularly of these indeterminate capacities. For these reasons, it is notoriously hard to teach *another* person to teach English. Method courses, helpful books, watching established teachers, sharing experiences with others, professional associations, the advice of colleagues, trial and error, have all been mentioned by some of our sample of teachers as contributing to their development. Nevertheless, teacher-tutors testify that it is difficult – almost impossible – to describe the knowledge that they have painfully gained over a period of time in such a way that others can share the experience. Looking back inevitably distorts; we oversimplify the process, imposing a shape on what was uncertain and tentative at the time. Some highly successful classroom teachers have been disastrous tutors of education students: there is no easy correlation between effective teaching and the ability to communicate it.

You can see the difficulty in conveying what it is like to be an English teacher by considering these ten responses to our questions: 'Why be an English teacher? Do you ever regret it?' What justifications do you detect beneath the enthusiasm?

1. I love teaching English – the subject is exciting and extremely varied and gives plenty of scope for new methods and new topics.
2. Classroom teaching is very pleasant and I never tire of talking to children and listening to them – that is the beauty of the job.
3. I get a tremendous kick out of it.
4. I love English. I love sharing things that I've enjoyed with others. My relationships with the pupils are the most important things. I want them to like English. I want them to get the enthusiasm.
5. Children enjoy most of the things that they are asked to do in English.
6. I like the contact with children . . . I like the idea of working with them on a book, passing on my enjoyment.
7. It gives me a good deal of satisfaction when I feel that I am doing my job well.
8. The job is often very satisfying. I enjoy it and feel that I have a good relationship with the children; it can be a most stimulating job.
9. It's a bit like a drug – if you can get your buzz out of a couple of lessons a week you've had your fix for the week.
10. Probably the biggest thing is giving the kids self-esteem.

What do you think of these comments? They testify to strong feelings that prove difficult to tie down. Careers in English are justified by those feelings (loving and liking, satisfaction and stimulation, the 'kick' or 'buzz') growing on the one hand out of relationships with children (working with them, talking and listening, sharing, encouraging) and on the other out of the subject itself (exciting, varied, open to novelty, popular with children). This shifting balance between a teacher's feelings for the subject and for pupils' learning is common to all subjects, but in English the emphasis seems to be much less on transmitting the material of the subject than on transmitting feelings, 'enthusiasm', 'enjoyment', by 'working *with* them' on books and activities that teacher and class both value. Such an ability is much harder to identify and to achieve than any mechanical expertise. What follows is a tentative suggestion of what our young teachers believe that they have learned and continue to learn in those crucial early years.

REFERENCES

1. Measor Lynda 1985 'Identities, choices and careers', in Ball Stephen J and Goodson Ivor F (eds) 1985 *Teachers' Lives and Careers*. Falmer Press, p 62

2. Merton Robert K *et al* 1957 *The Student Physician*. Harvard UP, cited Lacey Colin 1977 *The Socialization of Teachers*. Methuen, p 13

3. Atkinson Paul and Delamont Sara 1985 'Socialisation into teaching: the research which lost its way', *British Journal of Sociology of Education*, vol 6 no 3, pp 316–17

4. Kohl Herbert 1977 *On Teaching*. Methuen, p 15

5. Dale R R 1967 'Teachers who have had a good influence' and 'Teachers who have had a bad influence', *Education for Teaching*, February, pp 35–42 and Autumn, pp 25–32

6. Bernbaum Gerald *et al* 1982 *The Structure and Process of Initial Teacher Training within Universities in England and Wales*. University of Leicester, School of Education

7. Protherough Robert and Atkinson Judith 1991 *The Making of English Teachers*. Open University Press.

SECTION ONE

Towards the classroom

CHAPTER 2

First impressions

FROM STUDENT TO TEACHER

You will be conscious from your own experience and from that
of your friends that students do not enter training courses as
neutral, wholly malleable beings. They come as products of a
particular academic discipline and with firm perceptions about
the nature of teaching. Students arrive on secondary courses
primarily concerned to teach their subject[1] and this subject-
awareness conditions the way in which they view education. As
an English teacher you are likely to have different priorities from
teachers of other subjects. Lacey has shown for example, by
applying different scales to assess teacher attitudes, that English
students are at one extreme, with teachers of French, Physics and
Chemistry at the opposite pole.[2] In the NFER study of teachers'
behavioural strategies, it was similarly found that 'Teachers of
English are not typical of teachers in general in their respective
countries.'[3] Your perceptions about what is involved in
'becoming' an English teacher are also likely to have influenced
your choice of training institution (and *their* decision whether to
accept you). There is some evidence that a high proportion of
students on any English course will share similar ideas about the
objectives and organization of teacher education. This is rarely
overt, and a stir can be caused when it becomes explicit, for
example when one department publicly said it favoured English
graduates who were 'progressives' opposed to streaming, formal
examinations and authoritarian teacher roles, suspicious of the
political overtones of 'standard' English and predisposed to peace
education.[4]

Your existing attitudes and perceptions are continuously modified or reinforced by experiences during training and in schools.
Richard Smith has described how students are initiated into
particular ways of talking and thinking about educational issues,
and how repeated words, ideas and actions come to shape their
developing thinking about what is involved in 'becoming a
teacher', so that they believe 'that some things rather than others
are equated with common sense'.[5] Memories, observations,
instruction, videotapes and practical experience combine to
provide metaphors for what teaching is like, though inevitably we

believe that we work it out for ourselves. One of our teachers said, for example:

> We weren't really taught anything about discipline . . . the only way you learn your own style of conducting yourself in the classroom is through bitter experience and you have to make mistakes to realise what you *can* do: when to maintain a certain distance and when to maintain a certain control and calmness, when not to lose your temper and not to shout, whereas occasionally at other times that might be effective.

You might consider in what ways your own perceptions of the English teacher's role have changed and why. Do your experiences confirm those studies which examined students before and after their PGCE courses and suggested changes like these?

1. A tendency to rank job conditions more highly and idealistic motives (creativity, using one's talents, etc.) at a lower level in assessing reasons for becoming a teacher.
2. A decline in the importance attached to 'theoretical' studies and an increase in the significance attributed to educational administration, awareness of individual children and self-knowledge. (Understanding of the main subject and of methodology in that subject remain constantly important.)
3. A general shift in attitude towards a more progressive, liberal, radical and tender-minded stance.
4. A decline in the degree of commitment to teaching as a career.[6]

It would clearly be dangerous to over-generalize about a situation in which there are so many variables, especially in the models of student and of teacher that are acted out in colleges, departments and schools.[7] Different institutions may perceive the training role as essentially one of craft apprenticeship (imitating the style of an acknowledged 'expert', sometimes described as 'sitting with Nellie'), or of clinical practice ('interns' learning to diagnose and prescribe), or of academic reception (of approved principles and methods), or of personal discovery (developing an individual style). You may have felt that tutors on your course presented a particular model of a teacher as the ideal to aim at: the skilled classroom performer, the professional organizer and decision-maker, the practical psychologist interacting well with children or the facilitator with a bank of resource materials. This can prove to be quite different from the preferred role in the English department that welcomes you as student or probationer. Discovering your own teaching style tends to come by trying on others until you discover what fits.

In that *rite de passage* of training, students traditionally place a very high value on initial school experience and on teaching practice. That is when they see themselves as closest to the teacher role at which they are aiming. In summing up their courses, they repeatedly use phrases like: 'I learned much more from my actual experiences in the classroom than from any other part of the course' or 'Although the method course was interesting and practical, it was the actual experience of working with those methods that was important.' Certainly it is only when you have responsibility for a class that you *really* begin to discover what knowledge is essential, what help you need, what you have failed to think through and what resources are needed. Unfortunately, experience is not necessarily such a reliable guide as students may think at this stage. Only later do they discover the difference between the same activity when carried out as a student and as a full-time teacher (an 'infinite difference', according to one). 'As a teacher you learn differently from when you were a student.' Only then do they realize the need for 'the continuous learning that a teacher has to be willing to do to put theory into practice' if you are to make the transition 'from being a student teacher (i.e. a supervisor of work) to being a proper teacher, one who actually teaches'. The fundamental difference is that during the student experience you are working in someone else's classroom, building (or failing to build) on their structures, approaches and conventions, and judging your success at least in part by someone else's criteria (the teacher's or the tutor's). One recent American study has pointed out the truth that students cannot bring themselves to hear: 'Making it on one's own in student teaching is not the same as learning to teach or being a teacher.'[8]

Our Hull students rapidly came to realize that the generalizations they formed on teaching practice did not necessarily hold good in the probationary year and that their apparent successes and failures were not necessarily predictors of future success. Some of them blamed themselves for being imperceptive, but in fact their only real weakness was to expect too much of the practice. 'Classrooms are not set up for teaching teachers.'[9] Although they did not realize it at the time, virtually all our teachers later saw that as students in school they led 'a very sheltered existence', 'operating rather artificially', dominated by 'a need to perform' on particular occasions, planning 'in short bursts' and trying to satisfy the implied or explicit demands of tutors and supervising teachers. Ironically, it was when they were most uncertain of what they were trying to achieve and how to set about it that they were expected to be most explicit and detailed in their statements of aims and plans for the conduct of lessons. As students they were 'allowed' to make mistakes and could shrug off failures, whereas in school 'you have to live with your difficulties and mistakes for a full year', 'You have to learn to fail.' The shift was not essentially in methodology. Approaches introduced in method courses and tried out during training were described as 'extremely worthwhile', 'practical', 'imaginative', 'helpful with regard to methods and materials', 'informative and interesting'. The differences were structural and organizational: materials had to be 'radically reorganized' into longer-term sequences of work and to fit the developmental needs of individuals and groups. 'It takes much longer to get an overall picture and understand what development means', a topic that is discussed at greater length in Chapter 9. Feelings about the first year out were predictably ambivalent. On the one hand, many students felt like those who said: 'In my first year I felt I had little status – the tag of probationer is quite a stigma and I felt inadequate and conspicuous' or 'I found my first term extremely exhausting and somewhat disillusioning'. On the other hand there was a general feeling that becoming one of a department enabled you to feel 'established', 'accepted', 'belonging', with 'confidence in knowing the routine', and 'an opportunity to build up relationships' (as opposed to the 'temporary' feeling of teaching practice, when it is 'difficult to establish yourself in staffroom or classroom').

As these English teachers record, the ideas and skills developed during the period of training are – however useful – inadequate for the new role and its accompanying responsibilities. Theoretically they have 'passed', and no longer have the protection of being 'only a student', while simultaneously being acutely conscious that they still need to display L-plates. In particular, courses had apparently been least successful in preparing students for the sheer weight of work that would be expected of them in school. They record:

1. The diversity and sheer volume of the activities involved in a normal teaching day came as a real shock.
2. The main difference concerns the amount of non-teaching activities that most teachers are involved with in schools – form groups, pastoral work, inter- and intra-department meetings, discipline, getting on with difficult children (and staff!), ordering books and so on.
3. I had little conception during training of the sheer volume of marking, preparation, tutor group administration and so on that I am expected (and need) to do.
4. Sometimes teaching gets pushed to one side . . . by report-writing, form-mistress administration, exam setting and marking as well as extra-curricular involvement (magazine, English Society) and residential duties.

It would be possible to make a list of hundreds of items to which English teachers devote their time. There is no logical boundary to what *can* be involved in caring for the needs of a range of individuals within a school situation. This lack of clear definition explains why some young teachers work a seventy or eighty-hour week while others seem to confine themselves to 9 till 4 forty weeks a year. It seems unlikely that any formal contract will radically affect that. It has been fashionable – and too easy – to attribute weaknesses in *Teaching Quality*[10] simply to the selection and the training of students. It is true that a good school department can do something to remedy a poor probationary year or that a successful probation may 'compensate for apparent defects or omissions in training'.[11] On the other hand, besides being critical of themselves and of their training, our teachers also pointed to a whole range of factors in their first schools which seemed to decrease their effectiveness. Their perceptions are reinforced by the comments of Her Majesty's Inspectors.

The HMI report *The New Teacher in Schools* made clear some of the difficulties faced by newly trained teachers. In general, three out of ten were said to be working in conditions that would not 'promote their professional development and many of these are receiving little support from heads or fellow staff'. Many of the schools themselves were in a state of flux (nearly a quarter had been 'newly opened or reorganized in the last five years' and half 'had suffered a significant change in size over the last three years') and that proportion is almost certainly greater now. Over a third of the schools 'appeared to expect too much of newly trained teachers', indeed, one secondary head suggested that 'They should know all the tricks of the trade in the professional teacher's book.'[12] Unreal expectations are almost certain to be disappointed.

In detail, the report pointed to a close relationship between the quality of lessons taught by young teachers and the constraints within the school that affected them: 'in nearly all the least successful lessons, teachers were working under external constraints of one sort or another.'[13] These constraints (more fully considered in Chapter 8) were said by HMI to include:

1. Pressures towards narrow or unimaginative work, imposed by the department's expectations or policies (especially with examination forms), which affected a third of all lessons seen.
2. The difficulty of the class (sometimes notoriously troublesome, 'which other members of staff found difficult to handle') which affected 40 per cent of lessons seen.
3. The absence of clear guidelines, schemes of work or marking policies, which affected half of the lessons seen (and 70 per cent of the poor lessons).
4. The non-availability of suitable books or other teaching materials, which affected over two-fifths of lessons seen.[14]

Such constraints were intensified by the relative failure to provide adequate opportunities for probationers to see more experienced teachers at work (only 58 per cent of secondary schools claimed to arrange this in their own schools and only 34 per cent in other schools)[15] and by the frequent use of young teachers in subjects for which they were not qualified. In particular, 'More than three out of ten of those concerned with the teaching of English . . . had no academic basis for their teaching.'[16] However, the question of 'matching' teacher and group goes further than academic qualifications. It is sometimes assumed too easily that an effective young teacher can operate in *any* situation:

Where there is a reasonable harmony between the strengths and personal qualities of the teachers and the style of the school to which they are appointed, both the quality of work in the schools and the professional development of the teachers are helped. There are teachers who would be able to work happily in a relaxed, supportive environment and thus develop into good teachers, but who have been appointed to schools where a rigid or authoritarian style of organisation exists. In consequence they are both unhappy and unsuccessful. The reverse can also be true. This is an element of 'match' which tends to be neglected.[17]

GETTING TO KNOW THE SCHOOL

It is impossible *not* to start forming impressions and evaluating them from the moment you enter a school, whether it is as a preliminary to teaching practice, or on interview, or to begin work there. What we notice and what conclusions we draw from that vary according to our own backgrounds, personalities, expectations and experience. According to one partisan view, the tell-tale signs of a 'bad' school are CND badges, chairs grouped around tables rather than facing the front, and any references to 'sexism' or 'racism' on notices. We may look for clean and tidy classrooms, an absence of graffiti, a system of rewards and recognition for good pupils, and signs of regular homework as indicators of a successful school.[18] We may be chiefly guided by the way in which staff and students dress, or by the kind and range of out-of-school activities, by the accommodation and facilities available for English, or even by the smell of the place.

How personal the process is can be seen from the way in which half a dozen probationers recorded what first struck them about the schools in which they are now teaching:

The buildings retain the appearance and, in some ways, the atmosphere of a grammar school: large glass case full of trophies outside the Head's office, lists of former Heads on wooden panels in the entrance hall, etc. Examples of the old tradition include a Combined Cadet Force . . . inter-house Sports competitions . . . a chaplain . . . a school song.

My first impression was that it was fairly easy-going, rather run-down and in need of maybe half-a-dozen new staff who were willing to shake the place up.

I was very conscious of the academic atmosphere, the excellent exam results and the traditions . . . The atmosphere in the staffroom was not exactly frosty but it was not unlike a public library: polite whispers, favourite chairs, rustling pages from the *Telegraph*.

My first impressions were ones of awe: extremely polite pupils, no graffiti, a luxurious library, a well-stocked English department.

As a 'showpiece' school, its atmosphere is very pleasant: modern premises, pictures, plants . . . echoed by the corridor behaviour of the kids who are largely very pleasant. I have found this to be a fairly reliable indication of the general demeanour of the school. Another favourable point is that every child . . . has his or her own pen, pencil and rubber.

My first impressions of the school were that it was fairly peaceful and ordered, trying to convey a traditional image and keeping its Catholicism well to the fore . . . a crucifix was prominently displayed in each room. On my first visit the Deputy Head made a casual remark about them 'sitting quietly in rows and working – or supposed to be working', which gave me a good idea of what to expect.

Impressions cannot be dispassionate, because as you walk along the corridors and peer into classrooms you begin to 'place' yourself in the school: to imagine what it would be like working with that class, chatting in the staff-room, using those resources. You might try to recall impressions of your own. What were the chief signs that significantly shaped your first views of a school? Almost certainly you will have been influenced by the way in which you yourself were received, whether as a student, a probationer or a newcomer to the staff. How helpful and welcoming was the preliminary written information? How were you greeted and introduced to people? What opportunities were you given to put questions and to discuss your role? How adequate was the documentation you were given? How quickly were you able to make personal contacts and to feel yourself one of the group?[19] Particularly in cases where the initial information is inadequate, but to some extent in all schools, you will be left with the task of discovering the essential hard facts to place under your atmospheric impressions. Noting essential information during a preliminary visit, to be more thoroughly considered later, is a difficult task, especially when time is short and informants may be under pressure. (It is desirable to try to use several different people as your sources, rather than imposing on one.) Here is a check-list, adapted from one supplied to English students making their first visits to schools. You may be able to modify this to fit your own needs and interests, remembering that the purpose of this activity is not to amass inert information, but to help you to prepare yourself to work in that school by building up the clearest possible imaginative picture of what that will involve for you.

1. Background information about the school
   (a) How much of this is already available in published form? (Calendar of dates, staff lists, publications for parents or new teachers – acquire what you can.)
   (b) How would you describe the area served by the school? What kind of houses, shops, entertainment, recreations, places of interest? Where do young people seem to congregate out of school? What transport is available?
   (c) Any significant details about the school's history and recent development?
   (d) What is the school's geography like? Is a plan available? In particular, where are the rooms used for English? Library? Drama studio? School office? Resources centre? Staff room and toilets? Are there any obvious problems in getting between rooms to be used? What is the state of repair and maintenance? How are rooms furnished, equipped, laid out (rows, groups, other)?
   (e) How do pupils behave about the school? To a stranger? Is children's work displayed? What attitudes towards it? What sort of programme of out-of-school activities? What impressions from notice-boards?
   (f) What are the feeder schools? Any problems of variation in approach, method, materials concerning work in English? Any cooperation or liaison? Any staff interchange?

2. Organization
   (a) How are students grouped for English? For other purposes? (Setting, streaming, mixed-ability?) How much group, pair, class work? Any integrated working or team teaching? What kind of pastoral care? (Houses, year groups, tutor sets?) What provision is made for children with reading difficulties, from different language backgrounds, with special needs? (See Chapter 4 for fuller details.)
   (b) Is there a curriculum policy document? How is the National Curriculum implemented? What is the pattern of guidance for careers and Higher Education? (See Chapter 3.)
   (c) What modes of assessment are used in English (and in other subjects)? What tests have been developed for National Curriculum assessment? What is the policy for marking and corrections? Are Records of Achievement kept? Other records? To whom are they available, and how?
   (d) What is the pattern of external examinations and subject choice? Which syllabuses (and which Board) are

followed in English? What percentage of pupils stay on beyond leaving age? What range of courses is available to them (A-level, re-sits, CPVE, etc.)? What is the involvement of the English Department in all of these? (Chapter 6.)

(e) What arrangements are made for contacts with parents? With the wider community? What are the attitudes of the governing body towards English? Who are the teacher governors? (Chapter 8.)

3. Equipment and materials (see Chapter 5.)

(a) How are funds allocated to the Department and how are decisions made about spending them? What possibility is there for you to request specific purchases?

(b) Which items of equipment are owned by the school? Department? Individuals? What arrangements for borrowing and using? How much notice required? Where kept? How acquired for use?

(c) Arrangements for duplicating? Where are materials kept? Does the Department build up a shared stock of worksheets and other materials?

(d) What rooms other than classrooms are available for drama? Use of library for project work?

(e) Books – is there a department book list? Where is stock kept? Who has the key? Is there an allocation method? What is the school library like? Is there a private teacher's collection? Sets of examination papers?

(f) Other resources apart from books? Paper, scissors, card, felt-pens? OHP transparencies? Slides and filmstrips? Audio-cassettes?

(g) Does school or department tape-record and use school broadcasts? TV programmes?

(h) Are micros or word processors used in English teaching? What is their availability?

4. Professional duties (see Chapters 6 and 7.)

(a) What help are you expected to give with registration, general duties, meal supervision, substitution for absent staff, exams, parents' evenings? In carrying out general duties, what does one do *if*? Who is responsible for notice-boards? Discipline? Absentees?

(b) What are school rules? Approved sanctions? How much notice for detention?

(c) Personal relationships – who is the professional tutor, and where and when do you meet? What are the names of departmental and other colleagues (especially those whose lessons you teach)?

(d) Whom to notify and how if you are going to be absent or late?

5. English
   (a) Is there a syllabus, policy statement, scheme of work or book list? (Get copies where possible) If not, what are main emphases? How is policy decided? (See Chapter 3.)
   (b) Which forms will you work with? (Make notes on any forms or lessons seen.)
   (c) How are lessons organized? (Groups, pairs, individual assignments?) What are main ways of working? Related use of exercise books, rough books, paper (where obtainable) (See Chapter 4.)
   (d) What kind of work, standard achieved, ability spread? What has form done previously? What topics, themes, books already covered in school? (Get copies of books they are likely to be using)
   (e) What arrangements are made for departmental meetings? Individuals with specific responsibilities? Groups working on resources and curriculum planning? In-service education for teachers (INSET)? (See Chapter 7.)
   (f) What support is available beyond the school? English adviser? LEA courses? Local professional or teachers' centre? Facilities of local college or university and courses there? Branches of National Association for the Teaching of English, School Library Association, School Bookshop Association, etc?

WATCHING CLASSROOMS AT WORK

Observing an English lesson in progress sounds easy and is actually difficult. What is observed is coloured by the personality of the observer and by that observer's perception of the purpose of the observation. Their notes show that students in their first term focus on different elements in the classroom from those that appear significant to a young trained teacher. When two students observe the same lesson, they frequently respond quite differently to the same events. Because they must have some comparative norm, students draw on memories of their own schooldays and anticipations of how *they* will teach. Subliminally through what they record runs a tissue of implied judgements of the level of children's work, the style of organization and control, the interaction of teacher and class. As yet they are very unsure about what they are supposed to be learning by observing (and some may even think it a tedious irrelevance). Ironically, those more experienced teachers who might know better what to look for are rarely given the opportunity to develop observation skills because of a long tradition of 'private' classrooms. We can all gain from seeing others at work, and it is particularly important that probationers should *expect* to see a variety of classrooms (and request this if it is not offered).

Little training is generally given in observation apart from the slightly artificial use of videotapes. Students are frequently puzzled about what to select out of a welter of impressions. So much is going on simultaneously in an active classroom that it is easy to receive only a confused, general impression. There are many schedules and other record-making devices available to give some shape to these impressions[20] but they all tend to limit attention to what is measurable or analysable and omit subtler or more complex factors. Observation has to be accompanied by the ability to interpret what is heard and seen, in a situation that has no neat end-product. What is the focus of our observation?

Specifically, it is an active imaginative awareness of the *significance for the observer* of what is going on in the classroom. What need to be recorded are not neutral facts, but those practices, responses and routines that *you* will adopt, the alternative strategies and methods that *you* will try. Good observation develops the capacity to learn from and to adjust to future experiences. You may choose at different times and for different purposes to focus on the teacher, on the children, or on the resources employed. What are you looking for in each case?

The teacher

It is necessary to be quite clear about *why* you are in the privileged position of watching an experienced teacher at work. You are there to learn about *yourself*. It is all too easy to fall into false expectations of your role in the classroom:

1. To see a model of good teaching in action, which you will be able to imitate (but what works for this teacher, with a particular personality and a unique relationship with the class cannot simply be reproduced by anyone else).
2. To make a critical evaluation of a performance (but you are in no position to judge teaching ability, and to do so will only distract attention from the real purpose of observation).
3. To pick up methods and materials that you yourself will be able to use (but there are much more satisfactory and systematic ways of obtaining these than by random observation).

Your chief attention should be on the apparent (though ambiguous) relationship between the teacher's chosen strategies and the learning generated by them. Your thoughts should be: Why is it being organized in this way? Would I set this up differently? If so, how and why? What other material or activity might I substitute?

A very simple check-list (that would rapidly be outgrown) might include such items as:

1. First impressions: How did the teacher enter? What were the first words and actions? How long before the children were actively involved? How was this achieved? How was the voice used? What were the pupils' initial responses?

2. Organization: What sort of structure and sequence did the lesson have? What balance of English activities? How were transitions between activities achieved? What balance of whole class, group or pair, and individual work? Were the objectives made explicit?

3. How far were children of different abilities and backgrounds catered for?

4. Instructions: Given at length or in small units? Accompanied by specimen answers or reinforced by questions? Supported in written form on blackboard or ohp? Repeated?

5. Questions: What kinds (closed/open, factual/reasoning, etc.)? Directed to individuals or generally to class? Did pupils themselves ask questions? How did the teacher use mistakes?

6. Supervision: When students were working individually or in groups, how was the teacher occupied? How were difficulties tackled? How were praise and encouragement used? How was progress monitored? Were additional resources deployed? Where was the teacher positioned at different stages of the lesson?

7. Conclusion: Was there a specific planned ending? Was work drawn together or was there anticipation of future activities? What – if anything – was left to be completed later? How were materials collected? What routine was followed for leaving the room?

8. Homework: Was any set, and if so how? Was it common for all or self-chosen by pupils? Was there strict adherence to a school homework timetable or were pupils given longer periods to organize for themselves? Was any homework collected during the lesson? How was this done and how were 'offenders' dealt with?

9. Looking back: What kind of·preparation must this lesson have required? What previous knowledge or experience of the pupils must have been necessary? What kind of difficulties did any of them experience? Were there any unexpected events, and if so how did the teacher deal with them? How were behaviour problems tackled? How effective was the general style of management and control?

10. Relating to myself: What have I chiefly learned from this observation? If working with this class, what would I most need to remember? If teaching this lesson, what different materials, approaches, activities might I consider employing? What particular difficulties would I anticipate, and how might I overcome them?

The children

Observing children's behaviour in school is very much easier for young teachers who have recent previous experience of meeting them naturally outside school. Lesson observation can be supplemented by occasions at break and lunchtimes or in out-of-school activities when you are simply being *with* children rather than being their teacher. Some of the aspects that might be noted with groups that you will teach are:

1. What is the general attitude to work? How many seem bored? Resentful and antagonistic? Cooperative and enthusiastic? Resigned to failure? What methods seem best to motivate them?
2. Interaction: How do pupils in general seem to respond to the teacher? How do they address the teacher, and vice versa? How much interaction between children is there, and of what kind? What evidence is there of natural groupings? Isolated children?
3. Involvement: What sort of response is there to the teacher's questions? How long is taken in settling to a new activity? What variation is there in the amount of writing done? Do any seem reluctant to engage in pair or group work? What strategies seem to be practised by some to avoid doing work?
4. What seem to be standard practices? How do they enter a room? Decide where to sit? Behave on the arrival of the teacher? How far are they permitted to move about? Form groups of their own choice? Help each other? Leave the room? Do they put their hands up? Are they silent when the teacher talks? How are books and materials distributed and collected? Are pupils expected to have their own pens, rulers, rubbers, etc.? Is borrowing permitted? How?
5. How do pupils 'test out' the teacher, to see how far they can go? Asking questions and making comments? General uncontrolled talking and noise? Passivity and refusal to work? Interfering with other pupils, horseplay?
6. What is their experience of sanctions, and how effective do these seem? Reprimand given to individuals? To the whole class? Sending out of the room, or to another teacher?

Being asked to stay behind to talk with teacher? Detention? Extra work or imposition? Threats not followed up? Other . . .?

7. Which pupils present distinct, identifiable management problems? Who are the leaders? Grudgers? Isolates? Jokers?

8. What conclusions for your own teaching of this group do you draw? Which expectations and rules are you going to insist on? What 'testing out' behaviour do you anticipate, and how are you going to react?

9. How do you plan to learn their names? (Classroom map? Labels on desks? Specific name-using activities?) What policy do you have for getting to know and dealing with selected individuals? What do you think the class will learn about *you* from the first lesson you plan to take with them?

The resources

You might consider:

1. What range of resources was deployed? How much use was made of each of these?

   Blackboard, whiteboard, ohp, display charts, illustrations, exercise books, paper, files, notebooks, course books, novels, plays, poetry books, anthologies, reference books, cassette or tape recorders, gramophone records, video-recorder, film projector, slide/filmstrip projector, micro or word processor.

2. Where are these resources stored? How are they brought into use or distributed? (To individuals? To groups?)

3. How do the pupils respond to these materials? What difficulties do they seem to experience? What help is given to them?

4. What materials and equipment do pupils bring with them to lessons?

5. What routines are there for ensuring chalk and board rubber are available? Dealing with pupils who have forgotten books? Pen? Homework? Obtaining new books or paper?

6. To what extent do individuals or groups work with different materials from one another? How is this organized?

7. What kind of work is displayed in the room? Is any specific use made of the display?

8. At the end of the lesson: How are the materials and resources collected and stored? Is the blackboard cleaned? How is the furniture left?

YOUR FIRST LESSONS

Even in a well-organized school you are likely to find the beginning of a busy term difficult if you are a student, unfamiliar with the routine and nervous at what lies ahead. In such circumstances, it may be hard to remember that most teachers positively like to have English students in their schools. They say that:

1. Students bring with them new ideas and new materials that can help to update the department's repertoire.
2. The questions that students pose can help experienced teachers to re-examine their own principles and practice.
3. By working alongside teachers, students can make possible new approaches, and enable more attention to be given to selected groups of children.

Unless the school has a well-developed induction policy, then the start of the school year can also be a nightmare for you if you are a probationer, expected to have metamorphosed from student to capable teacher during the summer vacation. In a sense, the problems of the first lessons are not significantly different for the student, the probationer or the experienced teacher starting in a new school.

Being a new teacher in the classroom is inevitably a lonely and vulnerable situation. You alone seem unfamiliar with the routines, the personalities, the expectations. At times it can seem as though there is a kind of conspiracy to isolate you. It is natural to want to be liked, by pupils and staff. You may become abnormally sensitive to the messages or cues transmitted by word and expression. This can lead, with seductive ease, to shifting teaching styles towards those advocated by colleagues, to accepting their ready-made valuations of groups and individuals, to adopting a different stereotype of the teacher's role, rather than trusting one's own observations and principles. In any occupation, enthusiastic new entrants with fresh ideas pose a threat to established practices, and pressure is put on them to conform. In such circumstances it is dangerously easy to begin making simplistic distinctions between 'theory' (idealistic notions of tutors and advisers) and 'practice' (hard-headed, no-nonsense practices which 'work'). We are all inclined to revert to primitive 'safe' behaviour under pressure. Students who are highly critical of the poor English teaching they received at school frequently lapse into practising those methods they condemned if they find themselves in difficulty. One of our young teachers describes the situation like this:

I felt that many of my ideas were frowned upon by staff and pupils alike . . . It was difficult to resist the way in which the pupils almost imposed a traditional teaching style upon me. They seemed to want to be given notes, to be tested, to be told rather than offer opinions of their own. Consequently it was difficult at first to do as I had wanted and had planned.

There would have been a real danger of reverting to 'traditional' methods, but for one thing:

Fortunately my head of department, who arrived at the same time as me, was very supportive and tended to teach in the same way that I hoped to . . . I think it must be very difficult to adhere to your beliefs about teaching when a school imposes different principles by force of successful precedent and tradition.

Other comments of our sample of young teachers suggest that what surprised and disturbed them most on those first occasions in the classroom was the constant pressure of having to make choices: about strategies, about control, about the needs of individuals, and particularly about the unexpected events. In most cases, this was made harder by the fact that they were facing conflicting – often contradictory – pressures and demands.[21] Energy is consumed by trying to be sensible and consistent in an ever-changing situation where you are internally making up the rules as you go along.

The peculiar intensity of our first classroom experiences is caused by the fact that they highlight our personal weaknesses. Although we may have anticipated where we would be vulnerable, and although we shall also have discovered personal strengths, the experience is inevitably daunting. Remember, though:

1. This is virtually universal experience. Young teachers need regular contact with one another, if only to remind themselves that their problems are not unique. (The occasional confident beginner, sure of total success, is either self-deceiving or insensitive). Hearing from others who have previously taught your groups is generally helpful (though their opinions have to be treated with care).
2. As we tell the children in our classes: learning depends on error and failure. The inevitable mistakes we make are the signs that show us precisely how to become more successful.
3. Effective English teaching depends on knowing oneself as honestly as possible. Trying to pretend – to tutors, colleagues or oneself – postpones the necessary building on one's personal strengths and developing new abilities to deal with particular situations.
4. Early experiences are a time for reasoned experiment, rather than playing safe. Inevitably some materials, teaching approaches, forms of organization will be less successful in

particular situations than others. Analysing why there has been some degree of 'failure' is an essential element in increased efficiency.

5. What we regard as a 'bad' lesson may often be largely caused by factors outside the teacher's control: tensions within the group, trouble in a previous lesson, frequent changes of teacher, the 'last lesson on Friday' syndrome.

The actual problems mentioned as dominating their first term or so of teaching are extraordinarily varied. There is always a sense of pressure, but what is perceived as causing that pressure varies according to the probationers' personalities, the attitudes of the pupils and the nature of the school in which they are working. A few examples will help to give the flavour:

The major difficulty I faced in the first term was trying to get through the amount of work I was expected to do . . . to cope with a full teaching-load and to plan homework and the inevitable marking.

My main problem during my first term was getting the pupils to talk! I'd completed my PGCE course convinced of the value of small group discussion activities but found that the pupils were reluctant to participate.

I realise now how little direction or idea I had of the enormity of the task organizing a year's work involved. At the end of the first term I was so physically and mentally exhausted my social life dissolved. My week consisting of sleeping, eating and working with little else other than the foolishly large number of extra-curricular activities I undertook.

I had difficulties with my fourth and fifth year CSE classes. This was mainly because, to them, I was terribly middle-class, unsmiling and unbending. On TP I could deal with classes like that because I knew I only had them for ten weeks and didn't mind making myself fairly unpopular. What I didn't realise was that I would have to live with these people all year.

The one difficulty that overshadowed all else was sheer physical exhaustion. At several points in that first term I felt ill through tiredness. Not being aware of the full range of resources available contributed to this – much time was spent studying the contents of the stock cupboard.

I had rioting fifth formers, kids who escaped out of the window and little support from the upper echelon of staff, including the head who seemed as scared of the fifth form as I became.

The most difficult aspect of my first job was adjusting to the more intensive academic pace of such a school. With large sixth form groups much time had to be spent preparing and marking sixth form work. Oxbridge also took up a great deal of time and I needed to do much reading here.

I found this a very difficult start to teaching because of the negative atmosphere and the consequent discipline problems. Some pupils should really be removed to other schools after assaults on teachers . . . There is little or no parental back-up except in many parents encouraging the pupils to stay at home. Many . . . regularly miss two days schooling per week.

I had a foul low-ability fifth year class which contained a fair collection of the biggest villains in the school and I had to try and get them through 16+ English. Homework was a non-event . . . I think at first my expectations were too high, and I had to become more realistic in how much I expected to achieve with them.

It will be clear from the variety of these comments and (perhaps) from your own experience that much depends on the kind and amount of teaching that is expected. Some of the pressures of timetable allocation on young teachers are obvious enough. There are still schools where far from being given a lighter timetable, probationers have a heavy one and are given some of the most difficult classes or slower streams to teach. It is becoming increasingly uncommon for young teachers, however well qualified academically, to get A-level teaching until they have 'earned' it by a year or two in the lower school. They are more likely to be 'under pressure to 'fill in' by teaching other subjects (sometimes including ones for which they lack qualifications). There are also less obvious effects of the way in which English is organized. It is rare for anyone to teach right through the school at all levels, and some young teachers record that it is difficult to build up a clear developmental picture when they are not taking a second or a third year class. Because English lessons with a given year tend to be blocked, probationers rarely get the opportunity to work with *two* parallel first year or fourth year groups, which would lighten the preparation load, and enable them to compare different responses to the same lesson.

The next two chapters consider in practical terms how you can prepare for work in a new school. The first is concerned with what you teach, the curriculum, and the second with planning and structuring that work: assessing the constraints, devising sequences and planning lessons.

REFERENCES

1. Sikes Patricia J 1985 'The life cycle of the teacher' in Ball Stephen J and Goodson Ivor F (eds) *Teachers' Lives and Careers*. Falmer Press, p 35
2. Lacey Colin 1977 *The Socialization of Teachers*. Methuen, p 60
3. Paisey H A G 1975 *Behavioural Strategy of Teachers in Britain and the United States*. NFER, Windsor, p 82 (also see pp 69–73)
4. *Times Educational Supplement* 14 October 1983
5. Smith R 1979 'Myth and ritual in teacher education' in Pusey M R and Young R E *Control and Knowledge*. Canberra, pp. 98–9

6. Lacey, *Socialization of Teachers*, pp 106–14
7. See Zeichner Kenneth M 1986 'Content and contexts: neglected elements in studies of student teaching as an occasion for learning to teach', *Journal of Education for Teaching*, vol 12 no 1, pp 5–24
8. Feiman-Nemser Sharon and Buchmann Margaret 1985, 'Pitfalls of experience in teacher preparation', *Teachers College Record*, vol 87 no 1, Fall, p 60
9. Ibid. p 63. Also see Hadley Eric 1982 *Teaching Practice and the Probationary Year*. Arnold
10. DES 1983 *Teaching Quality*. HMSO
11. HMI 1982 *The New Teacher in School*. HMSO, 5.33
12. Ibid. 1.3, 5.34, 1.7, 5.4
13. Ibid. 2.62, 5.43
14. Ibid. 2.6, 5.41, 2.11–12, 5.13
15. Ibid. 5.19
16. Ibid. 4.28
17. Ibid. 6.3
18. Rutter Michael *et al* 1979 *Fifteen Thousand Hours*. Open Books
19. See Marland Michael and Hill Sydney 1981 *Departmental Management*. Heinemann and Cohen Lou and Manion Lawrence 1983 *A Guide to Teaching Practice* Second edition. Methuen pp 17–26
20. For example Walker R and Adelman C 1975 *A Guide to Classroom Observation*. Methuen, or Boehm A E and Weinberg R A 1978 *The Classroom Observer*. Teachers College Press
21. Horner Sue (ed) 1983 *Best Laid Plans: English Teachers at Work*. Longman, York, for the SCDC

CHAPTER 3

The English curriculum

SOME PROBLEMS OF DEFINITION

What does an English teacher teach? We live at a time when increasing concern is being shown for teachers' mastery of their classroom subjects and when we are told that 'the subject is likely to be perceived as being the most important part of being a teacher'.[1] If that is so, just what special knowledge and expertise do you possess and hope to pass on as an English teacher? Graduate students frequently remark how little direct relevance their degree courses in literature seem to offer to what they do in the classroom. The courses were valuable to them as people, perhaps, but what essential knowledge did they provide? What in turn do we try to achieve in those timetable slots marked English? Are you clear about it from the beginning, or do you claim – like one cynic – to make up the English curriculum as you go along? How aware are you of the principles and practices of others in your department – and do they coincide with yours? How do you explain to someone from a different discipline what English is about?

Professor Harold Rosen began his inaugural lecture at the London Institute by remarking on this curricular uniqueness. English, he said:

Is the least subject-like of subjects, the least susceptible to definition by reference to the accumulation of wisdom within a single academic discipline. No single set of informing ideas dominate its heartland. No one can confidently map its frontiers . . . the practices which cluster together uncomfortably under its banner . . . appear so diverse, contradictory, arbitrary and random as to defy analysis and explanation.[2]

It was hardly surprising, then, that when HMI produced the first of their Curriculum Matters series, *English from 5 to 16*, it received 'differing responses' ranging from 'approving' to 'condemnatory', and being welcomed 'for often contrasting reasons . . . with emphasis upon the relative merits of quite different items'.[3] However, it is not just those 'items' which are in dispute; there is a more deep-seated uncertainty about the very nature of the curriculum subject we call English.

That uncertainty is grounded in its brief history. You may find it hard to realize that this apparently dominant subject was in effect the last of the major elements of the curriculum to be recognized. English teachers were the last to be accepted as specialists in secondary schools, and their professional associations like the English Association and NATE were not established until well after those of other subjects. Whereas Classics or Mathematics had long been seen as organic fields of study, English gradually emerged as the title for a debatable cluster of activities. In 1900 the Board of Education's *Schedules* for each age group show Reading, Writing and English as separate subjects (and English is defined solely in terms of grammatical knowledge). Within schools these activities were broken down further into periods labelled Spelling, Recitation, Handwriting and so on.[4] The false assumption that by secondary or university level pupils should already have achieved mastery of the vernacular underlay the low importance that was attached to the teaching of reading and writing. These divisions lived on in the separation of English Language and Literature in the new Certificate (1917), maintained in the successive changes from School Certificate to O-level. Although GCSE introduces a unitary subject called English, with a literary element, it also maintains a separate additional subject titled English Literature. In the HSC or A-level, English came to mean almost exclusively English Literature. Although there are now two A-level examinations in language, these are still seen as *alternatives* to literature. Even within these two broad divisions there is no longer – if there ever was – agreement about the field of study. Deconstruction of concepts of 'reading' and 'writing' has shown how shaky are our apparently commonsense assumptions about the nature and field of these studies.

At a time when the establishment of English as a subject seemed to depend on its having a unique 'field' of knowledge, it was understandable that it came to be defined in terms of knowing *about* language and literature. Increasing dissatisfaction with such a narrow view has led to the claim for much wider frontiers: 'English is the sum of all the activities we engage in through language.'[5] Unfortunately this too faces us with difficulties. First, it presents English as a kind of training school for the rest of the curriculum and eventually for life itself – a service subject with nothing of its own to offer. Second, in curricular terms, it makes it virtually impossible to establish the priority of certain elements and activities over others: any interesting theme or topic will seem to do so long as students can read and talk and write about it.

Between the extreme views, narrow or wide, English teachers find it hard either to be sure what it is they should be doing or to convince others of the rightness of their diagnosis. A number of researchers have pointed to the different (and often irreconcilable) paradigms of English teaching that exist within the profession. Some of our teachers found, as you may do, that clashes of basic principle may even divide departments. The Cox committee said that in their work they were 'acutely aware of the differing opinions that are held on a number of issues that lie at the heart of the English curriculum and its teaching'.[6] They later identified five major views of English as a subject, saying that teachers 'differ in the weight they give to each of these'.[7] Other researchers have similarly found English a 'disputed area' with its teachers representing a 'complete spectrum' of opinion.[8] If you are not to be thrown into uncertainty by such 'disputes', you will need to be clear about the principles underlying these arguments over the English curriculum, and to realize that informed professional opinion has agreed in broad detail what that curriculum involves.

ENGLISH IN THE NATIONAL CURRICULUM

The history of the subject English has been marked by successive attempts to define more closely what English is essentially 'about' and how it should be taught. The most important of these – often establishing principles that have remained significant – would include the Board of Education's *The Teaching of English in Secondary Schools* (1910), The Newbolt Report entitled *The Teaching of English in England* (1921), together with George Sampson's *English for the English* (1921), John Dixon's *Growth through English* (1967), and the Bullock Report, *A Language for Life* (1975). Even though these (and other books and reports) had a formative influence on English practice, none established total consensus within the profession or bridged the gap in perceptions of the subject between teachers and the general public. Indeed, there was furious disagreement between different groups about attempts to formulate specific objectives for particular ages in the HMI document *English from 5 to 16*.[9] These disputes are grounded in the nature of the subject.

English has a uniquely important role because it is concerned with those abilities (talking, listening, reading and writing) that are required for learning in all areas and for the whole of life, as well as being responsible for more limited applications than are 'subject specific'. English is the subject preeminently concerned with what it means to be a human being in relationship with other individuals, growing within a culture. By language we create the world that we need to know about, we come to know ourselves and others, we discover how to learn and how to make choices or judgements, and at the heart of these processes is responding to literature.

Because of its wider role, many other groups will have a legitimate interest in what takes place in English: parents, industrialists, managers, institutions of higher education, the media, politicians, curriculum theorists – and not forgetting the children themselves. Those interests will not always necessarily be helpful or enlightened, as the Inspectorate have discovered.[10] Problems can arise as soon as any of these groups attempt to translate the standards *they* value, *their* principles, into universal curricular objectives for any age, and particularly when it is proposed to measure the attainment of those objectives. A school's English curriculum has traditionally grown out of the ideas and the activities of a group of teachers with different experiences, values and expectations, trying to formulate a policy unique to their situation. That has now changed abruptly, with the coming of the National Curriculum and its assumption that all subjects can be codified and assessed according to the same pattern. The publication of *English in the National Curriculum*[11] marked an essentially managerial attempt to tidy up varieties of practice into coherent, if artificial, shape: four key stages, five attainment targets and ten levels of attainment. That publication is at its best when endorsing good practice in schools and offering practical examples of appropriate activities; it is at its worst when struggling to differentiate sequential levels of performance (five different ways of saying 'read a range of books', six ways of saying 'write in a variety of forms'). We are not concerned here to debate the concept of a National Curriculum and the methods of its implementation, but simply to consider how you can best live with it.

Don't panic at the sight of the yellow and white looseleaf folders, with their regular updating sections from the National Curriculum Council. Most experienced English teachers will tell you that the Cox Report, *English for Ages 5 to 16*, which almost unchanged became the statutory instrument, essentially proposed what good English departments had been doing for some time. The Cox committee were quite clear that the curriculum statement should be 'enabling rather than restricting...a starting point, not a straitjacket'. They did not believe that it was possible to 'formulate definitive and unchanging truths about what English teaching involves', because views have been constantly changing and will continue to change.[12] If you pay too much attention to the statutory framework, you may fall into one of two misconceptions: first that this is something quite new, that supersedes your existing knowledge and training, and second that it provides a clear and systematic syllabus which you simply have to follow. In fact, English remains uncertain, tentative and personal.

Some suggestions for approaching *English in the National Curriculum:*

1. Begin by reading the introductory chapters of the Cox committee's report, *English for Ages 5 to 16* (*not* the yellow pages of attainment targets, which the Secretary of State for Education insisted on having printed at the front) and underline those principles that you find most important.

2. Next, in the English Curriculum folder, look at the programmes for study for each of the major activities (speaking and listening, reading, writing with spelling and handwriting), concentrating on those of the four "key stages" that cover the pupils you are to teach, but not ignoring the others.

3. Then turn to the attainment targets themselves. A useful way of familiarising yourself with these and simultaneously assessing them is to cover the left-hand column (statements of attainment), read the right-hand column ('examples' of actual classroom work), and see to what extent you can predict from these what the statements say that 'pupils should be able to do'.

4. The scissors-and-paste stage. You may find that your training institution or school department has already done this for you. The ten-level statements need to be reorganized in two ways to be of practical help for teaching. First, you need to see together all the targets for each level, to see how far talking, writing and reading (together with "knowledge about language", which is subsumed in the others) hold together coherently. Second, each broad target can be broken down into subsidiary targets at each level (for example, reading can be divided for convenience into three related concerns: with the actual range of reading matter encountered, with increasingly discriminating expression of response and judgement and with growing literary awareness manifested in greater technical understanding).[13]

5. Look at the packs of "non-statutory guidance" issued by the National Curriculum Council to support the teaching of English in the National Curriculum.[14] These give helpful guidance on planning and resourcing programmes of work with some specific examples (eg on storytelling, folktales, taking photographs).

Looking at the English curriculum from the *teacher's* end, however, involves converting such generalizations about objectives and criteria into what has been called *experiential* (or *practical*) knowledge, realized in particular situations: knowledge that dictates how and why we behave in particular ways, make particular decisions.[15] Our young teachers were obviously dependent on a theoretical base: the literary awareness and the critical stances of their English degrees, the principles acquired in professional training (a repeated comment is: 'I'd completed my PGCE course convinced of the value of . . .'), the subsequent reading of books and journals, the meetings and conferences of *NATE* and other groups. But to be converted into practical knowledge, these ideas have to be modified, synthesized and – in some cases – abandoned.

A teacher's definition of the English curriculum will be personal, experiential and contextual. Each of these comes out clearly and repeatedly in the responses of young teachers. First they are conscious that their own personalities, educational experiences, literary preferences, social assumptions and so on condition the way in which they each bring curricular knowledge into being. In a wider sense, teaching is essentially a matter of personal encounters, and the teacher's self-awareness cannot be divorced from the understanding of learners: 'The situation in any classroom grows out of the interlocking perceptions that teacher and taught have of each other and of the task on which they are engaged.'[16] Teachers shape their approaches and materials to take account of their pupils' interests, expectations, abilities, attitudes, backgrounds, feelings, beliefs. Freema Elbaz has argued vigorously that the teacher's ultimate responsibility ought to be more widely acknowledged:

> The teacher confronts a classroom full of waiting human beings; ultimately, the psychological sense of responsibility for what happens to these students in the course of the day devolves upon the teacher. In the practical context it is the teacher, not the learning theorist, who is the final authority on learning; the teacher, not the sociologist, who is the final authority on the social development of children; the teacher, not the psychologist or artist, who is the final authority on the creativity of children; the teacher, not the scientist, who is the final authority on the science kids learn. Whether or not such authority is actually granted him, the teacher is the only one in a practical position to discharge it.[17]

Second, they become aware that developing experience – sometimes simple trial and error – changes their perception of appropriate objectives, approaches or structures. This may be as basic as awareness of the stage of the day, week or term ('Is it a wet Friday afternoon?') or expectations of particular activities, books and styles, leading towards tentative generalizations ('Usually a lesson which goes well is . . .').

Third, they learn rapidly about the particular constraints imposed by groups of children, by departmental organization, by the resources available and by the school's particular social structure. What do you think are the implications underlying this probationer's apparently dispassionate description?

> The timetable is completely arranged in single 40 minute periods for English, with five periods a week per class . . . Years 1–4 read two Shakespeare plays, 2 novels and poems each year, which adds up to three lessons a week, with two language lessons. The textbooks are *Art*

of English C1–C3, Smith's *New Syllabus Tests* and Rhodri Jones' GCE coursebook.

Particularly for young teachers, learning what is required for survival, what is perceived as being 'successful', what will and what will not be accepted by the hierarchy, is crucial. One describes the tensions aroused by a style of working new to the school (a drama module based on S. E. Hinton's *The Outsiders*) which came close to being 'initially banned by one of the deputy heads' but which eventually proved 'both successful and much enjoyed'.

Operating from such a background of practical knowledge, an English teacher will consciously or subconsciously define the English curriculum in terms of a model, a set of images, that will interlock with a series of other models: of the curriculum as a whole, of what are imagined as appropriate styles of teaching and learning, of group dynamics, of development, and of the teacher role.

Any current curricular thinking has to begin from these principles about language and learning that were put forward as widely agreed in *The Curriculum from 5 to 16* (Curriculum Matters, No. 2, 1985) and supported by 'degrees of accord' in the published responses. In brief, these suggested that:

1. Teachers should build on the language experience and skills that children possess on entering school.
2. The key principle for English is promoting the interaction of the four language modes (talking, listening, reading and writing).
3. Language competence develops by being applied to an increasing range of and variety of real needs, purposes and audiences, through which something of genuine interest is conveyed.
4. Meaning-making is aided when pupils and teachers are working collaboratively and sharing learning experiences.
5. The English teacher's role is complex and responsible because it is not concerned with the simple inculcation of skills, but with the organization of those language activities for real purposes from which those skills are acquired.
6. Few aspects of English can be mechanically marked, and formal language exercises have little or no effect on ability to use language.
7. Literature has a place at the heart of the English curriculum, and developing personal response to what is read is of crucial importance.
8. More attention needs to be given to the place of the spoken word in learning.

What follows is an attempt to build on these principles, and is structured according to those aspects detailed in the National Curriculum, with the reminder that it is the interaction of these, not their separation, that is important. In each section there is a brief, point-by-point summary of what we know about pupil performance. The lists are short and unelaborated, but aim to substitute reliable information – drawing on the work of Her Majesty's Inspectors, the Assessment of Performance Unit (APU), Schools Council and Schools Curriculum Development Council reports and research studies – for the vague and frequently inaccurate prejudices critically reviewed by Geoffrey Thornton.[18] In each case this is followed by an equally skeletal suggestion of some of the implications for a teacher's classroom strategies. These are amplified in the notes which refer to works in which fuller and more detailed guidance is given.

In approaching each section, you might find it interesting and helpful to ask yourself (before reading further):

1. What expectations do I have of children's abilities (in talking, listening, reading, writing or knowledge of language)?
2. On what evidence do I base my expectations?
3. What principles and practices do I think help children's development?

You can then compare your own views with those of others that are summarized here.

TALKING AND LISTENING

'In a world where speech is more important than writing in everyday communication it seems to me ludicrous that people are still trying to insist that pupils should be seen and not heard.' The heritage of such insistence can make it hard for young teachers who want to encourage purposeful talking: 'I'm building up the spoken word in the lower years but can't risk it with the third year and above unless there's half a class missing for some reason.' These two comments from young teachers encapsulate their concern for oracy and their awareness of potential difficulties in the classroom. Their concern is echoed by some of the experienced teachers who find themselves faced in the GCSE with a requirement for new modes of oral assessment.

What expectations can we have of pupils' oral capabilities as they enter secondary school? The tentative findings of the APU, based on the first two surveys in 1982–3, were that:

1. Most 11-year-olds can modify the ways in which they talk and listen appropriately for the particular purposes they are trying to achieve.
2. Girls and boys perform equally well in the majority of tasks (which is not true of writing).

3. The standard of performance varies according to the task (and, predictably, children of eleven are more successful at telling stories, describing, instructing and recapitulating than they are at speculating, hypothesizing, justifying an argument or evaluating evidence).
4. Oral and written abilities do not necessarily match (there seems to be a lower correlation between oracy and writing than between reading and writing).[19]

If we try to relate from the one side our teachers' classroom experiences and from the other 'official' publications like those from the APU and from HMI, what basic principles and related practices seem to emerge?

1. Talk needs to be seen as a collaborative way of getting things done. Although it will serve many different functions, those closest to the purposes for which children normally use talk in everyday life should take precedence in the early stages. (Activities like formal debates or speaking for 60 seconds on unprepared topics are likely to be seen as artificial as well as intimidating.) Because oral effectiveness is so dependent on context, unthreatening activities with an obvious point are particularly important.
2. Listening and talking should generally be inseparable, so the emphasis will be on reciprocal activities in which pupils are both talkers and listeners. This implies that most of the work will be done in pairs or small groups, so that:
   (a) everyone is actively engaged as rapidly as possible
   (b) everyone has a chance to talk more and more often
   (c) there is no intimidating, external audience
   (d) individuals do not get bored waiting for their 'turn'
   (e) disagreement without noise or quarrelling can be handled more easily than in larger groups.
3. Although most of the talking and listening will grow out of the regular, daily conduct of English lessons, some oral activities may have to be planned to aid realization that we have to adapt our way of speaking according to the different purposes and situations in which talking goes on. These may involve, for example:
   (a) telephone calls (dissatisfied customer and shopkeeper)
   (b) giving directions (how to get to . . ., how to play . . .)
   (c) autobiographical anecdotes (partner guessing whether true or false).
4. When starting out with classes unfamiliar with active methods, certain strategies are probably wise:
   (a) develop pair work before working with larger groups
   (b) use clear, simple tasks at which everyone can have some degree of success

(c) provide concrete materials to talk about: pictures, maps, newspaper headlines, interesting objects

(d) work to stated time limits, and keep the time short at first

(e) pre-arrange and rehearse a signal to stop the talking

(f) avoid role-playing activities until you are sure that you can control the class.

5. Situations should ideally be those which are essentially self-assessed or where there can be general feedback of what has been learned, rather than depending on the teacher as assessor:

(a) describing a picture to a partner who cannot see it

(b) describing a route to be followed on a shared map

(c) completing a story when one of a pair has the beginning, one the end, and the middle is missing.

6. Although it will clearly depend on the topic, normally move from straightforward description through extension and empathy towards speculation and hypothesis:

(a) describing pictures, before 'bringing alive' by using other senses, then imagining *yourself* there, then creating a story set in that place

(b) describing people's appearance before working out their personality and history, then imagining them talking in a given situation

(c) giving your own views on a controversial issue, before imagining yourself someone of the opposite conviction, then creating a situation in which the two might meet and argue.

7. Role-playing activities can be particularly lively and productive. Conflict situations, in which characters can only achieve their objectives through talk (and in which they are unaware at first of the other characters' intentions), seem particularly effective, but remember:

(a) these situations are noisier than other talk activities, and the larger the groups the more noise is generated

(b) to avoid reinforcing particular character traits it is necessary to give and rotate roles, rather than letting them be chosen

(c) it is easier to begin with situations where movement is not required or minimal (shopper, assistant and manager; family argument around table about where to go for holidays; neighbours visit to complain about rowdy youngsters).

8. Although the teacher's role is less demanding than it is when trying to handle whole-class discussion, it is also more complex. It demands abilities:

(a) to establish contexts in which talk seems natural and purposeful

(b) to initiate situations which demand increasing powers of talking and listening
(c) to prepare appropriate materials
(d) to organize the pairs or groups in which the work is to be done (and modify them as necessary)
(e) to ensure that they all understand the lines on which they are going to work, and that appropriate preparation time is provided when necessary
(f) to monitor the work as it goes forward
(g) to give additional stimulation or guidance where necessary (possibly intervening in role in dramatic situations)
(h) to be prepared with controlled or quietening situations in case of need
(i) to guide concluding discussions of what were perceived as difficulties, helpful strategies etc.[20]

READING

I realize even more just now how vital reading is and how very important the development of reading for pleasure must be. When parents ask me how they can help develop Fred's English, I always tell them to encourage reading as often as they can. It is so obvious from a piece of writing which child reads and which doesn't.

Although such an awareness of the importance of reading ran through many of the young teachers' responses, a surprising number of them felt the lack of any coherent departmental programme to develop response. 'The reading policy in the Department is one of its weaknesses', said one, 'and we need more class readers or sets of books for groups'. 'The English Department is rather diverse', said another, 'and we don't really have enough idea-swapping sessions. Members of the department seem to have different interests and these are reflected in the choice of books available.' 'The ideas of developing response to fiction tend to be difficult to put into practice', reported a third, complaining of the 'imposed structure' of texts to be studied, with 'regular tests and exams' and 'no emphasis on response or learning *how* to read'. Not surprisingly, 'How to teach to mixed-ability classes books such as first year *As You Like It*, third year *Great Expectations* is something I'm still working on! The best solution may be persuading the school to change the books.'

What expectations can we have about children's reading tastes and abilities? (The two go together: negative attitudes towards reading tend to be associated with poor reading performance.)

1. The overwhelming majority of children will come from primary schools reading (in the sense of decoding printed

words) and enjoying at least some of the material presented to them.

2. Fiction is overwhelmingly their preferred reading matter (over 90 per cent of primary children say they like reading stories, and over three-quarters of the voluntary reading of secondary pupils consists of narrative) and provides the strongest incentive to read. From the teacher's point of view, it is necessary to be aware that the ability to respond to stories is important *functionally* (because of the evidence that reading grows on reading, that it enables children to handle the non-spoken language and that it helps to make them better language users) and *developmentally* (because story making and story hearing are uniquely human activities, tools of thinking, that aid our understanding of what it means to be human, socialize us into a particular culture and help us to judge between different courses of action).

3. Nearly a third say that they wish that books were easier to read, and feel that the books given them in school are too difficult.

4. Almost all children prefer reading at home to reading at school, prefer reading silently to reading aloud and prefer the books they choose for themselves to those given them in school.

5. All other things being equal, girls tend to read rather more than boys and to have a greater preference for stories (as opposed to non-fiction).

6. Between the ages of 11 and 15 there is a serious overall decline in the amount of voluntary reading done, especially by boys.

7. A significant developmental spurt in the ability to respond to stories and poems occurs, on average, around the ages 13–14.

8. The widest range of preferred reading styles and levels of response is found in the third year of secondary schools (with consequent problems for book choice and teaching strategies during that year).

9. 'Successful' readers are marked by their willingness to revise first impressions of a text, their ability to pick out relevant clues pointing to likely outcomes, their capacity to see events in stories from the viewpoint of different characters, their ability to synthesize relevant information from a text into a coherent pattern of their own, and their responsiveness to effects beyond the superficial level of facts or events (irony or symbolism).

10. The perceptions of reading which pupils come to form, and their developing preferences (partly in response to cultural

pressures), can significantly affect not only their performance but also their subject choices in the third year (and
thus their future careers). The APU surveys suggest that
girls' interests are increasingly biased towards English
activities (away from maths and science) while boys move
in the opposite direction (away from the subject teachers
who might be able to encourage and guide their reading).
Barrie Wade has pointed out that the pictures of early
reading schemes conspire to show book-reading (and
especially story-reading) as an essentially female activity.[21]

In the light of these factors and of our teachers' comments,
what principles and practices seem likely to be helpful in an
English classroom and beyond it?

1. The active encouragement of children's reading for
   pleasure is crucial, not least because of the correlation
   between negative attitudes to books and poor reading
   performance, and because of the evidence of diminishing
   voluntary reading in the secondary years. This encouragement will probably involve:
   (a) provision of adequate timetable time for reading
   (b) a plentiful supply of appropriate books in class collec-
       tions as well as in the school library, and the oppor-
       tunity to take books home
   (c) guidance in book selection and teacher interest in what
       individuals are reading
   (d) attractive book displays, 'tasters' of available books,
       systems for pupils to recommend books, visits from
       authors and other kinds of publicity
   (e) a school bookshop or book club
   (f) regular reading aloud of stories to children in English
       lessons
   (g) involving the help of parents in encouraging their chil-
       dren to read
   (h) concern that children should encounter very different
       kinds of story, poetry and plays
   (i) demonstrating that teachers themselves value books
       and reading.

All of these points have been mentioned by some of our group
of teachers.

2. As we all create meaning from texts in terms of our
   existing knowledge – of life, of language, of books – books
   chosen for reading should be accessible to the readers in
   respect of each of those three kinds of knowledge.
3. Because meaning is something constructed by individual

readers in their transaction with the text, time and opportunity need to be given for children to formulate their responses to what they have read (by jotting, or talking to partners) before wider sharing or any search for 'the' meaning takes place.

4. Pupils are likely to be helped by collaborative activities that 'act out' externally those processes which successful readers do in their heads: predicting likely outcomes, picking out words that point to a particular conclusion, rehandling events from a different viewpoint, converting information from the text into a picture or diagram (particularly working in pairs or small groups).

5. Talking or writing about stories is a form of learned behaviour, with students progressively working out what sorts of information are seen as relevant. The teacher exercises a powerful control over these perceptions of what is appropriate (by choice of texts, methods of discussion, questions and written assignments, as well as by direct comments). English teachers need to take care, therefore, that pupils gain experience:
   (a) of a variety of texts of different kinds
   (b) of a range of different reading strategies
   (c) of different ways of exploring and responding to those texts (in performance, in imaginative writing, in rehandling from different viewpoints or for different genres, as well as more formally).

6. Children's reading capabilities need to be diagnosed by something more sophisticated than standardized reading tests. The APU Primary Report (1982) said that the appropriate question is not 'Can they read?' or even 'What can they read?', but 'What sort of sense are they making of what they read?' (What kinds of 'active' or 'passive' reading styles can they display? What levels of response are demonstrated? By what criteria do they judge stories or other materials?)

7. Because reading grows on reading, a department should try to formulate some policy that will encourage the progressive development of reading abilities, and govern different sequences:
   (a) of texts to be read
   (b) of approaches to be used
   (c) of activities in a lesson or group of lessons.
   Such a policy depends on having some developmental model of how children can come to grips with and enjoy increasingly difficult and demanding texts; the stages by which they seem to 'naturalize' (internalize) different literary conventions.

8. To be realistic, such a policy will also involve record-keeping:

   (a) of children's progressive mastery of reading abilities
   (b) of those with special needs, identifying their difficulties and the kinds of help to be offered
   (c) of pupils' individual reading, noting the development of interests, as the basis for discussion with the teacher.

9. We should try to avoid a sudden change in the books studied and in the approaches to them when students reach the fourth year (the broken-backed curriculum). The same methods of formulating personal response that were used in years 1–3 are equally valid in the fifth and sixth forms (and, equally, literary approaches – discovering how books work – should be used from the very beginning).

10. Conventional 'comprehension' exercises (a passage followed by sets of questions) are dangerous in a number of ways:

    (a) they take the attention away from reading
    (b) they are perceived as tests rather than pleasurable experiences
    (c) they suggest, falsely, that there is a 'right' meaning and that all readers should come up with the same answers
    (d) they provide a dangerous model of how to read for information
    (e) they are extremely inefficient ways of testing understanding
    (f) they emphasize solo competition rather than collaborative making of meaning.

    If you are concerned to develop children's ability to comprehend, use activities like labelling and underlining, reducing text to diagrams, group cloze (discussing which words would best fill blanks left in text), prediction and sequencing, retelling to partners, groups framing *their* questions, revising the text, etc.

11. In addition to their 'literary' reading, children should be guided in reading for information, understanding the format of reference books, discovering how to use the resources of school and public libraries. This guidance should be given while carrying out 'real' research tasks, not by artificial exercises in 'how to use reference books'.[22]

WRITING

It is hard but necessary to maintain a balance between the encouraging of accuracy of expression and clear comprehension on the one hand and enjoyment and the imagination on the other.

I have still to reconcile my desire to make all of my pupils more fluent, expressive and effective writers with the conviction that a certain degree of technical competence is a prerequisite. Why should I feel that such factors are irreconcilable? Teachers tend to become entrenched in their 'traditional' or 'trendy' beliefs to the extent of suggesting that writing sensitively and writing accurately are mutually exclusive.

Have you ever shared this either/or feeling, fostered in the *Black Papers*? The author of the second comment felt that the problem might have seemed exaggerated 'because the traditional v. progressive issue has been so conspicuous at my school. As well as attitudes to the pupils' writing, assessment and marking have also caused a great deal of controversy.' It is the *permanence* of writing that makes it the centre for such controversies, which can be particularly worrying for young teachers. Despite all the evidence of a wide and varied writing curriculum, one teacher in his first year could worry simultaneously that with one form he had 'perhaps not done enough of the more obviously imaginative work' and that with another he '*should* have done more "nuts and bolts" work'. English teachers should be conscientious, of course, but they must also avoid unreal expectations. What can they reasonably anticipate about pupils' writing in the secondary school?

1. Only about 3 per cent of secondary pupils are in 'great difficulty' with writing, and the great majority can produce writing that is both readable and interesting.
2. The range of ability in any class is likely to be very wide. (For a graphic impression of what this means, see the APU folder *How well can 15-year olds write?*) Children come to writing by different routes and at different speeds.
3. The amount and maturity of what is written by most pupils increase with age but not at an even rate. However, at the bottom of the performance range little development of writing skills may be shown between 11 and 15.
4. Girls, other things being equal, write more, have more positive attitudes towards writing and get higher grades than boys at 11 and at 15.
5. Students who are 'matched' in terms of background and measured ability can still vary widely in written performance according to the nature of the particular task and the teacher's attitude.
6. Pupils' own perceptions of their writing ability and how to improve it are in general heavily concerned with neatness and accuracy rather than with subject matter, style or appropriateness of function and audience.
7. The great majority of pupils see learning to write as one of the most important activities in school and enjoy at least some forms of writing (fictional narrative in particular,

followed by project work). Reading habits tend to correlate with preferences for written topics. Predictably, dislike of writing is chiefly associated with those with less ability, particularly boys.

8. The writing tasks mentioned by pupils as being particularly disliked include copying, dictation, punctuating passages and comprehension exercises.

9. Contrary to conventional prejudice, the chief weaknesses in children's work are *not* inaccuracies in spelling, punctuation and syntax, but are demonstrated in what is being said, the way in which it is organized and the appropriateness of the styles (especially the last in the case of 15-year-olds).[23]

English only accounts for a small proportion of the writing that children do in school, and English teachers also need to be aware of the overall picture. The impression conveyed in *The Secondary Survey* and in the work of the APU can be briefly summed up. Far from needing more practice, pupils in secondary schools actually do *too much* writing, but the bulk of it is of the wrong kind:

1. in borrowed language
2. without clear aims
3. inadequately prepared and revised
4. on artificial tasks
5. written not for a real audience but as a test of learning
6. on a restricted range of topics and lacking in variety of styles and approaches
7. brief rather than extended.

For a number of associated reasons, the act of writing in secondary school may come to have unattractive associations, especially for those who are not proficient:

1. It is a slow, hard process and provides a lasting record of mistakes and errors.
2. It is sometimes associated with discipline in a punitive sense.
3. The attitudes of adults rub off, and children rarely see parents or teachers writing for pleasure.
4. Particularly in the examination years, the tasks set for writing are perceived as almost uniformly dull.
5. Students believe that in general they are given no real guidance in what is expected of them or how they might improve their writing.

What principles and practices seem to be helpful?

1. Establishing a context in which successful writing is likely to occur, by:

(a) making it clear that children's writing is valued by reading it aloud, displaying it on walls, making up booklets and magazines, recording work on tape
(b) regularly hearing and reading models of effective writing, seeing authors' drafts, meeting authors when possible
(c) the teacher being seen to write and to share what is written
(d) the teacher being seen as helper in the creative process, not just the setter and marker of work.

2. Consciousness that your own half-aware values (linguistic preconceptions, models of 'good' writing, preferred teaching styles and materials) will affect not only your judgement of their work, but also the way in which children will learn to respond to your assignments.

3. Awareness that children can only learn to write by writing, and therefore encouragement for them to write frequently on as wide a range of subjects as possible, and progressively to extend that range. This should include opportunities to write in different poetic forms, note-making, report-writing and journal-keeping. As well as ensuring progression in writing assignments, there should be some monitoring of individuals' linguistic, stylistic and structural development.

4. Establishing a purpose for the writing; placing it in a context that means something to the pupil; indicating an audience (real or imaginary) to whom the writing is to be directed. As far as possible, writing should be done in 'real' situations first (where there are actual rather than imagined purposes and audiences).

5. Helping children to gain access to what it is they most want to say: by the supportive activities of the English classroom – shared talk, the reading of related stories and poems – and by guidance as needed *during* the writing process, discussing problems and providing appropriate materials. Pupils should be helped to see the differences between spoken and written English, and the implications of this for the writing they have to do. Teacher-set assignments should be given adequate specifications, to answer the unspoken questions:
(a) Why are we doing this?
(b) For whom are we supposed to be writing?
(c) What am I going to be judged by?

6. Reducing the 'overload' – the number of simultaneous demands that are made by the complex process of writing. To intervene in that process helpfully means temporarily to remove some of those requirements by emphasizing others. For example:
(a) concentrating on drafting and rewriting can lessen the

concern with transcribing skills of surface accuracy and structure in order to stress generating ideas and expressing them effectively

(b) concentrating on pre-planning and structure separates the need to generate material from the concern with *how* to present it.

7. Encouraging some extended writing to be done over a period of time, and permitting as far as possible some freedom of choice about where and when that writing is to be done.

8. Providing opportunities to revise and redraft work, working on it until the writer is satisfied, rather than insisting on success first time. Because *drafting* or *conferencing* (one-to-one discussion of the text with a teacher or another) are now becoming cult terms, it is necessary to add some provisos:

(a) redrafting seems to work better with some topics (records of personal experience or factual, explanatory pieces) than with others. Redrafting fictional narrative is rarely popular (perhaps because the story has no external existence to which reference can be made, apart from the words on the page)

(b) redrafting does not have to be a private affair between pupil and teacher. Good results can come from authors reading their work aloud to others (who can ask questions but not comment) or from working in pairs with each revising the *other*'s first draft.

9. Receiving the work supportively and constructively:

(a) responding as an interested reader to the work as a whole, concentrating on the intended function

(b) discerning the strengths revealed as a basis for future development

(c) proposing positively how the work might be improved rather than negatively what was wrong with it

(d) interacting by asking questions, to lead the writer to look more critically at the work

(e) establishing an order of priorities for those errors of expression which the pupil might reasonably be expected to correct at this stage.[24]

KNOWLEDGE ABOUT LANGUAGE

The curriculum document *English from 5 to 16* said with confidence that in addition to the aims for talking and listening, reading and writing, there was one 'which applies over all the modes of language'. This was: 'to teach pupils *about* language, so that they achieve a working knowledge of its structure and of the variety of ways in which meaning is made, so that they have a vocabulary for discussing it, so that they can use it with greater awareness, and because it is interesting'.[25] Reasonable expectations in this area are more debatable and harder to define than those for reading or writing. This proposal and the objectives based upon it 'prompted a good deal of disagreement and division'. The rationale was felt by many to be 'unjustified' or 'justified on weak grounds', and the *kind* of knowledge about language was widely thought to be inappropriate.

This dissatisfaction centred on the formulation 'working knowledge of its structure' and·on the related objectives (knowing 'the functions and names of the main parts of speech' and being able to identify them; being able to 'distinguish between sentence, clause and phrase'), which recalled for many teachers 'tedious and useless' activities in the past.[26]

Language study in the traditional sense of sequential lessons on the structure of English, through analytic and modelling exercises of the kind used in classics, in order to achieve mastery of 'standard' English, has long been thought dead (though some books based on this model still live on in schools). Teachers who were unwilling to return to this kind of work detected a difference in the way that this final aim was expressed. Unlike the other aims, which dealt with what pupils should learn, this one emphasized *teaching*. It specified knowledge *about* language rather than knowledge *of* language (rather like giving knowledge about *Macbeth* precedence over knowing the play itself). It talked in the vaguest terms about *knowledge of its structure* (as though there was some kind of agreement about what this meant instead of there being over fifty systems of parts of speech and 200 definitions of 'sentence'). Worst of all, it rested the case on a series of highly dubious assumptions:

1. The idea that language knowledge improves language use ('learning about language is necessary as a means to increasing one's ability to use it'). Neither the classroom experience of teachers nor the weight of research evidence justifies this claim. Indeed, the document itself admits that 'It has long been recognised that formal exercises in the analysis and classification of language contribute little or nothing to the ability to use it.'[27] Some graduate students still wrongly believe that 'without a fairly comprehensive grounding in vocabulary, grammar and sentence-construction no child will be able to communicate lucidly'. They are in danger of behaving like Howard Jacobson's art teacher, who declined to give children paints or crayons 'until they have fully mastered the fundamental theories of line,

harmony and perspective'.[28] In fact, despite the recurrent horrors of engineering professors and others that children cannot write or speak 'properly', the APU found that when they are assessed, 'pupils overwhelmingly use the grammatical forms typical of standard usage'.[29]

2. The idea that knowledge of grammatical terminology is necessary for understanding and correcting mistakes. ('Many pupils are taught nothing at all about how language works as a system, and consequently do not understand the nature of their mistakes or how to put them right.') Unfortunately those pupils who cannot be helped to understand the nature of their mistakes are precisely the ones who cannot acquire the grammatical concepts needed for that understanding. As one of our young teachers said, 'If they can't understand grammar when they're eleven or twelve, they won't understand it when they're sixteen, whether or not I spend hours or weeks teaching it.'

3. The idea that knowledge about language 'is interesting . . .' Of course, all knowledge is potentially interesting. Unfortunately, the *kinds* of knowledge in the lists of objectives do not seem to be those likely to be perceived as interesting by *pupils*. A different kind of knowledge (of which, more later) might well be seen as both interesting and useful. The judgement of the subject matter, summarized in *Responses*, was: 'As for what should be taught, either to teachers or pupils . . . there were no clear trends except for the widespread and vigorous rejection of grammatical analysis and of teaching the terminology listed in the objectives'.[30] Although the disappearance of formal grammar teaching from some schools has had its dangers (a lack of developmental sequence, perhaps, and a lessened regard for accuracy), it has become clear that sequential teaching of grammatical concepts to whole classes (as for a foreign language) is at odds with current understanding of individual language development. There seemed a tension in *English from 5 to 16* between the formal knowledge required in the *Objectives* and the practical knowledge proposed in the *Principles:* 'Learning about language is not an end in itself . . . It should arise from the activities of talking, listening, writing and reading for real purposes: and take the form of encouraging children's curiosity about language.'[31]

Fortunately the Cox committee moved on from the so-called teaching 'model' advanced in the Kingman Report to say firmly: 'We believe that knowledge about language should be an integral part of work in English, not a separate body of knowledge to be added on to the traditional English curriculum' (6.2). The emphasis of chapter six in *English for Ages 5 to 16* is on pupils' sensitivity to their own use of language and their awareness of its significance in social life. Such reflecting on language is surely a daily feature of all successful teaching of English. Despite the popularising of another acronym – KAL (Knowledge About Language) – and the proliferation of "cascade" model training courses, teachers generally remain uncertain about the overlapping kinds of knowledge that are appropriate for their work:

1. The implicit, experiential knowledge which all children have and the explicit, theoretical knowledge that classifies it.
2. The specific knowledge of mother-tongue language and the wider knowledge of language that can include second (and sometimes third) languages.
3. The analytical knowledge of language structures and the socio-linguistic knowledge of how language is used for different purposes in different contexts.
4. The knowledge that is perceived as appropriate for pupils and that which is thought necessary for their teachers.

You will need to adapt and update the following brief list of principles in the light of your personal experience and of developing knowledge in this field.

1. What we are studying is the language itself, in the variety of its manifestations, rather than facts *about* language. The *Language in Use* team defined their agenda as 'ways of thinking about language and its uses' relevant to students who are users of language and who already have an established (though possibly implicit) knowledge of how it works.[32] Themes which are likely to be important both for development in English and for learning across the curriculum include:
   (a) the differences between spoken and written language
   (b) the effects and appropriateness of different styles and registers
   (c) the ways in which languages are acquired and developed
   (d) the varieties of language ('standard' and 'non-standard', dialects, the multicultural classroom), possibly including consideration of whether there are gender differences in conversation.

2. The subject matter therefore includes:
   (a) the class's own language, spoken and written, including anecdotes and jokes
   (b) textbooks and library books in all parts of the curriculum
   (c) the language of rules, instructions and forms
   (d) television, radio, film, advertisements, newspapers, magazines – indeed, any authentic language from a specific context, rather than the 'artificial' language of exercises.
3. The study should grow out of the natural talking, writing and reading of the group rather than being introduced as a separate element for its 'own' sake. Two of the draft questions (as yet unpublished) which HMI felt schools might helpfully apply to their own practice were:

   How much time do the children spend on exercises and assignments from textbooks and work cards and for what purpose? Are these exercises relevant to the current needs of individual children as evinced in their own writing? Do exercises and drills ever exceed continuous prose?

   If skill exercises are set, do they relate to a diagnosis of particular pupils' needs, or are they set to whole classes regardless of individual differences? What is their weighting as against other kinds of writing?

4. Teachers need to be aware of what their own views and prejudices about language are, and to recognize that there is no simple agreement about which syntactical forms are 'right' or 'wrong'.[33] We have plenty of evidence that one teacher's error is acceptable to another, and that teachers generally exaggerate the seriousness of errors (rather than seeing them as the means by which we learn).
5. Evolving 'language awareness' programmes[34] in schools suggests that the most helpful emphasis is on active discussion and discovery of language features (establishing patterns and categories, analysing different ways of marking sense units and emphasis in speech and in writing, say) rather than presenting 'rules' or language as a body of knowledge to be 'learned'. By looking at a series of 'jokes' ('Paintings of nudes over seventy years old wanted' or 'Don't kill your wife with work – let electricity do it'), principles can be established more effectively than by talking of 'erroneous placing of adjectival phrase' or 'ambiguous use of pronoun'.
6. Structure and sequence should not be imposed by a pretence that the mother-tongue is being acquired like a second language (i.e. with step-by-step grammatical explication and exercises). It may be more helpful to identify the different

functions for which we use language (Halliday's model of seven purposes,[35] perhaps), to examine language used in one of these ways, to set up real or imaginary situations in which students themselves use language in this way, and then to extrapolate principles from these experiences, becoming aware of the meaning of terms like *appropriateness*, *register* or *cohesion*.

7. Observation and guidance should be directed towards pupils' linguistic *self*-improvement. In Geoffrey Thornton's terms, language activities should be intended 'to promote pupils' awareness of, and insight into, what is required to achieve successful performance; and, to increase thereby pupils' confidence in tackling new tasks'.[36]

8. In a society where many children are brought up speaking different first languages in different cultures, any examination of language should aim to increase understanding and tolerance towards other languages and language-users (as well as towards different modes, accents and dialects of English).

9. Accuracy and competence should come less by whole-class instruction (still less by testing and exercises) than by a continuing process of monitoring and guiding the work of individuals. This does not mean that teachers are incapable of devising interesting and effective work for whole classes. Two of our teachers claimed that 'certain mechanical skills can be taught with vitality and humour' and that 'designing ways of teaching construction and punctuation that are both informative and fun . . . seems to be paying dividends'. Unfortunately it seems that teaching 'mechanical skills' apart from an individual's real need to use them fails to transfer (apostrophes are used correctly in an exercise but not in subsequent free writing) and is only briefly remembered. Some general principles might include:
   (a) teach similar language forms together, not those that are likely to be confused (i.e. teach *it's* with *that's* and *what's* rather than with *its*; teach *there* with *where* and *here*, not with *their*)
   (b) work *from* actual examples (where possible from the children's own work) *towards* linguistic concepts (not the other way round), reinforcing them by models and practice.
   (c) if you want the class to add punctuation to unpunctuated work, use *spoken* language as the basis (since this genuinely has no punctuation until written down) rather than artificial print with punctuation removed. Preferably work on punctuating children's own writing (as in the real world we almost never punctuate some-

body else's)
(d) keep a simple check-list of the language capabilities which individuals reveal in their work, for diagnosis and help as needed. (see pp 171–5).
(e) encourage the keeping of personal spelling lists, and give regular brief occasions when students can work together in pairs.[37]

REFERENCES

1. Sikes Patricia J 1985 'The life cycle of the teacher' in Ball S J and Goodson I F *Teachers' Lives and Careers*. Falmer Press, p 35
2. Rosen Harold 1981 *Neither Bleak House nor Liberty Hall*. University of London Institute of Education, p 5
3. HMI 1986 *English from 5 to 16: the responses to curriculum matters 1*. DES, pp 1–3
4. Paffard Michael 1978 *Thinking about English*. Ward Lock, p 14
5. King Peter 1985 *Teaching English: a teaching skills workbook*. Macmillan
6. *English for Ages 5 to 16* 1989. DES, par 1.17
7. Ibid, pars 2.20–2.27
8. Grace Gerald 1978 *Teachers, Ideology and Control*. Routledge and Kegan Paul, 1970. Ball Stephen J 1982 'Competition and conflict in the teaching of English: a socio-historical analysis', *Journal of Curriculum Studies*, vol 14 no 1, p 1
9. *English from 5 to 16*, pp 1–3
10. Ibid, pars 5 and 6.
11. DES 1990 *English in the National Curriculum No 2*. HMSO
12. *English for Ages 5 to 16*, pars 2.3 and 2.5
13. See 'Cox by Strands' in the *English Magazine* no 22, Summer 1989, pp 42–5
14. *English non-statutory guidance* 1990. NCC, York
15. Elbaz Freema 1983 *Teacher Thinking*. Croom Helm, pp 3–5
16. Protherough Robert 1986 *Teaching Literature for Examinations*. Open University Press, p 16
17. Elbaz, *Teacher Thinking*. p 17
18. Thornton G 1986 *APU Language Testing 1979–1983*. DES
19. See MacLure Margaret and Hargreaves Mary 1986 *Speaking and Listening: Assessment at age 11*. APU, NFER/Nelson, Windsor
20. *Recommended reading on talking and listening*. **For general understanding**: Farb Peter 1975 *Word Play: what happens when people talk*. Bantam. Wilkinson Andrew *et al* 1990 *Spoken English Illuminated*. Open University Press. **Children's development of oral abilities**: Tough Joan 1979 *Talk for Teaching and Learning*. Ward Lock. **Studies in young people's talk**: Adelman Clem 1981 *Uttering, Muttering*. Grant McIntyre; Barnes Douglas and Todd Frankie 1977 *Communication and Learning in Small Groups*. Routledge; Rogers Sinclair 1976 *They Don't Speak our Language*. Edward Arnold. **Suggested classroom practices**: Brown Gillian 1983 *Teaching the Spoken Language*. Cambridge; Knowles Lewis 1983 *Encouraging Talk*. Methuen; Self David 1976 *Talk: a practical guide to oral work in the secondary school*. Ward Lock

21. Wade Barrie 1986 'A Picture of reading'; *Educational Review*. vol 38 no 1 pp 3–9
22. *Some recommended titles on reading*. **For general understanding of the reading process**: Smith Frank 1978 *Understanding Reading* (2nd edn). Holt Rinehart; Rosenblatt Louise 1978 *The Reader, the Text, the Poem*. South Illinois UP; particularly chapters 2 and 11 in Corcoran Bill and Evans Emrys 1987 *Readers, Texts, Teachers*; Hayhoe M and Parker S 1990 *Reading and Response*. Open University Press. **Considering children reading**: Applebee A N 1978 *The Child's Concept of Story*. Chicago UP; Fry Donald 1985 *Children Talk about Books*. Open University Press; Ingham Jennie, 1982 *Books and Reading Development*. Heinemann; Thomson Jack 1987 *Understanding Teenagers Reading*. Croom Helm. **Books in school**: Lunzer Eric and Gardner Keith 1979 *The Effective Use of Reading*. Heinemann; and 1984 *Learning from the Written Word*. Oliver and Boyd; Whitehead Frank *et al* 1977 *Children and their Books*. Macmillan; Foster John L 1977 *Reluctant to Read*? Ward Lock. **Working with literature**: Benton Mike and Fox Geoff 1985 *Teaching Literature 9–14*. Oxford; Hayhoe Mike and Parker Stephen 1984 *Working with Fiction*. Edward Arnold; Jackson David 1983 *Encounters with Books*. Methuen; Stibbs Andrew 1991 *Reading Narrative as Literature: Signs of Life*. Open University Press. **Teaching the reading of fiction**: Bolt S and Gard R 1970 *Teaching Fiction in Schools*. Hutchinson; Parker Elizabeth 1969 *Teaching the Reading of Fiction*. Columbia UP, New York; Protherough Robert 1983 *Developing Response to Fiction*. Open University Press. **Teaching poetry reading**: Benton Peter 1986 *Pupil, Teacher, Poem*. Hodder and Stoughton; Andrews Richard 1983 *Into Poetry*. Ward Lock and *The Problem with Poetry* 1991 Open University Press; Tunnicliffe Stephen 1984 *Poetry Experience*. Methuen; Dias P and Hayhoe M 1988 *Developing Response to Poetry*. Open University Press; Hayhoe M and Parker S 1989 *Words Large as Apples*. Cambridge
23. See White Janet 1986 *The Assessment of Writing; pupils aged 11 and 15*. APU, NFER/Nelson, Windsor, the reports of the SCDC *Writing* project
24. *Recommended reading about writing*. **General**: Smith Frank 1982 *Writers and Writing*. Heinemann Andrews Richard 1989 *Narrative and Argument*. Open University Press. **Ways of looking at children's writing**: Bretton Language Development Unit 1981 *A policy for writing 9–12*, pamphlets. Bretton Hall; Dixon John and Stratta Leslie 1986 *Writing Narrative and Beyond*. CCTE, Ottawa; Wilkinson Andrew 1986 *The Quality of Writing*. Open University Press. **Writing in the classroom**: Graves Donald 1983 *Writing: Teachers and Children at Work*. Heinemann; Harrison Bernard 1983 *Learning Through Writing*. NFER/Nelson; Medway Peter 1980 *Finding a Language*. Writers and Readers; Moffett James 1981 *Active Voice: a writing programme*. Boynton/Cook, USA; Thornton Geoffrey 1986 *Teaching Writing: the development of written language skills*. Edward Arnold. **Initiating writing**: Brownjohn Sandy 1980 *Does it have to rhyme*? Hodder and Stoughton; Styles Morag 1989 *Collaboration in Writing*. Open University Press; chapters 4–6 of Protherough Robert 1983 *Encouraging Writing*. Methuen. **Revising and responding to children's writing**: Andrews Richard and Noble J 1982 *From Rough to Best*. Ward

Lock; Cooper C R and Odell Lee 1977 *Evaluating Writing: describing, measuring, judging*. NCTE, Illinois; Dunsbee Tony and Ford T 1985 *Mark my Words*. Ward Lock; chapter 7 of Protherough Robert 1983 *Encouraging Writing*. Methuen; Stibbs Andrew 1979 *Assessing Children's Language*. Ward Lock

25. HMI 1984 *English from 5 to 16*. DES, par 1.6
26. *English from 5 to 16*, pars 3.7 and 4.5
27. *English from 5 to 16*, 3.8
28. Jacobson Howard 1986 *Redback*. Bantam Press, p 33
29. Thornton, *APU Language Testing*, p 27
30. *English from 5 to 16*, 3.9
31. *English from 5 to 16*, 3.7
32. Doughty Peter *et al* 1971 *Language in Use*. Edward Arnold, p 14
33. See Mittins W H 1970 *Attitudes to English Usage*. Oxford
34. See the NCLE Working Party report in *Newsletter*, no. 6, June 1986
35. Halliday M A K 1973 *Explorations in the Functions of Language*. E Arnold
36. Thornton, *APU Language Testing*, p 44
37. *Recommended reading on knowledge about language*. **General**: DES 1988 *The Kingman Report*. HMSO; Mittins, Bill 1991 *Language Awareness for Teachers*. Open University Press **Understanding children's development and use of language**: APU *Language Performance in Schools*. HMSO Surveys, 1982 onwards; Perera Kathleen 1984 *Children's Writing and Reading*. Blackwell, Oxford; Wells Gordon 1987 *the Meaning Makers*. Hodder and Stoughton. **Language in the classroom**: Barnes Douglas 1969 *Language, the Learner and the School*. Penguin; Chilver Peter 1982 *Learning a Language in the Classroom*. Oxford; Stubbs Michael 1976 *Language Schools and Classrooms*. Methuen. **Developing language awareness in English lessons**: Currie William B 1974 *New Directions in Teaching English Language*. Longman; Doughty Peter 1974 *Language, 'English' and the Curriculum*. Edward Arnold; Hawkins Eric 1984 *Awareness of Language: an introduction*. Cambridge; Moffett James 1968 *Teaching the Universe of Discourse*, Boston. **Improving accuracy**: Shaughnessy Mina 1977 *Errors and Expectations*. Oxford, New York; Smedley Don 1983 *Teaching the Basic Skills*. Methuen; Torbe Mike 1978 **Teaching Spelling**. Ward Lock. **Materials for use in language awareness lessons**: *Language in Use* thematic packs such as *Women and Men* or *About Teenagers*, pupils' booklets associated with *Awareness of Language* (see above), English Centre publications like *The Language Book* and *Writing*, the periodical *English Today*, McCrum *et al The Story of English*, courses like Michael Newby *Making Language*, Forsyth and Wood *Language and Communication*, or Richmond and Savva *Investigating our Language*

Planning the work

Faced with a new post, or a new school year, how do you set about preparing to teach in an as yet unknown situation? You will have a timetable on which your classes will appear as anonymous and oddly labelled groups, to be taught in rooms which may be unfamiliar to you. You will probably have received a document from the Head of Department and several lists of names, books and instructions which out of context may mean little to you.

This chapter will consider how, from this starting point, you might establish principles for planning work with the classes allocated to you, and how these principles can be put into action.

YOUR TIMETABLE

You should receive your timetable well before you begin to teach; if you don't get it well in advance, don't be afraid to ask for it. Remember that the individual timetable you receive is only part of the larger department timetable which, in its turn, forms part of the whole school's. You may find aspects of yours which dissatisfy you – a difficult fifth year group for the last two periods of Friday afternoon, a group of thirty-two in a small room, or only four periods instead of six with a Third Year – and it is important to see how planning like this comes about and why difficulties may sometimes be unavoidable.

Practice varies in different schools, but generally the whole school's timetable is the responsibility of one member of staff, perhaps the Deputy Head in charge of curriculum, who will consult the Head of English at an early stage about the department's particular preferences and problems, and about staffing for the following year. In the light of consultations across the departments and bearing in mind school policies for the whole curriculum, the timetabler will draw up a framework. At this stage Heads of Department are often brought back into the planning and are then responsible for staffing and rooming their department timetable. Departments are rarely completely satisfied with the final result, because issues which are important to them may have to give way to the larger concerns of whole-school policy. The following are examples of some of the factors which put constraints on timetabling for English:

1. Policy for time allocation to different subjects varies from school to school; provision of time for English can vary between two and eight 35-minute periods a week.
2. Double periods of 70–80 minutes are considered essential by many English departments, yet timetables may, for example, link English with Maths, the other non-option subject, which may demand single periods, so limiting English to the same arrangement.
3. The advantages of 'blocking' for English (that is, time-tabling a year or half a year at the same time) are considered later, but as blocking creates difficulties for overall time-tabling it is rarely completely achieved.
4. Very large or split-site schools add further complexity for timetables and may, for example, limit teachers to one site, or require them to move from one building to another between lessons and thus restrict the sequence of lessons that can be offered.
5. Allocation of non-teaching time varies greatly and the placing of 'free periods' may often be unsatisfactory (not uncommonly, for example, teachers have four of their six 'free periods' on the same day, leaving three days of the week without breaks).
6. Ideally, departments should be able to meet during the working day, particularly to moderate GCSE work, but in large schools it is rarely possible for the timetabler to free up to sixteen staff at the same time.
7. In schools where English 'suites' of rooms have not been established, specialist rooms for subjects such as Art, Science and CDT are often allocated first and 'non-specialist' subjects, such as Maths or English, last. This may mean that individual English teachers cannot work in their own room and, at worst, may have to teach some groups in a variety of different rooms (room provision for English is considered at greater length in Chapter 5).

In deciding on the final form of the English timetable, your Head of Department will have a series of further considerations to take into account. Each member of the department will have particular wishes, professional needs, strengths and weaknesses. It is the Head of Department's job to balance these in allocating groups to teachers. Most full-time staff will want and need to teach across the age and ability range. In schools where setting or banding takes place, there will need to be further decisions to ensure fair distribution, to give staff experience of different kinds of groups and to make best use of particular strengths with, for example, slow-learning pupils or students pursuing a chosen course for GCSE Literature. Not all staff will wish to teach A-level English, and the Head of Department will need to weigh up how to employ the different capabilities of those who do. In a young department, most of the staff will move on to other schools and their first few years of teaching should continue their professional training. In your first year, you *ought* to be given a special, lighter timetable, in accordance with government policy. No reasonable Head of Department will object if you ask for one – though whether you get it is another matter. Her Majesty's Inspectors say that to meet the dual demands of induction *and* probation requires 'a more flexible form of timetable than is normally provided, and a programme of teaching for the probationer which is to some extent differentiated in the course of the year'.[1] Indeed, they go on to suggest that perhaps a year's probation should *follow* a year's induction. At the moment, however, you are unlikely to be offered a timetable which offers regular opportunity for team-teaching, observation and consultation, and which gradually increases the amount of teaching as the year goes on. In fact, HMI record that over a third of schools 'appear to expect too much of newly trained teachers'.[2]

Despite the assertion of government policy, that 'Teachers in their first posts need, and should be released part-time to profit from a systematic programme of professional initiation and guidance, and further study where necessary',[3] you are unlikely to find that your teaching load is significantly lighter than that of others on the basic scale, and very unlikely to be released part-time for further study. At the time of the *Secondary Survey*, probationers had virtually the same teaching load as other assistant teachers, and financial pressures have ensured that the tripling of the release rate planned in 1972 has never materialized.[4] For staff in stable departments from which there is little movement, the timetable needs to widen teaching experience and provide challenges which will provoke/inspire teachers to re-think their ideas.

In deploying staff, the Head of Department is also responsible for meeting the needs of particular classes and individual pupils. The department will have to discuss (for example) how best to meet the special needs of particular children: they may perhaps decide to take advantage of blocking by merging seven mixed-ability groups into six and releasing a teacher to work with pupils on difficulties with writing or as adviser for GCSE Literature pupils working on wider reading assignments. The Head of Department will also need to provide in the timetable teaching for pupils in small groups, such as those preparing for Oxbridge exams or following a CPVE course.

If you have only been given your own timetable, try to discover at an early stage how it relates to the rest of the department. In particular, discover whether English is 'blocked', i.e. whether a whole year or, in large schools, half a year is timetabled for English at the same time. You will find this organization has many advantages for you as a new member of the department. It provides the opportunity for you to plan programmes with colleagues and to follow this up with team-teaching. During your first year it may be comforting to know that more experienced colleagues are taking parallel groups at the same time; you will be able to share similar problems but also sometimes have positive help with difficult pupils. Sharing resources is also more easily organized, and discussion about rotas, book boxes, library periods and class novels will draw you into the team of staff assigned to each block.

Before you begin to plan your programme of work it is worth studying your timetable to try to assess how it might affect your teaching. Look for days which may be tiring because you have very different groups and no non-teaching periods, and for the relationship between homework times and your marking programme. In planning you may need to assign at least one double period each week during your fullest day to activities that will conserve your energy, perhaps individual reading. You may be teaching parallel groups, two mixed-ability second year classes, for example. Consider whether it might be useful to prepare the same scheme for both, so cutting down on preparation but also using the opportunity to evaluate how differently composed groups react to the same material. If you are working in a split-site school, think through beforehand the implications for class control and organization of resources at times in the week when you change sites in the course of a day. As rooms and resources are so important, find out about the rooms you have been given and take into account any particular features which might affect your teaching; for example, storage facilities, whether the furniture is suitable for group work, how far you will have to walk to the stockroom or whether the room is big enough for the group.

HOW DEPARTMENTAL POLICY STATEMENTS CAN HELP YOUR PLANNING

When you receive your timetable you will probably also be given a department document called *English Department Syllabus* or *Scheme of Work* or *Guidelines*. There has been a reaction against the old-style syllabus which prescribed books, topics for writing and grammatical concepts to be learnt for each half term. In its place have come documents with more tentative titles which sometimes confine themselves to giving information about department organization or which express general aims without necessarily suggesting how they can be put into practice. A special kind of reading is required if your study of a school syllabus or policy statement is to be fruitful. Remember that this document was not written just for *you*. Its peculiar nature is explained by the fact that it has simultaneously to achieve different functions for different readers. Such a paper will be designed to impress the head with the importance of English and its need for resources, to indicate to the advisory services that the department is up to date, to remind members of the department of consensus achieved in meetings or the findings of working groups, and – increasingly – to satisfy the demands of the National Curriculum and its assessment. This does not mean that you will not find such a document helpful, but that you need to read it critically – perhaps marking those passages that raise questions in your mind. It is particularly helpful if you can make a comparison with similar documents from other schools (compare notes with friends, or those with whom you trained).

To take a simple example, consider the formulation of aims (or objectives, or goals) which normally comes at the beginning of any such statement. You can learn a good deal about the department by looking beneath the surface of the bland prose. A study of some twenty such documents suggests that you might, for example, consider:

1. The sequence in which aims are presented (do they start, 'to teach basic skills'?).
2. The emphasis of dominant verbs (*train* and *instil*, or *teach* and *ensure*, or *encourage* and *develop*?).
3. The stated purpose for education in English (to reach certain *standards*, success in *examinations*, for *work*, *leisure* and *citizenship* – all suggesting the *future* – or to fulfil children's potential *now*?).
4. The force of the metaphors ('language is a tool', 'ability to handle language', 'provide in-depth language experience' or 'broaden their imaginative horizons', 'stimulate the imagination', 'develop imaginative power'.
5. The extent to which the aims are seen as absolutely to be achieved, as developmental processes, or to be realized in children marked by certain qualities.

The evidence from new teachers suggests that those documents seen as helpful are marked by some of the following qualities:

1. Expressing principles which are shared by the department, which have been agreed upon and which (you will discover) inform their teaching.

2. Written by several members of the department, not just by the Head of English.
3. Describing characteristics of development in different aspects of English so that your work with particular year groups can be seen in perspective.
4. Describing the kinds of activities and listing the books the department has agreed are appropriate for different age groups.
5. Outlining approaches to structuring schemes of work and giving examples of department practice.
6. Including explanations of department policy for marking, GCSE organization, class libraries etc.
7. Including up-to-date information about departmental organization.
8. Showing evidence that the document is kept up-to-date, has been modified through use and is in a usable form, perhaps loose-leaf.
9. Giving an insight into the approaches and teaching methods which are characteristic of the department.

A good document should give you a sense of the 'feel' or atmosphere of the department, which will help you to anticipate what the pupils will expect of English lessons and teachers.

What do you do if you are presented with a syllabus, course outline or book allocation and find yourself unhappy with it? Before doing anything, you need to be clear in your mind about:

1. Precisely what it is that you are objecting to, why you object, and how strong that objection is.
2. The extent to which you can yourself modify what makes you unhappy without adversely affecting anyone else.
3. Whether your feelings need to be discussed with others and, if so, how.

Your reservations may be about points of detail or about major items of department policy. Young teachers have objected, for example, to 'teaching' parts of speech to First Years, to using *The Chocolate War* with Third Years, to the regular use of standardized reading tests and to the organization of a school's English programme into six-monthly thematic units (myself, family and friends, etc.). In each case they have to face the fact that they are objecting to a decision made by other, experienced teachers. Are their convictions strong enough to enable them to ignore or to challenge those decisions? It will usually be possible to substitute one book for another, it is not too difficult to adapt teaching methods so that concepts like *noun* and *verb* can emerge from practical work, but if the whole department works thematically then the most that can reasonably be done is to supplement the theme with whatever other activities seem to have been squeezed out. If convictions are so strong (about reading tests, say) that the probationer feels unable to support established policy, then there are stages through which those convictions can be shared and considered: talking informally with colleagues; discussing the matter with the Head of Department; raising it formally for debate at a departmental meeting: making the criticism in written form (which may go beyond the department). However, you should guard against the idea that the strength of your convictions is itself a necessary argument in favour of your case. In any department it is necessary at times for individuals to modify their views in the movement towards consensus. Ultimately, if you cannot accept this, then the only answer is to look for a post elsewhere.

FIRST APPROACHES TO PLANNING

Embarking on plans for work with each of your teaching groups is the next stage. Although you will know from previous experience that plans have to be modified in the light of your growing knowledge of your classes, it is still important to have a clear idea of what you want to do.

Before starting to plan more systematically, it is generally helpful to jot down roughly some of the ingredients that will later be brought together in your recipe for a particular group. It is particularly helpful if you can talk about this while doing it with a more experienced colleague, so that it becomes a brainstorming activity. You may want to consider some of these questions:

1. What learning processes and experiences are going to be particularly important for this group this year?
2. What materials are going to be especially useful?
3. What topics need to be introduced?
4. What assignments are going to be essential?
5. What key considerations and constraints are going to shape my planning for this group?

Avoid being too systematic at this stage. Identifying a book you very much want to use may lead to ideas for a thematic unit and that in turn to projects that the group might carry out; or the associative process may be the reverse of this, starting from an activity and working towards supporting stories, poems and audio-visual materials. If you want to see examples of some ways in which experienced teachers rough out their preliminary ideas, look at *Best Laid Plans*.[5]

One young teacher describes his general approach to planning in this way: 'I make a general plan of my intentions for a half term with all my teaching groups. I invariably depart from my plan, but it is a source of comfort at the beginning of another demanding bout of teaching. I make more specific and detailed plans every weekend for the following week.' Apart from the importance of providing the 'comfort' this young teacher recognizes, it is essential to take a long-term view of planning. In taking an overall look at a term or half a term it is possible to see how the pupils can be presented with a balance of the different English activities and it enables you, and the pupils, to be aware of progress. Planning in blocks or units avoids a wearing and directionless succession of one-off lessons, and although it requires initial time and effort, it conserves your energy in the long run because each week is a continuation from the last rather than a fresh start. If you work in a department in which shared sets and materials can be booked in advance, long-term planning is essential for the system to succeed.

Making the 'more specific and detailed plans' within each block of work is probably best done near to the lessons themselves so that you can modify your ideas after you have seen how they have 'gone' in the classroom. Some teachers feel that each week of English lessons should follow a similar pattern – a structure for teaching considered in more detail later. They feel that pupils work best when they have a routine. Although this may be true, a strict pattern of this kind has many disadvantages both for the pupils and for you. One young teacher sees it from both sides: 'I desperately try to avoid a set routine – this has disadvantages in that pupils are more likely to forget books etc., but it does preserve my sanity and usually pupils are eager to find out what the activity will be.' Apart from some regular sessions, which will be considered later, it is valuable to give pupils variety, but more importantly, if you wish them to progress through a unit of work, individual lessons should serve your overall plan rather than a weekly routine.

As an example, here is the outline of a unit of work:

Time: 2 weeks covering six 75-minute periods
Class: Fifth Year GCSE

Lesson 1:	Class read *The Pedestrian* by Ray Bradbury
	Discussion of how to film the story
	Pairs begin work on their filming plans
Lesson 2:	Pairs complete work
	Each pair gives brief presentation of ideas to the class
	Class discussion of findings
Homework:	Each pair reads two other short stories; suggestions:
	The Rain Horse, Ted Hughes
	Jamie, Jack Bennett

Fever Dream, Ray Bradbury
There Will Come Soft Rains, Ray Bradbury
The Wedge-Tailed Eagle, Geoffrey Dutton
The Landlady, Roald Dahl
Lesson 3: Pairs discuss which story to use for filming
Pairs begin work on planning with guiding
worksheet
Lessons 4, 5, Pairs continue and complete write-up of filming
6: plans
Pairs mount display
Homework: Individuals continue own reading and spend
time on GCSE journals

HOW TO GIVE STRUCTURE TO SCHEMES OF WORK

Aims and objectives

Whatever pattern you decide to adopt for your schemes of work
you will always need to begin by expressing for yourself what in
a general way you *aim* that your pupils should achieve – at first
during the whole year, then through a block of work within the
year and, finally, what your shorter term and more precise *objectives* are for each lesson within a block. When you are teaching
to a demanding timetable and have a heavy marking load, it
might be tempting to save time on this part of planning. Articu-
lating aims and objectives requires more strenuous thought than
the listing of activities and resources, but without this underpin-
ning schemes and lessons will lack direction and purpose. One
teacher, after returning to her career, looks back in dissatisfaction to this aspect of her first years in school: 'In the 60s I was
never encouraged to think out ultimate aims and reasons for my
pieces of work. Looking back, I would have liked to be pushed
much harder to think about why and how I was teaching as I
was.' As she recognizes, teaching can only be thoroughly effective if during planning you think about 'why and how'. A teacher
of two years' experience has discovered this from practice: 'I'm
a great believer in having something down in writing, deciding
the purpose of each lesson forces me to think clearly. I also ask
myself what I want the pupils to gain from the lesson.' Both these
teachers, in their use of the phrases 'pushed much harder to
think' and 'forces me to think', express the sense that framing
aims and objectives requires strenuous thought, but that the
effort is essential.

Here, as an example, are the general aims and more precise
objectives which underlay the fortnight's block of work on
filming short stories which was outlined in more detail at the end
of the previous section.

Class: Fifth Year   *Time*: Six 75-minute lessons
Aims: for pupils:
    To read three very different short stories
    As part of the year's work on looking at the structure of
    stories, to consider how events are narrated and how the
    world of the story is established, using the activity of
    adaptation to a different medium
    To deepen understanding of structure through discussion
    To explore through activity the filming of narrative
    To find language and visual forms to express ideas to
    others
    To continue ongoing novel-reading and journal-writing

Activities	*Objectives*
Lesson 1: Whole class read *The Pedestrian*. Class discussion builds up ideas of how to film the story. Pairs begin to create their filming plans	1. Whole class to discover how to set about looking at storyline and atmosphere through adaptation for filming by working on the same short story. 2. Whole class to begin considering the techniques of filming narrative.
Lesson 2: Pairs complete work. Each pair gives brief presentation of ideas to the class. Follow-up class discussion of findings	1. Through reading out and listening to each other's ideas, to discover possibilities of different interpretation through adaptation.
Lesson 3: Pairs read two other short stories. Pairs discuss which story to film. Pairs begin planning with guiding worksheet	1. To discuss and come to a decision about the suitability of a story for film adaptation. 2. To work together to agree on the overall plans for adaptation. 3. To take individual responsibility for communicating parts of the plan to readers.
Lessons 4, 5, 6: Pairs continue and complete write-up of filming plans. Pairs mount display. Individuals continue reading and spend time with Journals (GCSE)	1. To collaborate on producing 'public' explanation of filming ideas. 2. To give time and opportunity for continued individual reading and reflection.

PLANNING A YEAR'S WORK

Although this is not always a realistic proposition, it is valuable
to begin thinking about a new class with a long-range view of

what you hope to achieve with them. Planning in outline for the whole year gives you the opportunity to build in progression, for example, in introducing a highly structured thematic block in the first term followed later in the year by theme work requiring greater pupil selection and organization; you can choose class novels which make progressively greater reading demands. Seeing the year in perspective also allows you to plan the balance between different aspects of English, ensuring, for example, that poetry appears frequently and that drama sessions grow out of or into the rest of the English programme.

PLANNING A YEAR'S WORK IN ENGLISH FOR A FIRST YEAR CLASS

Autumn term

Week
1. ⎱ *The Family* guided writing with choice allowing the
2. ⎰ teacher to get to know individual children.
3. Group work–poetry reading and performance.
4. *Our animals*–teacher-guided thematic block.
5. ⎫ Individual writing, poems and short stories read
6. ⎬ and written, group reading and talk (planning
7. ⎭ zoos), drama.
8.
9. ⎱ *The Battle of Bubble and Squeak* by Philippa Pearce
10. ⎰ – shared novel and activities.
11. ⎱ Writing a long story in 3/4 chapters, plot mixing
12. ⎰ reality and fantasy. Structured writing at length.
13. ⎱ *A Christmas Carol* by Charles Dickens – reading
14. ⎰ and drama; picking up the idea of reality/fantasy.

Spring term

Week
1. ⎱ Group work – projects designed and presented for
2. ⎰ using wasteland in a town.
3. ⎱ Myself – thematic block of self-chosen work, based
4. ⎰ on ILEA English Centre booklet.
5. ⎱ Individual writing, reading poems and autobio-
6. ⎰ graphical writing.
7. ⎱ *The Turbulent Term of Tyke Tiler* by Gene Kemp
8. ⎰ – shared novel and activities.
9. ⎱ Short stories with surprise endings, e.g. *Boys will*
10. ⎰ *be boys* (in *Mischief Makers*) – reading and talking.
11. Group script-writing for taping – 'surprise' plots.
12. Individual/group work on changing fairy stories.

Summer term

Week 1. Group composition of booklets for feeder primary
2. school – 'Moving to . . . . School'. Writing
3. for an audience – explanation, instruction, enter-
4. tainment, reporting on personal experience and
opinion.

5. Reading and writing poems – looking at different
6. shapes, playing with words.

7. *Tuck Everlasting* Natalie Babbitt – shared novel
8. and activities.
9.

10. Writing a long story in chapters.
11. Adventure/quest/journey structure.
12. Looking back at the year.

Activities continuing throughout the year

Individual reading
Students making entries in their reading journals or diaries
Regular individual follow-up work on technical aspects of written
work.

POSSIBLE STRUCTURES FOR UNITS OF WORK

You may find yourself teaching in a department which suggests
or imposes the content and structure you should give to your
schemes. Some may work exclusively through themes, so that the
whole department will take the First Year through, for example,
'Myself' linked with a relevant novel in the autumn term,
'Animals' in the spring term and 'Mystery and Adventure' in the
summer. Others may issue particular sets of books for each term,
the situation discovered by this young teacher: 'I cover certain
set books for twice yearly school exams in January and July. The
language work for each class I have based on the text books *Art
of English*. It's useful but can be repetitive.'

For many English teachers, however, no structure is imposed
and they will need to make decisions for themselves about how
best to give shape to their work.

You will find it helpful before you begin to remind yourself of
the nature of the different 'jigsaw pieces' – the lessons – that will
go together to make up whatever schemes you adopt. Individual
lessons will have different characters because they serve different
purposes. In broad terms, they are of three kinds:

1. Key lessons:
   (a) a lead lesson to launch a theme

(b) a self-contained drama lesson
(c) a self-contained simulation
(d) reading a short story with follow-up activities.
2. Work in progress:
   (a) reading an instalment of a shared novel
   (b) individuals working on extended pieces of writing
   (c) individuals pursuing chosen programmes of work as part of a theme
   (d) groups working on a shared project.
3. Pupils' lessons:
   (a) reading chosen novels
   (b) poetry 'read-ins'
   (c) writing journals
   (d) working on pupils' own projects.

Discussion of the four most commonly used structures for English through which you will bring these different kinds of lessons together may help you to give direction to your long-term plans for your classes.

Lesson by lesson

Describing the structure

In this method of planning, each lesson is seen as a discrete unit, perhaps concentrating on a particular English activity. Some teachers choose to match each lesson to a particular period in a weekly or fortnightly cycle, for example:

Tues.	Class novel
Wed.	Comprehension and related writing
Fri.	Oral work
Tues.	Class novel
Wed.	Writing
Fri.	Drama or oral work

Why teachers choose this way of structuring work

1. Each lesson can be a satisfying whole in itself.
2. It avoids too many potentially untidy 'carrying on' and 'finishing off' sessions.
3. If the lessons form part of a regular cycle, pupils can adopt an organized attitude to their responsibilities in bringing books and materials, meeting homework deadlines etc.
4. Self-contained lessons can be used for important on-going activities which might be overlooked if not given a regular 'slot'.

The problems you need to be aware of

1. It is difficult to give pupils a sense of progress if lessons are not linked.
2. As the different elements of English are interdependent, self-contained lessons, particularly if devoted to discrete activities, can make artificial divisions.
3. Self-contained lessons do not allow for pupils' very different work speeds, particularly when you are teaching a mixed-ability group.
4. Both at the planning stage and in practice it is more energy-consuming to see each lesson separately rather than as a part of a sequence.
5. If the self-contained lessons form part of a regular cycle, the routine may become tedious rather than helpful for the pupils and rigid for the teacher.

Planning

At its most extreme, planning lesson by lesson can produce the following kind of pattern, taken from a departmental syllabus:

From an autumn term's programme in English

1 Sep.	Phrases and sentences (e.g. 'As cold as ice' is a . . .)
3 Sep.	Idioms ('They fought tooth and . . . to repel the invader')
8 Sep.	Sentences ('In spite of his tiredness he could not . . .). Choice from list
8 Sep.	Comprehension
10 Sep.	Common mistakes Vocabulary ('New College is a . . .') ('Dr Spooner was a . . . of his college')
15 Sep.	Comprehension
17 Sep.	Letters (copying a model; painting a house). Proper and common nouns (Plymouth, plumber)
22 Sep.	Letters. Another model

More profitably, you could combine the use of individual lessons as separate units with the longer-term blocks described later. In this way you ensure that two important elements of your English programme are included: (1) regular time for on-going activities, and (2) space for unexpected 'one-offs' which are a response to a particular situation.

1. (a) a lesson once a week or fortnight for individual reading of books from the class or school library, perhaps accompanied by times for recording responses in reading journals

(b) a lesson once in a while (perhaps once a month) spent reading poems, e.g. individuals browsing through a selection of anthologies before choosing one poem to read to their group, or the class; groups choosing a poem to rehearse, then perform to the class: individuals choosing one poem to learn, one to turn into a poetry poster, one to read out, one to write about

(c) a lesson, or pair of lessons, which needs no link with a longer programme and focuses pupils' attention on work you consider important at a particular stage in their development, e.g. intensive writing from observation; experimenting with particular kinds of poetry-writing; precise spoken explanation

(d) a lesson in the drama room on a regular basis if you teach in a large school in which the drama facilities have to be shared through a rota

(e) a lesson once a half term, or term, in which pupils take stock of their own progress – read back through their writing, bring reading lists up-to-date, swap reading suggestions, help each other with spelling lists, look back through reading or self-assessment journals, write their own reports.

2. (a) a lesson of talk and follow-up work after a striking/impressive programme watched the night before

(b) a lesson of talk and writing in response to a news item which has aroused emotion in the class

(c) a lesson of activities in response to an event in school, e.g. announcement of a radical change which will affect the class; visit by a writer or local celebrity; a pupil's unusual experience

(d) a lesson in response to an unexpected event, e.g. going outside to experience then write about thick fog; having a lesson in a chemistry laboratory because of heating failure in the usual classroom

(e) a lesson growing out of a suggestion which seems too good to miss, e.g. making up inventions for a television children's programme competition; writing letters as part of a scheme or competition.

Thematic units

Describing the structure

Lessons are linked together by activities designed to explore a chosen theme. The theme itself will be wide and unspecific (e.g.

the sea; growing up; the world of work) to allow for pupils to read, write and talk about it in many diverse ways.

Many young teachers find themselves in departments which employ this method of structuring work: 'We all work through thematic blocks in the department and this enables us to plan far in advance and to compare ideas and methods.'

Why teachers choose this way of structuring work

1. The exploration of a theme gives a sense of continuity and purpose for pupils which a series of self-contained lessons cannot give.
2. As a way of organizing a sequence of English activities, it allows the teacher to plan a balanced variety of work linked by the common theme.
3. As pupils will explore the theme through talking, reading and writing, this structure promotes the interrelation of the different aspects of English.
4. Because this structure allows for extended spans of working time, it gives space for pupils to work at different speeds.
5. This way of organizing work is particularly valuable with mixed-ability groups as activities and resources can provide for a variety of different individual needs, yet at the same time the group as a whole is united in its exploration of the subject.
6. Pupils are given the opportunity in reading to compare how different writers interpret different aspects of the theme, and in writing to discover the various forms and styles they can use to explore the theme themselves.
7. In departments in which individual teachers make up their own programmes of work, they have the opportunity to choose a theme to match the particular character or needs of a class, or of a time of year, or of a current pre-occupation.
8. In schools in which departments work together both to plan and to team-teach, thematic units are particularly valuable: at the planning stage, collaboration can build up a wide range of ideas and resources; and in practice, teachers can draw on particular strengths and interests.

The problems you need to be aware of

1. Unless the theme itself is chosen thoughtfully for a particular age range, with the needs of a single-sex or mixed class in mind, and for the character of a particular class, it may fail to engage some pupils' interest and you may feel

that detailed and time-consuming preparation has been wasted.

2. You need to be committed to and genuinely interested in the chosen theme yourself as you will be devoting considerable time to planning and teaching it. (If you feel unhappy about the choice of theme imposed by a department, follow the suggestions made earlier in the chapter.)

3. In searching for appropriate resources during planning there is a temptation to choose written material because its subject matter is relevant rather than for its merits as a piece of writing. At its worst this can mean that pupils are presented with a series of extracts from literature, rather than with complete stories, plays and poems, and are encouraged to respond only to one aspect of the complex of meanings which is the subject matter rather than to the writing's whole impact on the reader.

4. For a unit of this kind to be a success, you need to spend considerable time and energy on preparations:

   (a) to provide both for teacher-directed key lessons and for pupil-chosen activities, you need to find and prepare a wide range of effective resources

   (b) for pupil-chosen work you need to compose and produce worksheets

   (c) to ensure the smooth running of the unit you need to organize well ahead the help you will need from outside agencies, e.g. block loans of relevant books from libraries; arrangements for pupils' trips and for visiting speakers; bookings for tapes, the video recorder, the drama room, computer and software

   (d) to ensure the success of the unit in the classroom you need to plan how the room will be used, e.g. where pupils will find resources, store work in progress, tape group scripts, give in finished work for marking; and how sessions of pupil-chosen activity will be organized, e.g. how pupils will be guided in choosing, how they and you will keep records of individual work programmes and of assignments completed, how homework will be used, how you will deal with different finishing times, how you will organize both individual and group work at the same time.

Planning

Unlike the two kinds of planning units described in the following two sections, thematic blocks are difficult to time at the planning stage because:

1. With a big element of pupil choice, the success of the unit will be partially dictated by the involvement and enthusiasm of the pupils, which is always unpredictable – they may ask for and need more time than you had planned, or equally the work may soon lose its momentum and need drawing to a close or 'feeding' through a key lesson with the whole class to focus and rechannel interest.

2. There is a difficult balance between giving enough and too much time to pupils' on-going work. You may underestimate how long, for example, a group script and taping will take but, equally, if you give too long the activity will lose its momentum if the pupils have no sense of a deadline.

3. The unit may lose a sense of cohesion for the whole class, so it may need sessions for individuals and groups to report back and/or perform their work, and it will certainly need end products to be completed for a given deadline so that pupils know what they are working towards, e.g. a class wall display, playback of tapes, performance of plays and readings of stories and poems.

It is, therefore, important to remember that your allocations of time at the planning stage will need to be modified in the light of practice.

To consider in more detail how a block of thematic work might be planned, here is a particular theme as an example:[6]

'Adventure' with a First Year class

First ideas

As described on page 61, the first stage is to 'brainstorm' or jot down everything relevant to your aims for the unit, to the activities you will plan for the pupils and to the resources you will collect together.

Your first jottings might look like this,

Aims	*Activities*	*Resources*
Remembering own adventures.	Play on tape with sound effects. Maps.	Pictures.
Creating new ones.	Writing log books/	Scott/Amundsen diaries etc.
Thinking about why people go on adventures.	diaries of explorers. Reading adventure fiction and factual	*The Stone Book, Odysseus, Treasure Island.*
Reading about them.	accounts. Reading and writing adven-	Short stories: *Power, The Tree, Proudly*
Employing a range of writing styles.	ture poems. Exploration	*My Son, The World's Highest Tray Cloth*
Exploring ideas through talk and drama.	through drama. Stories of own adventures.	etc. Poems: *Breathless, Ancient Mariner, Boy*

Aims	*Activities*	*Resources*
		on top of a Green-house etc.
		Tape of sound effects.
		Video of play or exploration
		Software programme.

Starting to give the unit shape

These are the kinds of questions you will need to ask yourself in drawing up plans (answered in this case with the decisions made for the 'Adventure' theme):

1. What will be your general aims for this unit?
   (a) for pupils to create or re-create stories of adventure in writing and acting
   (b) for pupils to think about and discuss ideas raised by the theme
   (c) for pupils to compare fictional and factual accounts of adventures.
2. What kinds of activities will the pupils be involved in? Individual only? Individual and group? Group only? Self-chosen? Teacher-directed? Both?

   'Adventure' is the first thematic block for this First Year class, so half the time will be spent on teacher-directed activities (arising from key lessons) and half in self-chosen activities with teacher guidance. There will be both individual and group work.
3. How will you ensure that a balance between different activities is achieved?

   Teacher-directed lessons will involve reading, talking, writing, drama. Three worksheets will be designed for (1) writing stories and poems; (2) explaining things; and (3) working together; and pupils will be directed to choose at least one from each sheet. An 'Adventure' book box will be used throughout the unit for individual reading.
4. What will the end-products be?

   Display? Individual folders of work? Tapes or perform-ances? Wider publication? Display of poems, comic strips, travel logs, maps etc.? Individual folders? Tapes and performances?
5. How long should it last?

   Teacher-directed block: 3 weeks or 9 double lessons. Pupil-directed block: 2 weeks but may need to be 1 week longer, i.e. the unit would then last for half a term.

Drawing up a 'map' of the unit

In brief outline, this is the way activities are matched to lessons for 'Adventure', with comments on implications for resources and classroom organization when they are raised during planning.

Lessons	Resources	Organization
Week One		
Lesson 1		
Lead lesson: Drama room	*The Hobbit*	Book the drama room
Pupils listen to teacher reading account of exploring Gollum's cave from *The Hobbit* and to tape of underground sound effects	Tape recorder Tape from school resource centre	
Pupils explore a cave to repeated sound effect tape. Groups build up cave exploration, accident and rescue		
Lesson 2 Talking/writing from lead lesson – individual assignment		Writing to be finished for homework
Lesson 3: Groups of 3/4 are explorers about to set out on a voyage; they have: list of equipment from which they can take only five items; a map with two alternative routes; a deadline by which they must make their first report. Group make decisions about equipment and route and collaborate in writing first report which is then read out to the class	Make up worksheet	Room arranged for group work. Insist on deadline for finishing report. Room rearranged for class report-back

Lessons	*Resources*	*Organization*
Week Two		
Lesson 4: Teacher reads short story to class: *Proudly My Son* by E. A. Gollschewsky (in *Story – the second book*, Penguin). Pairs consider elements of the story, e.g. structure, relationship to their own experience, through various activities	*Story – the second book* Follow-up activities written up on the board	
Lesson 5: Teacher reads the Polyphemus story from *The Odyssey*. Pairs work to consider the story, e.g. comparing two 'heroes' in the two stories. Individual work to present one of the stories in comic strip form	Duplicated copies of Polyphemus story	Comic strips to be finished for homework
Lesson 6: Teacher introduces books in 'Adventure' library. Individuals choose, read and check out their book so that it can be taken home	Book box – made up from school and local library sources	Organize library borrowing system
Week Three		
Lesson 7: Drama room. Groups build up dramatization of Polyphemus story		Book the drama room
Lesson 8: Groups of 3/4 read several poems linked to the theme before	Anthologies and list of suggestions on the board	Room arranged for group work and rearranged for performance

Lessons	Resources	Organization
choosing one to rehearse and perform		
Lesson 9: Teacher introduces and explains the use of the worksheets. Pupils begin work on first chosen assignments. Three worksheets build on work already done in previous key lessons, e.g. writing a suspenseful story; writing poem to suggest fear, physical excitement; carrying on with travel logs and maps from Lesson 3: reading other Odysseus stories followed by maps, re-writing, scripts	Three worksheets with open-ended assignments expressed in direct terms so that all pupils can begin work without needing to consult the teacher. Box of pictures, books, objects referred to in worksheets. Tape recorders and blank tapes	Routine established for collecting and replacing resources and work in progress. Folder on teacher's table for completed writing. Routine established of pupils noting down their intended programme and having it checked, and of recording work completed. Teacher recording work completed to keep track of individuals. Routine established of pupils indicating which parts of their work are done for homework. Teacher assessing how to organize group and individual work – either combining both or creating some individual and some group sessions. Teacher ensuring that individuals continue private reading
Weeks Four and Five *Lessons 10 to 15* (or longer if necessary): Continuing with individual and group work. As concluding key lesson, listening to tapes, performances, short stories	Near the end of these sessions: card, glue, scissors etc. for folders and displays	

Lessons	*Resources*	*Organization*

and reading displays and folders.

Throughout these sessions the 'Adventure' library is available. Each pupil should have read at least one complete book by the end of the unit and recorded impressions as part of the final individual folder

Topic-based units

Describing the structure

While the subjects for thematic units are wide and general to allow for a diversity of activities, the subjects for topic-based blocks are more focused and particular, e.g. writing a group newspaper; introducing the school through group booklets to pupils of the same age in a different area; looking at dialects; studying stereotypes in advertising; writing a desert island diary. The nature and scope of assignments will also be different. During a theme, individual pupils will complete several pieces of work (which are different in kind): during a topic they will probably complete for themselves, or contribute to, a single 'product' like a newspaper, a tape, a survey or a debate. Group collaboration towards a final 'product' is frequently an important part of a topic. One young teacher describes work of this kind that he has planned and organized:

The project (which lasts on and off for a whole year) involves a fictional village 'somewhere in England' . . . every child takes a character in the village and keeps the character throughout . . . describe places of work, homelife, typical working day etc. . . . we have had a bonfire night celebration and will be having sections on Christmas and some incident at sea . . . next term will see some historical work, the castle, the village in the plague, the haunted house. . . .

Why teachers choose this way of structuring work

1. Like thematic units, topics give a sense of continuity and purpose to pupils.

2. The elements of English are interrelated in the pupils' activities.

3. Activities typical of topic work, such as problem-solving, decision-making and interviewing, promote purposeful oral work and collaboration.

4. There are opportunities for pupils to use language for real purposes as in oral work (e.g. to persuade or explain a case) and in writing (e.g. to inform or argue).

5. Collaborating towards a group end-product provides the double audience of group members and teacher, which can stimulate pupils to produce their best work and encourages drafting and proof-reading.

6. Topic work, like theme work, is particularly effective with mixed-ability classes because it can call on a range of skills including those not traditionally 'academic', for example, leading a group; keeping a check on progress; interviewing: working on tapes; taking photographs. Through group collaboration, it also provides opportunities for pupils to learn from each other.

7. For the teacher, keeping control over the progress of a topic can be simpler than it is with a theme because the activities are less diverse, pupils are working in a more closely defined area and often in similar ways.

The problems you need to be aware of

1. In common with theme work, topics need careful preparation if they are to be successful:
   (a) in preparing resources you need to find or create good source material – remembering particularly that much factual writing will be too demanding for weak readers; if questionnaires are used to elicit information they need to be carefully framed; instructions on worksheets need to be clear and unambiguous
   (b) you will need to contact sources of information such as libraries, travel agents, Citizens' Advice Bureaux well in advance; set up interviews with relevant people; organize trips and audio-visual resources such as tape recorders and cameras
   (c) as with theme work, you will need to think ahead about the implications for classroom management.

2. As topic work is often carried out in groups, you will need to consider how to form them so that members will work effectively together.

3. If groups are to collaborate towards a shared end-product, you will need to be prepared to check that jobs have been chosen or allocated fairly and appropriately.

4. If the extracting and summarizing of material from research

is to be part of topic work, you will need to supervise and help pupils who find this difficult and take refuge in copying out material word for word; you might introduce activities which demonstrate the necessary skills within work on the topic.

5. It may be difficult to check on and assess individual progress during a topic when the 'product' is not necessarily readable and markable work.

6. You need to decide beforehand how homework can be used during the unit:

    (a) for group work done in class there may not be a profitable link with homework, and other tasks should be set

    (b) during individual extended writing, e.g. novel in several chapters, detective's diary, it may be difficult to check what writing has been done at home.

Planning

To consider how a block of work of this kind might be planned, here is a particular topic as an example:[7]

'The Burnet Park Development' with a Fourth Year class

First ideas

As the content and pupil activities involved in a topic are precise, your first thoughts in planning will be affected by the nature of your particular group and the stage they are at during the year and in your overall programme for them. For example, if a Second Year group have worked on a desert island diary using the Avon Resources Booklet in the spring term, you might want them to try a different extended writing structure in a topic during the summer term such as '*Running Away* – a long story in chapters'. Or, if a Fourth Year group have taken part in a media topic comparing different newspapers' presentation of the same events during the autumn term, you might want them in the spring term to put their findings into action through a topic in which they report on an event they experience, in different journalistic styles. This example from the Fourth Year was the thinking behind the 'Burnet Park' topic and the next stage was to jot down possible ideas for the 'happening' which pupils would later report on. In the end, an article in *The Observer* provided the final idea – of considering the effects of commuter belt building on a small village community.

Drawing up a 'map' of the unit

It is possible to move straight from your first jottings to building up the outline of the unit because, unlike a theme which requires so much material and involves so many different activities for the pupils, the structure of a topic is usually sequential and requires less organization.

The *aims* of the 'Burnet Park' topic were for pupils to:

1. Create an event through the simulation of a public hearing.
2. Extract information relevant to the presenting of a case.
3. Present opinions and argue a case in writing and speaking.
4. Order material in writing for the purpose of informing and reporting with the needs of particular newspaper readers in mind.
5. Consider differences between newspaper and television reporting.

Lessons	*Resources*	*Organization*
Week One		
Lesson 1: Each pupil given (1) fact sheet, (2) character card	Prepare and duplicate factsheet and character cards	Prepare resources
(1) Factsheet shows plans to turn a quiet village within commuting distance of London into a 'township'. Developers claim to be respecting the environment in planning to extend a National Trust property and grounds into a public park, build marina on the river etc		
(2) Character cards are all different and give brief details of people involved, e.g. farmer eager to sell his land, representatives from Ministry of Environment, lady novelist who has chosen to live in the village etc: (a) each pupil to		

Lessons	*Resources*	*Organization*
prepare speech expressing character's views on plans; (b) pairs to draw up a poster from one point of view – to display before the hearing		
Lesson 2: Teacher presides as impartial chair over public hearing – each pupil makes a speech in role, general debate and vote to decide whether the development should go ahead		Room arranged for hearing
Lesson 3: Pairs, in turn, interview each other in the roles of journalist and character from previous hearing. Individuals begin work on two articles: (1) For the local newspaper two weeks before the hearing, a report of the Burnet Park proposals with maps and comments from the developers (2) For the local newspaper dated the day after the hearing, a report of the meeting and its outcome, including extracts from the previous interview	Copy of the school's local newspaper to remind class of layout, headline use and style	Room rearranged to allow interviews. Arrange for pairs who are not friends, to give formality to the situation. Writing to be completed for homework

Lessons	Resources	Organization
Week Two		
Lesson 4: Work on newspaper reports		Second half of writing completed for homework
Lesson 5: Teacher explains that dispute has continued despite decision of the hearing. Groups of five/six to prepare a 5- to 10-minute slot for local or national news programme on television, about the continuing Burnet Park debate – decide on 'ingredients', write and rehearse	Suggested 'ingredients' of programme on the board	Arrange room for group work. Think about the composition of the working groups
Lesson 6: Preparation and rehearsal		
Week Three		
Lesson 7: Performance and follow-up discussion		Arrange room with performance space

Book-based units

Describing the structure

A block of lessons is devoted to shared reading of a novel, a play or several linked short stories or poems, or a combination of these. Before, during and after the reading, pupils will work alone or together on activities to help them to respond to what they read and to express their responses in a variety of forms.

From the evidence of students and young teachers, this kind of structure plays an important part in their planning: 'I tend always to work to some extent round a novel or class reader'.

Why teachers choose this way of structuring work

1. As most books are stories, concentrating on them intensively allows pupils to behave like 'real readers' or 'a real

audience' in 'finding out what happens next' as soon as possible; whereas reading books in instalments over a long
period of time artificially holds up the narrative and risks
losing the pupils' interest.

2. Despite the breaks between lessons caused by secondary
school timetables, concentration on the shared experience
of a book can generate the kind of enthusiasm in pupils
which leads them into living in the world of the book.

3. The richness of the subject matter and form of books can
lead pupils into related enquiries, related writing of their
own, related creation in other media and related reading,
so that, although reading and responding are at the heart
of the unit, the other elements of English are also brought
into the activity.

The problems you need to be aware of

1. As you and the class will be spending several weeks with
the book, it is important, if you have the opportunity to do
this, to choose thoughtfully and not just take what is in the
stockroom, e.g. how does the book serve your overall plan
for the pupils' development as readers? Will it suit the age,
sex and character of the class?

2. You will need to give thought to the process of reading the
book, e.g. who will read it? Will you supplement live
reading with tape or television adaptation? How long will
reading last during a lesson? Will the pupils read any of the
book silently for themselves? If so, when? And how will you
cater for weak readers? Will you read the whole book or
will you select?

3. Books 'spark off' so many related English activities that you
risk the books becoming merely springboards; it will be
important at the planning stage to have priorities sorted out
– activities eliciting and enhancing response come first,
followed by other directions suggested to you and the pupils
by the book.

4. If you intend to introduce activities during the reading of
the book you will need to do some preliminary work to
divide it up into what seem the most natural phases of
narrative.

5. In common with thematic and topic units, book units need
careful preparation, particularly if you are going to build
pupil choice into the planning of activities:
   (a) if you are going to watch television adaptations, use the
   drama room, invite speakers, recommend related
   reading, tape radio versions etc., arrangements and
   bookings need to be made well ahead

    (b) you may want to prepare worksheets and related
        resources

    (c) the timing of the unit may be difficult – if you spend
        too long with a book you risk the 'overkill' which may
        destroy pupils' enthusiasm.

Planning

To consider how a block of work on a book might be planned,
here is a particular example of a unit built around a novel[8].

The Machine Gunners with a Third Year class

First ideas
In jotting down first ideas you will want to consider what is
particular about your chosen book as you work towards
expressing your aims for the unit. *The Machine Gunners* has
many interesting features: Chas' growing up during the novel; the
children's developing attitudes to each other and to Rudi the
German pilot; the presentation of violence; the role of Audrey;
the gradual breakdown of the community; the mixture of excitement and fear. It is also important to attempt to foresee problems
with the book: *The Machine Gunners* might not appeal to girls
in a mixed class, and although the narrative is generally taut it
seems to lose momentum just before its conclusion and might,
therefore, lose some readers' attention. In beginning to consider
what the pupils should do, *The Machine Gunners* suggests that
there should be plenty of talk to bring out issues; activities which
require empathy with and evaluation of characters and their
behaviour as well as related work on what it was like to live
during the Second World War.

Starting to give the unit shape
In firming up your first ideas, it may be helpful to ask yourself
the following questions. They are answered by the decisions
made in relation to *The Machine Gunners*.

1. What will be your general aims for this unit? For pupils to
   enjoy the novel and enter into the world of the book; to
   empathise with but also to look objectively at the chief
   characters and their actions; to form a picture of the world
   created in the book; to become aware of the narrative shape
   of the book.

2. How will the book be read? Teacher will read it aloud to
   pupils who have their own copies, because it reads out well.
   Some sections will be summarized, e.g. the passage about
   the Polish soldiers near the end. Pupils who are good
   readers will sometimes take the parts of main characters.
   Sometimes reading aloud will last for a whole lesson as the

novel is 'gripping' – sometimes half or whole lessons will be
spent in related activities.

3. How will you achieve a balance of activities? There is a
   temptation with this novel for pupils to do too much
   'Second World War research' – so local memories will only
   be tapped before and after reading. Majority of activities
   will take pupils back to the book.
4. How will the book be divided up? The novel divides
   naturally into about five 'instalments' without breaking the
   flow of the story.
5. What resources will you need to prepare? Pupils will need
   warning that there will be a Second World War exhibition
   at the end of the unit so that they can begin interviewing
   and collecting.

Pupils will be given a workbook for use throughout the unit
giving instructions for activities.

Drawing up a 'map' of the unit
This is how activities could be matched to lessons in a unit based
on *The Machine Gunners*. Remember that timing may have to
be modified as you go along because reading out loud sometimes
takes more, or less, time than you anticipate.

Lessons	*Resources*	*Organization*
Week One		
Lesson 1: To prepare for reading: visiting speaker already known to the class describes her childhood during the Second World War in Hull. Pupils ask questions. Teacher and visitor share in reading Chapter 1	Give pupils notice of exhibition in four weeks' time – suggestions for collections and research	Arrangements of class in informal clusters round speaker
Lesson 2: Teacher, with pupils reading parts, continues to end of Chapter 6		
Lesson 3: Each pupil given work booklet. Activity 1: to write an account of a		

Lessons	Resources	Organization
1940 air raid as though it were happening to the pupil's family – half the lesson.		
Activity 2: groups of four talk about Chas's and Boddser's fight, using guide questions	Work booklets outlining activities and addressed to the pupils	Complete writing for homework Rearrange room for group talk

Week Two
Lesson 4: Read Chapter 7.

		Record impressions and thoughts so far in reading journals for homework

Activity 3: individual drawing of the fortress from the description
Lesson 5: Read to the end of Chapter 10.

Activity 4: groups of four talk from questions, e.g. about first impressions of Rudi, of Chas' reasons for building fortress etc. – referring back to comments in journals

		Rearrange room for group talk

Lesson 6: In drama room. Preliminary work.
Activity 5: groups choose scenes from story so far and build up during lesson, e.g. Chas, Cem and Audrey meet Fatty Hardy by the wood; police sergeant inquiring at McGill house

Lessons	Resources	Organization
Week Three		
Lesson 7: Read to the end of Chapter 13.		
Activity 6: to write Clogger's account of the fight with Boddser, including his thoughts about Chas's part in it		Complete writing for homework
Lesson 8: Read to the end of the novel (selecting parts from Chapters 16 and 17).		
Activity 7: individuals jot down responses to the ending in reading journals – then in groups, share thoughts and feelings		Rearrange room for group talk
Lesson 9: Individuals to choose one assignment from three: (1) four or five extracts from Chas or Audrey's diary; (2) sequel to the novel – immediate, or set at the end of the war; (3) long lead article with detailed interviews about the fortress and Rudi – for the Garmouth paper. Groups to choose one assignment from three: (1) adapt a scene for radio, rehearse and tape; (2) research Second	Resource box of newspaper cuttings, library books, objects etc for group activity	Organize furniture when it is clear how pupils have decided to work

Lessons	Resources	Organization
World War in Hull; present display, comparing with Garmouth during the war; (3) present filming plans for a half-hour instalment of the novel adapted as a television serial. Pupils to decide for themselves on the order of their work		

Week Four

| Lessons 10, 11, 12: Continue and complete two assignments. Pupils given booklists of related reading suggestions | Provide tape recorders, tapes, video camera, paper. *Lesson 12*: remind pupils to bring in contributions to exhibition | Work on assignment for homework

Organize storage of work in progress, materials etc. |

Week Five

| Lesson 13: Put up exhibition of work and Second World War research for visit from feeder primary school classes | | |

MATCHING SCHEMES OF WORK TO CLASSES

When you sit down to plan schemes of work before a new job or a new school year you are to a certain extent planning in a vacuum. For example, 3W1 will be a labelled group of people whose names will probably be listed for you, but about whom you will know little. You may have been able to read departmental records about each individual and to talk about the pupils and the nature of the group as a whole with their previous teacher. Even so, until you meet the class for yourself you cannot be sure that work you have planned for them will be effective. This means that you must always be prepared to adapt and modify, or abandon, plans if you discover they are inappropriate to the pupils once you know them.

This has implications for your plans for the first few weeks with any new group. As the main priority is to get to know the 'feel' of the class and the particular abilities and needs of individual pupils, it will be important to make a variety of demands on them which will help you to assess them and then to evaluate your projected plans for the group. Try in the first two or three weeks to put pupils in situations in which they can do a piece of extended writing, take part in group talk, read aloud or take part in an activity to test their abilities to understand what they read and to talk briefly in front of the rest of the class.

Another way of ensuring that your schemes will match your class is to discover details of their work programme for the previous year. This may be unnecessary in schools which have set programmes of work for English (although it is still worth checking that the previous teacher followed the programme), but when departments have the policy of individual teacher autonomy it is essential that records should be passed on from year to year. On a visit to the school try to talk to the teacher as well as asking for a written record of books read, themes and topics covered and subjects for extended writing. After a consultation like this you should avoid the demoralizing experience of introducing a cherished book to cries of 'We've done it, sir'. (Other reasons for joining in liaison discussion of this kind are considered in Chapter 7.)

Preparing work for a mixed-ability class will add another dimension to your planning.[9] Although you will be thinking about a particular group, the fact that it is made up of a heterogeneous collection of very different children needs to affect the way you plan. These are some of the considerations you should take into account when you plan programmes for mixed-ability classes:

1. Whole-class lessons should form a small part of the total unit.
2. When tasks are framed for individual work and, perhaps, written down on worksheets, you need to decide whether they should be:
   (a) open-ended for interpretation at a variety of different levels
   (b) precisely targeted to individuals or
   (c) aimed at a group of similar ability within the class.
3. In preparing resources you will need to find written material to match different reading abilities.
4. The importance of timing units to allow for different working speeds is heightened.

5. Units should contain spells of extended individual or group activity to give you the opportunity to move round the classroom working with different pupils.

Bringing the pupils into the planning

After you have spent time creating a scheme of work and collecting exciting resources, and have invested energy in launching it, it can be frustrating when the lessons are not as effective in practice as you had hoped and you feel the need to make radical changes or even abandon the whole unit. Conversely, it is often exciting and challenging when you feel the need to modify your plans because the pupils' reactions have led the work in directions you did not anticipate. It is important to be prepared to adapt plans, for whatever reason, as this new teacher discovered: 'I plan my lessons carefully but I depart from the plan quite often. On T.P. I tended to feel that something had gone wrong if I hadn't been able to follow my plan.' Or to make this a positive feature of your approach, as this teacher has done: 'Although planning work in advance, I try to be sufficiently open-minded to change mid-stream or accept a lead from the pupils as to where the future lessons go.' You might find it valuable to read an experienced teacher's description of modifying original plans in *Continuity in Secondary English* (Methuen, 1982, pp 23–36). David Jackson gives an account of the ways in which his class's responses transformed their work together on Betsy Byars' *The Midnight Fox*.

Once you recognize the value and importance of the 'consumers' ' contribution it will begin to change your practice. Teacher and pupils will work together to direct their learning. The following sequence of quotations may help to show how attitudes to giving pupils responsibility can shift. The first three statements come from young teachers, and the last two from more experienced staff:

I always like the pupils to be aware of what they will be doing during the week rather than coming to lessons in a cloud of uncertainty.

I have found it essential to plan well in advance but to keep 'avenues' open to avoid too rigid a plan and help flexibility. I also ask the pupils to think of things that they would like to do in a particular topic. This helps to give the class the feeling that they have some say in what they are learning.

I now ask them what they've gained at the end of the lesson.

You must allow children to function as autonomous and independent people – we seriously undervalue pupils in schools.

We negotiated – 'Have we done enough of this or can we usefully go further? What can we look at next?'

The author of the first statement has realized the importance of informing pupils of the teacher's plans so that they can be aware of the direction lessons are taking and in a position to think about the aims and processes of their own learning. The second teacher is prepared to take the further step of bringing pupils into the planning, of asking them 'to think of things that they would like to do in a particular topic'. However, the final sentence of the statement expresses a young teacher's doubts about giving a genuine share of responsibility to pupils – they will be given 'the *feeling* that they have some say'. The third statement represents a more decisive step of confidence for a new teacher. In inviting pupils to make spoken or written comment on what they consider they have learnt from a lesson, the teacher is encouraging pupils to look responsibly and critically at their own performance and be aware of the progress of their own learning. This requires confidence because the pupils will, in assessing themselves, necessarily also be assessing the teacher's lesson. That this requires bravery from a new teacher is suggested in another comment: 'I've never dared to ask *them* what they think they've learnt.' The two more experienced teachers are able to speak from observation and knowledge, and show recognition that children are people with potential to take a responsible and independent share in their own learning. The teacher's role is then to create situations in which that potential can be realized. As the final teacher writes, in describing a drama lesson, she 'negotiated' with the pupils, bringing them into active collaboration with her in deciding what course the lesson and later sessions would take.

Experienced teachers, however, would not give a large share of responsibility to pupils at the beginning of their time with a new class. For teachers and pupils to share in determining the course that learning will take, they need to trust each other and trust grows from knowledge. It will only be when you know a class well that you can move from thinking of schemes of work as 'yours' to considering them as 'ours'. These are some of the steps you might take in training a new class to take responsibility for themselves:

1. In framing tasks, give choices whenever possible, and/or give hints or guidelines from which pupils can move to create for themselves.
2. In some situations when you give assignments for writing, or tasks related to reading, or instructions for group work, add the invitation for individuals or groups to work on their own alternative ideas after first explaining and checking them out with you.
3. In whole-class talk, learn quickly to recognize 'red herrings', but if a genuine 'new lead' is introduced be prepared to

extend the time you have planned for talking, perhaps showing the pupils how their ideas have opened up the discussion and changed your mind.

4. During sessions of work-in-progress, e.g. during a thematic block, ensure that individual pupils' 'projections of work to be done' become genuine consultation points with you and are not a meaningless routine.

5. Encourage pupils to be responsible for their own progress in, for example, spelling, by ensuring that personal spelling lists are kept up-to-date and are regularly used for testing with classmates or at home.

6. In writing comments on written work, ask pupils questions about their writing and encourage them to write answers which will explain, for example, why they made a particular decision about a story.

7. At the beginning of a year (or a term), establish regular use, perhaps weekly or fortnightly, of a 'self-assessment journal'. However, give pupils guidelines so that you guard against it becoming a channel for moans, or fulsome praise, about lessons, for example: 'You could write about: new ideas you have had, new ways of writing you have tried, your experiences in talking in your group or in front of the class, reading a new book, changes in your attitudes to spelling/poems/acting etc., your opinion of what you have achieved in a lesson or piece of work, what you hope/intend to do in following lessons.'

LOOKING FORWARDS AND LOOKING BACKWARDS

Anticipating problems

Lesson plans are 'imaginative rehearsals' of what will happen in the classroom and, as well as giving you the opportunity to anticipate success, they should also be used as a time for foreseeing possible problems: 'I feel it can be unwise to be over-expectant and unprepared for failure.' Some sources of possible 'failure' are unforeseeable, for example: noisy lawnmowers outside the window during the reading of a poem; eye-tests; the double-booking of the drama room; your bad headache; the absence of an essential pupil. For situations of this kind it is always wise to have an alternative plan of a lesson which will work, rather than to battle on, spoiling a promisingly planned session. It is sometimes sensible to plan two alternative structures for a lesson, with the same beginning and ending but a different 'development' section. As one student said, explaining a lesson note, 'If the oral work goes well then we will follow it up with these pair and small group activities, but if it does not then I have prepared these individual work-sheets to be completed before the final shaping of ideas.' Particularly when you are unsure of the timing of a lesson or anticipate that the planned lesson may have to be abandoned for some reason, it is well to travel about the school with an 'emergency kit' (essential when you are new to a school). Such a kit will include at least some of the following:

1. Half a ream of paper and a supply of ball-point pens (to overcome 'I've left my book at home' and 'I've got no pen').
2. The texts of half-a-dozen short stories (that you *know* are generally effective and not widely used in the school) for reading aloud.
3. Enough poem cards to engage pairs or small groups in reading, discussion and preparation for performance.
4. A supply of mounted pictures as a basis for oral and written work.
5. Portable cassette recorder and cassettes of two or three lively schools programmes.
6. Your own list of '20 ways to spend 5 minutes at the end of a lesson': word games, quizzes, improvisations.
7. A set of sheets with self-contained reading and writing activities: cloze, sequencing, supplying the missing middle of a short narrative, etc.

At least you should never then be out of material and praying for the bell to go!

The avoidable sources of failure can usually be anticipated when you know a class well if you plan thoroughly, thinking about the implications of decisions you make, preparing resources well in advance and foreseeing how the classroom will need to be managed. It is never wise to spend inadequate time on planning, as this probationer teacher discovered in the first year: 'I try to avoid planning work under pressure. I don't enjoy going to a lesson having no idea of what is going to happen next.'

As well as planning conscientiously for the pupils, it is also essential that you should think of yourself. Throughout this book teachers' comments echo the sense that there is never enough time and that tiredness is, particularly at the end of term, a common problem. By looking carefully at your long-term programme you should be able to take steps during the planning stage to try to avoid exhaustion:

1. Plan to 'stagger' your marking, e.g. balancing up a batch of intensive GCSE marking against topic work towards a display or performance with another group:

Another difficulty I faced was how to cope with a full teaching load and to plan homework and the inevitable marking accordingly. I realized that homework would have to be 'spaced out' in order to give me time to mark it and that the setting-up of project work over a two or three week period cut down on the amount of planning that needed to be done.

2. Work out your priorities, e.g. at different times in the year different groups will have more pressing needs than others, an A-level group just before final examinations, for example, and you should plan to focus on them. Although it is important to hand back marked work quickly while it is fresh in pupils' minds, if you have to choose between preparing an essential resource and marking, the preparation is a priority and you should explain to pupils why marked work will be returned to them later: 'When I had too much to do I overcame this difficulty by deciding upon an order of priority. You do learn how to apportion your time after the first year and to realize your limitations.'

3. Anticipate pressure times and try to plan for them:
   (a) during a week, avoid days when every period is a 'key lesson' and instead balance up teacher-directed sessions with individual reading times or pupil-directed periods
   (b) during a term, foresee times of stress, e.g. during mock-exam marking, report-writing, play-producing, the end of term, and plan with them in mind. 'I tend to rely on the advantages of routine to see me through the demanding final weeks before the end of term.'

Looking back

The evaluation of lessons and units should not be a feature of teaching practice which you shed as soon as you begin to teach. There continue to be advantages in looking back critically at the way your plans have taken shape in the classroom:

1. You only learn from experience if you articulate your reactions and thoughts, e.g. the understandable reaction to a failed lesson is to try to forget it, but as you have to continue to teach the class and to succeed with them it is essential to work out coolly the reasons for the failure if you are to plan to put them right.

2. You will probably want to keep your lesson plans from year to year so that you can perhaps use them again, but the plans will only be thoroughly useful in a year's time if you have also recorded some evaluation of the strengths and weaknesses of the unit.

Evaluation need not always take a written form. In a supportive department you will be able to discuss individual lessons and longer blocks of work with colleagues who, through questioning, suggestions and advice, will help you to look clearly at the successes and failures of the work you plan.

It will be the aim of the following chapters to consider how, when you start to teach your groups, different aspects of school life will affect the way you carry out the plans you have made. Chapter 5 will examine the effects on your teaching of relationships with the pupils and colleagues you will meet, Chapter 6 will look at how the physical surroundings of rooms and resources contribute to lessons, and Chapter 7 will consider ways to evaluate and assess the work your pupils do.

REFERENCES

1. HMI 1982 *The New Teacher in School*. HMSO, par 6.9
2. Ibid. par 5.4
3. DES 1983 *Teaching Quality*. HMSO, par 8.4
4. Ibid. par 17
5. See Horners (ed.) 1983 *Best Laid Plans: English Teachers at Work*. Longman for Schools Council
6. For further reading about planning through themes and topics: Summerfield G 1965 *Topics in English*. Batsford; Adams A 1970 *Team Teaching and the Teaching of English*. Pergamon, Oxford; Mills R W 1987 *Teaching English for All*. Robert Royce, pp 55–99
7. For further ideas see Taylor Gordon and Daw Peter 1987 *The Stanford Ebborne File*. Blackwell
8. For further reading about planning work with books: Jackson D 1983 *Encounters with Books*. Methuen; Protherough R 1983 *Developing Response to Fiction*. Open University, Milton Keynes; Hayhoe M and Parker S 1984 *Working with Fiction*. Edward Arnold; Benton M and Fox G 1985 *Teaching Literature Nine to Fourteen*. OUP; King P 1985 *Teaching English – a teaching skills workbook*. Macmillan, pp 41–3
9. For further reading about planning work for mixed-ability groups: Horner S 1986 'Providing for the ability range', Chapter 3 in Blatchford R *The English Teacher's Handbook*. Hutchinson; Mills R W 1987 *Teaching English for All*. Robert Royce

In the classroom

CHAPTER 5

The people involved

During the first months of teaching I felt very much as if I was suffering from an identity crisis, as well as the fatigue brought on by the war of attrition with certain classes. I often felt, and still do feel, that I am split into two people, as if I have a twin sister who is much more successful than I am.

When she enters a class she looks around ready to begin the lesson and silence descends like a friend rather than an enemy. She can demand and receive full attention whenever she pleases. Her pupils rarely forget homework or equipment and many of them have shown great improvement even after such a short time of teaching.

On the other hand, when I enter the classroom there is an unruly bunch before me, bags on desks, very few ready to begin work. I have to shout and nag to get the class to pay attention, hand out lines, threaten extra work, for those who misbehave in class.

Even stranger than this split personality is that the method and procedure I (my twin sister and I) adopt is not drastically different. Some you win, some you take a lot longer to beat!

You may well have shared this probationer's identity crisis in your own early classroom experience. Not only may you be unsure just what sort of person you are as a teacher, you will also be conscious of revealing different aspects of your personality with different groups of children in and out of school. Consciously or unconsciously, you will find yourself playing different roles with those adults that you encounter: colleagues, Head of Year, professional tutor, caretaker, adviser, parents, head teacher. Teaching requires elasticity: the ability to adapt yourself with bewildering speed to the various roles you have to play, the functions you have to fulfil, the demands that are made upon you. Consider this outline account of one actual day in the life of one of the authors: the events in one column and the accompanying thoughts and feelings of the teacher in another.

The day is a real one, lived through in an 11–18 comprehensive of 2000 pupils. The school is in a residential area near the edge of a city in the north. The pupils are taught on two sites a mile and a half apart. They come from the privately owned houses which surround the sites and from a large council estate a mile or so away. Although the city is a port, few of its inhabitants come from different cultures; in this suburban school the pupils are predominantly white and there are very few for whom English is their second language.

Wednesday – three weeks before the end of the spring term

8.30   Arrive at the Upper School on a grey rainy morning to catch the Head for a brief word about the shortlist for English interviews next week and to pick up post.

8.40   Drive through cyclists, usually three abreast, to Lower School – to Room 19 to take 2P3's register – only time to question Stephen quickly about an incident during a Games lesson yesterday before they leave for house assembly.

Must remember to see J. about Lower School Drama Group.

Worry that he won't meet my eye and wonder whether to keep him behind – decide not to – must talk to full-time tutor.

9.00   As I'm not their regular tutor, stay behind to finish register and read post – a request to do a teaching practice at the school from a former pupil, inspection copy invoice, information about a Sixth Form day conference, poster for a poetry competition – quick initialling of the various papers to pass on to colleagues at break, if I have time. As Room 19 is my Lower School teaching room, get out folders, worksheets, paper and look through work for handing back as I wait.

Who do I need to pass these on to?

Who is it important to see in today's lesson?

9.25   1W3 come in breathless and wet – they're late after assembly in the other block – bumping bags against legs and thump onto desks. Diane asks 'What we doing today?' Some rearrangement of unwieldy desks

She always asks that question but doesn't really want an answer – just wants to make contact. Need to focus the energy.

into groups by Keith and Martin who've remembered what we're doing today; the others noisily unpack their bags.

Call for silence and explain as briefly as I can that we're carrying on from last Friday with the group booklets for the top class at a local feeder school. 'Work in progress and everything you need on the side, send one person to fetch things. Sort yourselves out.' Diane immediately claims my attention again as others begin to fetch folders and get into huddles. Remind her that her first job is to talk with the rest of the group. Wait at the side of the room for a few moments, then pick up my folder of stories about life in school, comic strips, maps, instructions, jokes, self-portraits etc. Alan, forgetting where he is, sweeps round instinctively with a question: 'Mum – oh, I mean miss – can Simon and I write a play together, about Break?'

Manoeuvre my way round haphazardly sticking-out chairs, handing back work and hearing today's programme from each group. Pull up a chair next to Keith, who spends part of each week with the Special Needs Dept, and write down the questions about cyling and school that he thinks the new First

Straightaway aware of my usual irritation with her – try to quell it.

Need to assure myself that each of the six groups has begun.

It's a pleasure to see that all are absorbed in what they're doing.

It's time to focus on particular people who I know have problems.

Years would want to ask.
Leave him to make a first
draft of his answers.

Matthew's problem is
different: he's written a
careful but dull account of
his first day at secondary
school – he's reluctant to
modify it at this moment
because he's now enthu-
siastic about listing Lower
School sports teams,
fixtures and kit.

> He's a lively boy – there's
> nothing of him in the
> writing – I need to prompt
> him to improve on it in re-
> drafting.

Diane has painstakingly
noted and acted on my
suggestions from last lesson
and the drawings she's
added, making fun of her
own fear about a new
school, are great. Her
smile broadens.

> Pleased that I'm able to
> praise her account.
>
> Wonder why I ever feel
> irritated with her!

9.40   After the raised voices of
the first 5 to 10 minutes,
there's now a subdued
babble as people write and
draw, until Sarah – who's
asked if she can 'do a
survey' and has worked on
and checked her questions
with me – begins her trek
round the room. Exagger-
ated excitement from Alan
about the relative merits of
Spam fritters and Cheddar
butteries, a buzz from
other groups as the idea
catches on and others want
to 'do surveys' too.

> Should have known!
>
> Don't want that amount of
> disruption to the working
> atmosphere.

Make a statement to the
whole class, 'Only surveys
if you prepare them thor-
oughly, check them with
me and think hard about
how you're going to present
your findings – and only
one interviewer in the
room at a time.' Return to

working with individuals and exhorting the one group who're flagging and arguing with each other.

10.15 There's 15 minutes to go, so remind everyone to take paper for homework and make sure they've achieved what they set out to do this lesson. Read out the list of those who 'owe' me work and jog their memories about swapping book-box books. Until packing-up time stand by the book box and talk to the four who bring novels back. Packing up is swift, they're used to the way we work. As I put things away Diane and Sara linger to talk – about Sara's greyhound and Diane's cookery.

10.30 No time for coffee, into the car to 'commute' to the Upper School – traffic jam in the Square.
Re-orientate to *Romeo and Juliet* as I drive down the hill.

10.50 5P/W are in W6 already – in un-uniformed huddles talking animatedly about anything but *Romeo and Juliet*. Breathless from hurrying from the carpark, I'm only just through the door when Sharon comes swiftly across to apologize because she won't be giving her homework in. Remind her that at this stage in the GCSE course she should be apologizing to herself! Arrange to see her tomorrow – the other two

Cross with myself that I didn't intervene earlier
– I know they find cooperation for a whole lesson difficult.

Wish I could spend more time and give them all my attention.

Won't be able to hand on post. Will there be a parking space? Will the assignment 'work'?

Thinks I'll be more forgiving if she says she's sorry. As this always happens, I'm irritated.

'homework hard cases' are lying low and hoping I won't notice. Class straggle back to their tables – in this room facing the front. This is the last book we're reading together as part of a GCSE Literature Continuous Assessment course. Today I'm about to set the definitely last piece of coursework – it's important, but they're tired of folders and deadlines.

Take up my stance at the front for a brief collection of homework and interrogation of the 'hard cases'. 'Now I hope you'll remember from last Thursday that we're halfway through reportbacks from groups on different aspects of the play. Bring your chairs and books into the middle.' W6 is an enormous room: light tables and chairs always move to the sides, leaving a large 'hole' in the middle. I sit on my desk and the class makes a rough circle of chairs near me. Jane's group is to start with a talk about the Nurse. She is brisk, taking the class through relevant scenes; Joanna's quiet American drawl is difficult to hear but they've obviously thought about her relationship with Juliet; Jane covers embarrassment with swoops of giggles and compares the different Nurses we've seen in performance – biggest giggle reserved for

It's gone well so far but I'm still not satisfied that the assignment's right as the culmination of several weeks' work.

the statement, 'We three think the Nurse reminds us of you' – uproar of raucous laughter, slightly shocked giggles and nervous glances to see how I'm taking it from the earnest girls. Then Richard, as always, to the rescue, 'You're not quite as old as the one we saw at the New Theatre.'

Makes me laugh, although I'll need to watch Jane, she's a giggler who sometimes can't stop.

As that subsides, ask if the rest have questions or further observations – Rosemary wants to know how people feel about the Nurse advising Juliet to marry Paris – as automatic reaction, although we're sitting near to each other, hands go up and people make suggestions.

Think they're all skirting round the Nurse's attitude to sex.

As a follow-up I ask, 'Why does she give that advice?' Nicola, who rarely speaks, makes a quiet, pointed answer. Two more groups report back – on staging the duels and the final scene – ask them to return to their seats while I search for chalk and a board rubber.

Wish I'd been that mature when I was her age!

Reflect that thoroughly efficient teachers always carry chalk with them.

11.30 Write up the title for their assignment, 'Describe the views of love and marriage held by each of these characters: Lord and Lady Capulet, the Nurse, Mercutio, the Friar, Romeo, Juliet. Whose view do you share?', to offstage groans. It's getting near lunchtime and concentration could slip away – ask class to work in pairs to discuss the views of each

Need to exert myself to bring 32 people to think.

character in turn and to jot down relevant words and incidents. 'As we talked about the Nurse earlier on you were really beginning to think about this already – so try to build on it. Your notes will make the basis for the writing – we'll spend part of tomorrow on talk and preparation, then start it in class and it'll be your weekend homework to finish it. This will be your last opportunity to write about the play – and your last assignment.' A few ragged cheers before they settle down in huddles.

Need to spot the pairs who're taking the opportunity to have a quick chat.

In the middle of the room Tom with his Rowan Atkinson face is telling Jofi, and then me, for the umpteenth time this year that he can't see the point of this: 'I just want to read a book or see a play and that's it.' Reply that we've been here before; Jofi nods his head energetically – as Tom's friend the debate's familiar to him too – tell Tom to postpone our 'daily jangle' and start work. 'I'll never go and see this play again, you know.' Jofi winks at me and they turn to the play. Enough time for everyone to work on at least one character.

After two years I'm weary of this – it's a familiar wrangling point – he means it but at the same time it postpones getting down to work.

I fear he may not. I know that Rosemary, for example, is now 'hooked on' Shakespeare and some have made the play their own – but Tom is a valuable thorn in my flesh.

12.00   The bell rings – copies of *Romeo and Juliet* pushed into bags and a quick exit. To the staffroom for gulped sandwiches, and quick exchange of bits of paper and news.

12.30 To the A-level English room. Three prospective Oxford candidates from the Lower Sixth already there – it's our second session and they're still wary. Give out two poems for us to talk about and compare.

Aware that there's only 30 minutes, so it's a delicate balance between encouraging exploratory talk and giving a point to the session.

Chris is ready to have a go and that provokes Steve, but Sally sits looking at the paper and not meeting our eyes – I ask her a direct question and she blushes but her answer is sharp and perceptive.

I'll have to make a deliberate effort to bring her in, her writing is full of insight but she's painfully shy. It's hard work – I'm not sure we've achieved anything.

1.15 To a Physics Lab. for registration – sort out a problem with one boy's Work Experience placement for the summer term.

1.30 Back to the Sixth Form Block for 6C; Chris and Sally's group – already in the room – 16 of them round three sides of the square – me on the fourth side. Eve has another new hair colour, mottled this time like a leopard, and Paul's added an earring. The sun's out by now – ask for a window to be opened.

Aware that the small room is already stuffy.

Return of the Native's going badly – it's an interrupted half-term, field trips and university visits.

Knowing that we've lost momentum with the book, I'm on edge.

Dave wants to know if I watched a TV programme about *Death of a Salesman* at the weekend. I didn't – so five minutes of those who did telling us about it.

Pleased that they were interested enough to watch.

1.40 People have prepared to talk about impressions of Eustacia Vye: I don't want

It's time to bring things together.

prepared talks, just contributions and they're slow to come – we're all sleepy, it's warm and after lunch. Richard says, 'I think she's a spoilt brat.' Chris is incensed, others delighted, several moments of animated talk illustrated with 'You know that bit where . . .'

Relief – it's typical Richard, meant to be provocative and often our salvation in afternoon lessons.

2.00 Bring this to a close and ask them to change the focus and think about Clym – they're to work in threes and look at different individuals' or groups' expectations of Clym's return to the Heath.

I'm working towards giving them some writing next lesson which will explore the relationship between Eustacia and Clym.

Sit back for a few minutes and look out at the trees and the carpark, keeping an ear on what's going on.

Wonder if *Things Being Various* will be in W6 stockroom next lesson.

Get up and join each group, ask questions, explain a phrase to Dave, ask Eve about missing work – remind them of the time left.

Pleased with the level of discussion I'm eavesdropping on.

2.20 Ask one of the groups to report back: Andy and Paul interested in Clym's socialism and harsh about Mrs Yeobright's expectations; Chris disagrees and I sit back and leave them to it – everyone makes a contribution, even Sally. With an eye on the time, bring it to a close and set some preparatory work for next time.

At last I think the book's taking a hold on the group – pity it's happened so near the end of the lesson.

2.40 Back to W6 in the main block. *Things Being Various* are in the stockroom – sign them out and take them to the back of the room as

Worrying now about the set of books I need. A relief I don't deserve as I should have checked yesterday.

4R/S straggle in taking little notice of me. Lee obligingly offers to hand out books to people – 24 in this group so they're spread out in this big room, looking listless or over-excited.

It's going to be a struggle to do what I've planned.

To the front and I've got their attention when the door bursts open at the back – Karen, stormy-browed, plastic bag in hand. 'You're late Karen. Where have you been?' 'That Maths teacher kept me back didn't he.' Door crashes shut, bag is thumped down and chair hauled over – Karen glowers at me but at least doesn't turn to tell Elaine about it.

I'm angry, it's taken an effort to hold their attention, but from a look at Karen's expression decide to sound unrattled – I know her reputation for erratic behaviour and I know her Maths teacher.

Say that I'll speak to her during the lesson, then ask the class, who're still silent and watchful, to turn to the photograph in their copy of a boy kneeling to cradle a bird in his hands: 'Don't say anything for a few moments – just look at everything in the picture as I take you through it.'

Swiftly decide not to make an issue of it – it's a gamble but she's never given me real trouble before.

Wary myself as I know Karen may still have ruined the atmosphere – it's important to create the right 'feel' for this lesson.

Even Karen appears to be involved. I ask for their impressions – 'Who might he be? Where is it? Who's in the background? What's the story?' They're full of ideas. They're to work in fours or fives – first to agree on their story arising from the picture, then to act it out. 'Great' from Lee, 'Do we have to?' from Jon whose pose is to

Perhaps it'll be all right after all.

pretend that he hates everything. In fact he loves acting, but wouldn't admit it.

The room's easily re-organized and soon they're working. I lean against the cupboard at the back and wait before going round to hear their stories. They're working with friends and only one group is mixed – Karen's in this, she enjoys acting and 'that Maths teacher' is apparently forgotten.

Decide to postpone speaking to her until during clearing-up time.

3.10 All are on their feet – there are family rows, isolated boys being sneered at by gangs, in one corner Lee kneeling down to pick up the bird. When they pause I ask him and the group how it would feel in his hands – explain I don't know because I'm frightened of birds. 'You're not are you, Miss?'Between them they describe the claws on your skin: 'It'd be scared so you'd feel it throbbing', 'You'd have to hold it so it couldn't flutter'. Lee tries it again and the expression on his face matches the cupping of his hands. Glance up and see a teacher in the Sixth Form Block looking across from his room.

His hand movements look wrong, he could be scooping up a football, decide to intervene.

Aware that I'm enjoying myself and a lesson I thought would drag is racing past.

As a concession shut two of the windows, but he's smiling.

Suppose with the windows open that W6 is noisy. Probably wishes he was an English teacher.

3.45 All the groups have worked through their scenes at least once. I stop them, thank them for their hard work and ask them to put back tables and chairs – during this, take Karen aside and explain why she made me angry; refuses to meet my eye so ask her to look at me, and can just hear a grunted 'I'm sorry, Miss.'

Mustn't forget Karen – she's worked hard.

3.50 Bell rings and within seconds of my dismissing them they've gone.

3.55 To the staffroom for a coffee before returning to W6 for a department meeting – ring through to Lower School staff room and talk to 2P3's regular tutor about Stephen.

Reckon that's as much as I can expect – I'll have to watch her carefully in the next few lessons.

Glad I caught her, I was worried I hadn't followed up my concern about Stephen.

4.10 Colleagues from Lower School have arrived – hand over to second-in-department who's got a lot to say about GCSE admin. General worries aired about folders and oral moderation, plans for Open Evening in final week of term confirmed – despite grumbles about its timing people have obviously given it thought – several suggestions and offers of material and help, report back on recent meeting of feeder school representatives, senior colleague passes on one primary head's reservations and worries, 'Are we moving too fast?' Ask colleague to act as 'mediator'. Fix date for next meeting and suggest

5.15 we all go home.

I'm relieved and pleased as several Heads of Dept. have reported reluctant support from their staff.

Tired by now, I'm irritated that the dept. finds itself holding the delicate balance.

Chapters 3 and 4 considered how you might plan English lessons effectively; this chapter looks at the effects your own school, with its individual pupils, classes and colleagues, might have on the process of putting those plans into practice in the classroom. The outline account of one teacher's day is the starting point for examining how the complex network of relationships in a secondary school will affect your teaching. As the teacher is experienced you may feel that aspects of her day do not reflect your life in school. During the following sections, elements of her day, therefore, will be set alongside comments from teachers new to the profession, followed by suggested strategies for coping with the problems highlighted by the account. As you read you may find it useful to refer back to it.

ADAPTING TO DIFFERENT SITUATIONS IN A SECONDARY SCHOOL

Taking on different roles

In any day's teaching you will be called upon to fulfil a variety of different functions and so to play a series of different roles – often moving from one to another with confusing speed. To carry them all out with equal success is demanding and sometimes difficult. During her day the teacher had to call on different aspects of her teaching personality to meet exuberant 11-year-olds of all abilities, intelligent 16-year-olds weary with exam pressures, Oxbridge candidates warily testing the ground in a new learning situation, sleepy A-level students needing rousing to think, and 'middle band' 15-year-olds with little interest in school. In her role as form tutor she was administrator, disciplinarian and counsellor. Outside classrooms she met the Head as Head of Department, briefly discussed business with colleagues in the Staff Room and acted as chair to a large group of tired staff in the department meeting. At almost no stage during the day was there any time to make the adjustment from one role to the next.

Young staff find this kind of 'quick change' equally tiring, but also encounter problems in moving from one situation to another. One tension between different roles that several perceive is between acting as tutor and as teacher. On one hand, tutors are placed in the position of 'checking up' and then 'dealing with' offenders; lists of tutors' duties seem mainly to fall within this area:

Registration, inspecting rooms and desks, reading reports, delivering and collecting letters.

Reply slips to collate, lists to prepare, a '7-point' checklist every day on uniform and equipment, files to complete.

On the other hand, particularly as part of Personal and Social Development (PSD) or Guidance programmes, they are expected to be counsellors, able to encourage pupils' trust. Pupils themselves can become confused by these role shifts and sometimes take advantage of staff they meet both as tutors and English teachers.

Teachers at the beginning of their careers also find it difficult to gauge when, and indeed whether, to come out of role altogether and to 'behave naturally' with pupils – a problem perhaps unique to English in which informal talk and sharing of personal experience plays a large part. Several realize that it's easy to get this wrong:

I began teaching with too relaxed and informal an approach.

I realize now that I should have distanced myself from the class.

I was too friendly altogether.

Equally the adoption of a formal role as teacher, particularly in schools where pupils are used to a relaxed atmosphere, can be testing to handle: 'I did have difficulties with my Fourth and Fifth Year CSE classes. This was mainly because I was, to them, terribly middle-class, unsmiling and unbending.' Some young staff begin their careers teaching other subjects alongside English and find a clash between their two subject 'personae': 'Another major problem occurred through teaching PE. I enjoy sports but didn't have much idea how to teach them. I feel that my ineptitude and inexperience tarnished the relationship I had established in my English lessons.' A similar tension can be caused by the different demands of extra-curricular activities and lessons. Working closely with pupils during productions or during team-training is, as one teacher says, 'very valuable', but the familiarity generated by these activities cannot be carried over into lessons.

At the same time as adjusting roles in relation to children, young teachers will be trying to establish contacts with other staff: 'I always felt "new" during my first two years because nobody else joined the school during that period.' They find it difficult to cope with curiosity about or even hostility to English teaching from colleagues in other disciplines: 'When scientists and mathematicians say, "What are you doing in English?" we should have good answers for them in year one of teaching not by year five or six.' (More about this in the final chapter.)

What to do

Acknowledge to yourself that you will have to behave in different ways according to different situations and on some occasions explain this to pupils: 'I eventually dealt with this problem by becoming two teachers – an occasional PE teacher who admitted his failings and an English teacher who was on top of his subject. They responded pretty well to this.'

Adapting to different individuals

During her day the teacher encountered about 125 pupils and 19 staff – all of them in different ways making demands on her and all expecting her to respond successfully. The Head, for example, required informed professional advice and the tutor group pupil had to be questioned and a quick decision made about his answers. During lessons, Diane's insecurity showed itself in her repeated appeals to the teacher, and Tom's love of argument for its own sake in his new re-working of the 'why study books' debate. At lunchtime Sally began falteringly to talk and share her insights and at the end of the afternoon Jon needed cajoling to drop his bored pose and join in the drama lesson. During the department meeting the concerns of a variety of individual colleagues needed bringing out and channelling.

The sheer pressure of this range of demands can be daunting. Young teachers add to those already described: the delicacy needed for distressed children; the understanding and patience for slow learners; the attentiveness for pupils for whom English is their second language and tactfulness for pupils new to the school. They agree that their training did little to prepare them for demands which sometimes inevitably leave them feeling inadequate:

I was left to guess how to counsel a teenager whose parents had split up.

I showed a video on alcoholism. How was I to know that one of the girls had a father who's an alcoholic? What should I have done?

The nature of pastoral contacts in tutorial time and of talk often arising naturally in English lessons can lead to pupils confiding, sometimes disturbingly, in English teachers. One young teacher feels strongly that this should not be part of his work:

I guess that what I resent most is the need to be a pseudo-sociologist, a pseudo-psychiatrist when attempting to 'understand' the problems of children. I don't expect children to leave their problems from home at the school gate, but I think it dangerous for unqualified teachers to dabble in these complex and difficult areas.

The problem for an inexperienced teacher is to know where to draw the line.

What to do

1. Cultivate patience if it doesn't come to you naturally, but at the same time learn to recognize when a show of impatience is necessary to check someone who is making unfair demands on your attention, e.g. as the teacher did with Tom's attempts to rekindle a time-wasting debate.
2. Listen attentively and watch carefully for 'body signals' which will give you information that a person's words might not express, e.g. Stephen's inability to meet the teacher's eye which alerted her to trouble.
3. In the classroom make it clear by your practice that each individual is entitled to an equal share of your attention, and try to be consistent in the way you talk to members of a class – children are very alert to signs of 'favouritism'. Diane, for example, with her appeals for attention was not allowed to monopolize the teacher's time.
4. If, as the result of your teaching, a pupil confides in you and you feel unsure of how to respond, ask for advice from an experienced colleague without necessarily betraying the child's confidence. It is important to accept that there may be other people or agencies who will be better equipped to meet the pupil's need than you are.
5. Try to combine professional care with the ability to distance yourself from individuals' needs. Absorption in the apparently more demanding situation of one pupil means that you will be neglecting several others. Keith in the First Year class, for example, had pressing needs but it was important to give him a short spell of concentrated but *constructive* attention so that he could begin to work independently, and then the teacher could pass on to Matthew whose needs were less apparent but just as real.

WORKING WITH DIFFERENT KINDS OF TEACHING GROUPS

The nature of a teaching group will have an important influence on the way you relate to pupils and organize their learning.

Mixed-ability groups

As the whole class lesson has limited effectiveness with a group representing a wide range of academic ability, the more common classroom scene will resemble that described in the First Year lesson of the teacher's day. The pupils were involved in a variety of different activities and, apart from giving brief instructions to the whole class, the teacher spent the lesson working alongside the children. She was part of their activity and often forgotten when pupils were absorbed. In talking to individuals, she adjusted her teaching to the known needs of each pupil: challenging an able boy like Matthew, giving Keith help with elementary organization of ideas, reinforcing insecure Diane's success with praise, talking about books to individual readers.

The particular demands made by mixed-ability groups present more problems to teachers returning to the profession than to those at the start of their careers. They are aware, for example, of the need to adopt what is for them a new teaching style: 'With mixed-ability classes I have had to learn not to teach in the 'old' way, i.e. telling and then supervising, but to learn how to stimulate the pupils so that they learn as *they* think, plan and explore.' The presence in one class of highly able and slow-learning pupils poses one teacher with her most difficult problem: 'I am worried by the fact that, because I have to spend a disproportionate amount of time with the pupils who are in difficulties, I fail to stimulate and inspire sufficiently the most able pupils, especially the 13-year-olds.'

What to do

1. To free you to carry out the most important part of teaching a mixed-ability group – working with individuals – careful planning and preparation of worksheets and resources are essential so that pupils can work independently. (Remind yourself of the relevant section in Chapter 4.)

2. To avoid spending 'a disproportionate amount of time with the pupils who are in difficulties', there are various strategies you should adopt. Through collaboration with colleagues in the Special Needs Department, find out the precise nature of each individual's problems so that you can give particular and constructive help. Make sure that the pupil has help in addition to yours – either through support or partial withdrawal schemes. Create situations on some occasions in which less able pupils can collaborate with and so learn from other members of the group. During the course of each lesson, and over the course of a unit of work, keep a check on your movements round the classroom, making a mental, or written, note of who should be seen in each lesson so that you share your time as evenly as possible between all the pupils in the group. (You will find more about working with the Special Needs Department in Chapter 8.)

3. Be aware that individuals will require very different kinds of teaching when you work with them, and that your

approach and particularly your vocabulary needs adapting for the needs of each pupil.

Streamed or banded groups

When a block of work is in progress your relationship with a group of pupils streamed or banded according to ability will be similar to that described in the previous section. There are occasions, though, when your role will be different. A streamed group, particularly in the examination years, is homogeneous when all pupils are working towards the same goal, often in similar ways. The teacher directing a lesson on *Romeo and Juliet* was often the focus of attention, addressing the pupils as a class, using a variety of means to stimulate interest, acting as chair of class report-backs and discussions, framing questions to open up new lines of thought.

The role of whole-class teacher, more often called for with a streamed or banded group, requires a variety of skills (those related to control are considered later). One which poses a problem for young English staff is the extent to which a teacher should talk *to* the group. Some discover that they have the skills to do this, becoming 'performers' to an enthralled 'audience', but doubt the value of the skill:

An older colleague could understand my worries as regards talking too much – but he said, 'Don't be afraid to stand there and "teach", that's your job.' This was comforting and worrying.

The point I'm trying to make is – I *know* I can sit on the desk at the front of the class and talk at length without too many of them getting bored. But I daren't do this too often or for too long. My concern is that sometimes I might be over-anxious about 'teacher talk' and stop talking too *soon*.

This young teacher's confusion is compounded by the advice he received from a colleague, which might be seen as offering a model of teacher as knowledge-imparter and instructor, and who was apparently unaware of the limitations of that model for an English teacher.

What to do

1. Be aware that, although a streamed/banded group may appear to be homogeneous, it is always, through differences in need and personality, a collection of individual pupils as heterogeneous as any mixed-ability group. This awareness should direct you in your planning, when you balance whole-class lessons with individual and group activities, and in your relations with individual pupils.
2. Think carefully about the functions of different kinds of

'teacher-talk' in English and only employ each when it serves a valuable purpose.

3. Whole-class discussion requires sophisticated skills from the teacher – knowing when to intervene, how to question, how to encourage the shy and discourage those who dominate, how to steer the direction when necessary, how to time and how both to excite and to control debate, all techniques which the *Romeo and Juliet* discussion called upon. Create structures to help you gain experience, e.g. starting with group talk which is then reported back, followed by *brief* general debate.

4. One result of streaming is the development of unhelpful group identity, particularly in the lower groups. You need to be aware that the 'sink-group mentality' may demoralize pupils, making them truculent or apathetic or pessimistic about their own progress. Be prepared for this and for the need to adapt your role and manner according to the response and age of the group.

A-level groups

At first glance it may seem that an English teacher who has been 'on view' with groups of twenty-five to thirty children can afford to relax with a group of up to fifteen students who have opted for the subject and are at the age to be trusted to act maturely. It was clear that the teacher with her Sixth Form group had a more relaxed manner but, equally, in mental terms it was the most testing period of the day. Although part of the lesson was spent in pair work, when she was called on as adviser or as another voice in a discussion, most of the time was taken up with the group as a whole sharing their responses to their reading. In this kind of exploratory talk, her role was a difficult one. It was necessary to create a climate in which students would feel safe to express individual feelings and ideas and to make tentative suggestions. When the discussion on Clym Yeobright 'took off' she had to know when to intervene with words which would steer without imposing, which required complete concentration on students' contributions and alertness to the direction of the discussion. At the same time she needed to be aware of the hesitancy of pupils like Sally, and prepared to use strategies to bring her into the discussion.

What to do

1. As the steering of sharing and discussion is difficult and improves with experience, build up your expertise through planning different kinds of structures for talk, e.g. pair pres-

entation followed by questions, mock trials of characters and situations, sharing the 'chairmanship' with students.

2. Be aware that the adoption of a more informal manner with older and more academic pupils has its dangers, particularly for a young teacher. It may produce an encouraging atmosphere for the sharing of personal response to literature but may work against you in situations·which require you to assess, rebuke or even discipline.

3. In the first lessons with such a group, be conscious that they may be very resistant to offering ideas that they feel may be 'wrong', different from the teacher's or unpopular. Prepare strategies to deal with this, such as jotting, pair work, discussion of non-academic texts etc. (For more ideas, see Robert Protherough's *Teaching Literature for Examinations*.)[1]

CONTROL AND DISCIPLINE

For teachers of all subjects, the ability to control classes is an essential skill without which it is impossible to work productively with children. It is a skill about which colleagues and training courses can advise but in the end each teacher has to find personally effective methods that become part of a characteristic classroom style. Each teacher is alone in the last resort as this young one rather reluctantly has to admit: 'I suppose to some extent there is no way you can prepare someone for that experience of walking into a class of thirty people who aren't necessarily going to listen to you.' The nature of English teaching poses particular problems because the range of classroom activities is so wide and offers such apparent freedom. There must always be control for them to be successful, though it may not always have to be formally imposed: 'Many of the activities I hoped to make a part of my English teaching – group work, discussion, pupil self-help – I see as being "high risk". I am loath to try them until I have my classes exactly as I want them, and I am still battling to achieve my primary goal.'

In considering control and discipline, this section will look at its different elements. The 'What to do' lists are necessarily short but if you wish to read in more detail there are several books available.[2]

Establishing routines

As every classroom is a small society in its own right, it needs rules and routines so that class members and teacher can work productively together. Some of the rules will reflect those of the school as a whole, e.g. taking off coats, not eating, not writing on desks, whereas others will be the ones you establish to create an ordered environment. Most important among these are the routines for starting and finishing lessons, the rule of listening to whoever is addressing the whole class and the collection of work, particularly when it has been set for homework. Advice has already been given in Chapter 1 about how to use observation in your new school to discover which routines have been set up and adopted.

There is evidence in the account of the teacher's day for the importance of establishing all these routines. By the end of the spring term they have become accepted aspects of the class's life in English lessons, but only because they had obviously been spelt out at the beginning of the year when classes and teacher were new to each other. Lessons began in different ways but in all of them the teacher was 'setting the agenda' and indicating the pattern she had chosen for a particular lesson and its activities. So, although the First Year pupils appeared to organize themselves, the teacher's call for silence and explanation of deadlines reminded them of her expectations. It was clearly more difficult to obtain silence and make a firm start with the Fourth Year, who drifted in from different parts of the school, than with the Fifth Year, who were already assembled. All three large classes were clearly used to packing up in an organized way and all three were dismissed by the teacher. It was made clear to pupils in three of the classes that the handing in of homework was being checked and that 'offenders' would be followed up. The routine of putting hands up to indicate a wish to speak in discussion was so well established that Fifth Years continued to do it almost as a reflex action.

What seems easy for an experienced teacher can often cause probationers real problems. The elementary step of creating silence in a room filled with pupils seems one of the hardest to make. 'I used to waste too much time getting classes "settled" – could there not be more instruction for beginners in effective "quieting" techniques?'

I can hear my voice nagging,
'Don't do that'
'Stop talking – NOW'
'Stop muttering'
'LISTEN'.

What to do

1. Involve a class in work quickly and keep up impetus without spending too long trying to 'settle' them. The longer you delay, the harder it is to achieve silence or quiet.

2. If a class arrives in the room after you and straggles in, don't try to speak to the group as a whole until all pupils appear to be there. As they come in use the time either to distribute material as the teacher did with the Fourth Year class or, if you expect control to be difficult, watch them to their places. A group in the middle of a piece of work can begin straight away, as the First Years did. If you are inconvenienced by a few pupils arriving late, check with their previous teacher that they left on time and make an issue of lateness with the 'offenders'.

3. In the end the only genuinely effective 'quieting technique' is an instruction for the class to stop talking and listen, delivered in a loud, firm voice with a tone which implies that you expect to be obeyed. Saying 'Please be quiet' and 'Ssh!' are ineffectual because they are imprecise instructions and sound weak. Children may not obey immediately and you should be prepared to wait firmly with plenty of eye-contact until silence has been established. Make it clear to the class that in English in particular listening, whether to the teacher or to each other, is an essential part of learning to communicate. It may take persistence over days, weeks or even months, but if you are determined you will achieve silence, the sign to you and the pupils that you have succeeded in imposing your control over the class. 'Walking into a Second Year class and saying "Stop talking and listen" the other week, I nearly fell over in amazement when they *did* – immediately – not after much furrowing of brow and chastising. The silence was deafening.'

4. Once you have established routines of the kinds described in this section, be consistent in upholding them. Sloppiness from pupils about handing in work, for example, may be a reflection of sloppiness in your record-keeping and 'chasing-up'.

Focusing and channelling energy

One aspect of class control is perhaps the result of English teachers' own success. Pupils nearly always enjoy the subject, particularly in the early years of secondary school, and bring considerable energy and enthusiasm into the classroom. If this is not focused and channelled, pleasant, energetic classes can change during a year to boisterous groups who are difficult to handle. The teacher's First Year group, for example, showed the potential to behave in this way. There were several extrovert pupils – Alan with his First Year wit; Sarah, a lively girl who obviously provoked equal liveliness in others; and Diane with her nervous chattering – and they arrived already excited and noisy.

Focusing this kind of liveliness is seen as a problem by one probationer, who welcomes the exuberance and keenness of one of her classes, but found difficulty 'in creating a working atmosphere that was sufficiently self-disciplined to permit them to work and me to give individuals my personal attention'.

What to do

1. Prepare resources and organize their distribution so that activity can begin promptly, not allowing time for excitement to begin or build up.
2. Build into your lessons structured choices and goals or deadlines so that pupils are trained to become self-disciplined and responsible for their own programmes of work.
3. Keep the class 'on their toes', either with a variety of activities during the course of one lesson – none of them lasting too long – or, if there is on-going work, with reminders of deadlines and regular reports on progress from individuals or groups. The teacher punctuated her First Year lesson with reminders of this kind.

Controlling noise

As many English lessons involve talk and group work, classrooms are rarely silent, or even quiet. This does not mean, however, that noise should not be controlled. During her day the teacher had several noisy lessons and intervened in one, with the First Year, because she felt the noise was too great for pupils to concentrate. In another she worried about the volume of a drama lesson because it seemed possible that it was affecting classes in surrounding rooms.

For new teachers, considerations like these loom large. Although sure that this is how they wish to work, they feel vulnerable to criticism from staff in other 'quieter' departments and from members of the 'hierarchy'. 'My ears have been transformed from simply being receptors of sound, to become a sensitive sound level monitor. Once a particular level of noise is reached, warning bells start ringing in my head and a claxon-like voice emits instructions which eventually reduces the noise level to "safe".'

What to do

1. Learn from experience the differences in the character of noise in the classroom and how it varies according to the activity. Purposeful pair or group talk is subdued, chat raises the tone and the volume, irrelevant excitement

produces 'spurts' of noise. If you judge that the noise is unhelpful to the work in hand, call for silence and remind the class what's expected of them, as the teacher did during her First Year lesson when Sarah's survey caused excitement.

2. When individual writing is the main activity in a lesson some pupils are helped by talking with their neighbours but, equally, some need silence for concentration. Try to build an extended period of silence into a lesson like this, explaining to pupils why it's necessary and taking steps to ensure that the silence is kept.

3. Pupils need training to approach group talk responsibly. Part of this is for them to learn to respond to your signal that talk should stop so that a new activity can be started. They should not, for example, ever be talking too loudly to hear your signal whether it be a command or clap of your hands.

4. The right arrangement of furniture for various kinds of talk is crucial to its success. This is considered in more detail in Chapter 6, but it is always important to remember that pupils must sit close enough to each other to be able to talk and listen without the need to raise their voices and that this may involve rearrangement of the room. Equally, pupils will become restless during class discussion if they cannot hear what's being said, which often happens if all the class are facing the front. Again, you should consider creating a different arrangement so that pupils are facing each other and have no need to project their voices to be heard, as the teacher did with her Fifth Year group for their report-back session.

Dealing with situations which threaten your control of a class

Individual pupils

However effectively you may have established control over a class or a particular lesson, you will always find there are individual pupils who will frequently, or once in a while, challenge the situation. Some of these challenges will be quite unexpected – a pupil you think of as pleasant and cooperative may have had a row at home and may express pent-up feelings through a flash of bad temper or a truculent response to criticism from you or, as often happens in English lessons, a subject you propose for writing or talking about may re-awaken raw feelings. Other challenges may be half-expected. Karen, the latecomer to the teacher's Fourth Year lesson, was obviously known to her as a potential troublemaker. If at the end of the spring term she had given no real trouble in English lessons it was probably because this was one of the few subjects she enjoyed and/or succeeded in. From the teacher's commentary on the situation Karen caused, it's clear that her response was a complex one and, as you may find it valuable for your own practice, it will be considered in some detail. She had chosen to embark on a lesson which needed an atmosphere of silence and concentration. At the start of the lesson her own confidence in her ability to create that atmosphere seemed sapped by recognition that she'd made a mistake in planning – this was not the lesson for the end of a busy day at the end of term. Already tense, her feelings quickly changed to anger at Karen's deliberately noisy entrance. At the same moment, though, she had to make a swift rational decision about the whole situation. If she gave way to anger and forced a confrontation with an already stormy Karen – the first they would have had – the class would have transferred all its attention to what could have been a protracted wrangle and the teacher would have had to work even harder to recreate the atmosphere she wanted. On the other hand, as Karen was clearly well known by the children for her staff-baiting, the teacher risked losing face in front of the class in letting the challenge pass apparently unpunished. Deciding in a split second not to force an issue out of the situation was a gamble which paid off – Karen simmered down, perhaps glad in her anger with the Maths teacher to have a few moments to recover, and the class, after two terms' relationship with the teacher, accepted her handling of it and returned to work. If the circumstances had been different, reaction to the situation would have had to be adapted, for example if Karen began making a habit of late entrances she would obviously be spoiling for a fight with the English teacher and the issue could not be allowed to pass. Or if this had taken place at the beginning of the academic year, the teacher would have needed to sacrifice the atmosphere of the lesson in order to establish authority over Karen, and therefore a show of authority over a new class. Although not unique to the subject, this kind of situation is common to English. Karen's dramatic entrance into the teacher's introduction to a Chemistry experiment would break the mental concentration of the people in the room, but an atmosphere combining feeling, thought and imagination is delicate and can much more easily be shattered by a disruptive individual pupil.

Learning to deal with the variety of challenges posed by individual pupils takes time, probably a whole teaching life, and not all challenges are soluble! Some young teachers are frightened by them: 'I had rioting fifth formers – one kid who regularly "escaped" out of the window. Other staff seemed as scared of some of them as I became.' Others seem bewildered because they haven't as yet succeeded in distinguishing between real and 'try-on' challenges from pupils: 'They argue over things when they are clearly in the wrong, or over things which will make no difference to them, but not when they are genuinely being treated unfairly.'

What to do

1. Try to remember in the heat of the moment that your chief aims are to guard against an individual affecting a whole class's learning and to avoid that individual attracting support from other pupils and becoming, or remaining, a ringleader. If you are in any doubt about your success in confronting and dealing with an individual, don't risk failure in the classroom. Remove the pupil from the room or, in a school with a back-up system, arrange for the pupil to be taken out and supervised until both of you have 'cooled down' and you have the opportunity to think how to act.

2. Although you must be seen to 'win' in the eyes of the individual and the class, don't avoid asking more experienced staff for advice and/or active help. You will probably find you are not alone in having problems with a difficult child.

3. At the moment when a situation 'blows up' it is important that you should remain calm – or seem to act calmly. If the teacher had given way to her instinctive anger with Karen the situation would probably have escalated, and the work on the picture of the boy sensitively cradling the wounded bird would certainly have suffered.

4. Although this is difficult to achieve, try not to take challenges personally. For example, the teacher, despite her experience, was rattled by Tom's insistent questioning of her literature teaching. She needed the combination of his friend's complicit wink and her conscious remembering of her 'successes' to bring Tom back into perspective. One young teacher has succeeded in this: 'Now I don't let pupils get to me personally – I can handle it by distancing myself.'

5. You will lose credibility with individuals and classes if you fail to follow up and carry out threats. Although Karen worked well throughout the lesson, the teacher insisted on following up her promise to 'see her' at the end. As she obviously recognized that Karen had not genuinely intended to challenge the teacher of a subject she liked, her 'punishment' was deliberately low-key – an insistence on the girl doing something which she found difficult and embarrassing, meeting the teacher's eye and apologizing.

Small groups

A young teacher quoted earlier saw group work as a 'high risk' activity which she was not prepared to embark on until she had complete control of her classes. She had clearly not yet discovered that a class working in small groups is in many ways easier for the teacher to control. When pupils are turned in on themselves with plenty of well-structured work to do, the teacher is no longer the vulnerable focus of all the class's attention. Problems can still arise, however. One of the working groups in the First Year class, for example, spent much of the period arguing and if this had got out of hand it could have poisoned the otherwise pleasant working atmosphere.

What to do

1. If more than one of the groups in the room is working badly together, e.g. arguing over allocation of jobs or refusing to collaborate on an important activity, it's probably worth disbanding two or three groups and reforming them yourself. Make your displeasure very clear if you are forced to do this, as learning to collaborate is an important aspect of English.
2. If only one group is unsatisfactory, or if difficulties emerge late in a unit of work, check up on their progress more overtly, spend more time with them and be prepared to intervene if the pupils are not reaching agreement by themselves.

The whole class

The experience of planning what seem interesting lessons on paper and having them fail through the indifference, apathy or misbehaviour of the majority of a class is common to all English teachers. Although in her day the teacher had no lessons that 'failed' in this way, the final period with the Fourth Year had the potential to disintegrate into mutual frustration. Even without the interruption from Karen the class are described as 'listless or over-excited' and it took considerable expense of energy and will from the teacher to make the planned lesson come alive.

When a whole class works badly without commitment or uses its energy actively to spoil a lesson, young teachers are understandably demoralised:

I feel wasted and dissatisfied when I have a difficult class and the work we do has to be limited in order to keep them working quietly and busily all lesson. I think 'I'm worth more than this' when I'm marking their incomplete, untidy and careless work.

Many members of the class were either silly, disruptive or lacking in discipline, or all three; I felt angry at the conditions in which I was having to spend my life, and felt out of control.

With experience they came to realize that the planned lesson had the potential to be a good one. This discovery is sometimes made when teachers use the same plans with two parallel groups – it 'works' with one, but not with the other. To a certain extent, the failure is not in the teacher. Other influences of the kind described on pages 92–3 may have affected pupils on one particular day. Or, a more difficult truth to accept, the group may be an awkward one which doesn't gell or is dominated by strong characters and which may never or only rarely be taught without a struggle:

I think the key thing to remember is that no matter how good a teacher you are, there will still be groups who won't respond to you or your ideas, no matter how long or carefully you've planned your lesson and that you must accept it without feeling a failure or at fault.

What to do

1. Accept that there are no easy answers and that in the end the only truly effective solution is a refusal on your part to be defeated by the situation. This sentiment is echoed in many young teachers' reflections on their first few years:

   You cope or go under! I chose to cope and I suppose I'm a very much better teacher because of it.

   I overcame my discipline problems with this group by constant battling and repetition.

   I just kept plugging away at it persistently (and not sending out conflicting signals) and for no apparent reason everything calmed down in the second term — I wasn't doing anything different. It was probably just an unspoken feeling among the boys that 'we haven't managed to make him crack so we're stuck with him'.

2. Try to remember that most of the individuals in the class prefer an ordered atmosphere and interesting work – only a few actually enjoy disorder and wasting time. They may be making it hard for you but in the end they will respect and like you when you succeed in establishing control.
3. After a dissatisfying or distressing lesson, try not to think about it in a defeatist way, nor forget it. Analyse it coolly, perhaps in discussion with a colleague, so that you can see where faults lie.
4. There are many control strategies you can try, which are described in more detail in books listed at the end of this chapter. Experienced colleagues will be able to give support

and advice, so discuss your problems frequently with other members of the department and with sympathetic senior staff.

5. Although like one of the young teachers quoted earlier, you may at times have to resort to planning 'control lessons' with the sole aim of keeping pupils 'working busily and quietly all lesson', don't be forced by a difficult group into abandoning the kind of English teaching you want to do. Continue to plan what could be enjoyable, active and valuable lessons, so signalling to the class that you intend to teach in your way.

6. Try to avoid the temptation to keep trying new approaches and techniques in the hope that one will provide the magic answer. The main result is to give the impression of inconsistency so that the class keep testing you out to discover what the 'pattern' is. Learn from the teacher quoted in (1) above not to send out 'conflicting signals'.

Making mistakes

An unresponsive, unruly group will often, though, be the product of a teacher's mistakes in planning, organization or class management. An experienced teacher looks back to a failed lesson which combined mistakes in all three:

I was trying to teach a rather poorly motivated group how to punctuate sentences. I now realize that such things were anathema to them but I pushed on. I was in my first year, they were a difficult class and the result was that I finished the lesson minus four kids whom I had been forced to have 'snatched' from the lesson by a member of the hierarchy.

Another mistake which young English teachers can sometimes make is to feel that the emphasis in the subject on talk and sharing of experience requires an informal, friendly manner. They fail to realize that pupils can interpret this as weakness and that after the preliminary 'weighing up' period they may begin to test the teacher's control: 'When one is on teaching practice the "backlash" for being too lenient or "soft" is after three to four weeks. Now I have found the crucial period to be seven or eight weeks.'

What to do

1. In planning make sure that the material and activities are pitched at the right level for the group so, for example, take into account the short concentration span of younger and less able pupils. The teacher quoted above realized afterwards the inappropriateness of his class-taught lesson on punctuation.

2. Don't compound mistakes in planning by persisting with a

failing lesson. Have the courage to abandon one plan and move to another. Chapter 4 on preparation suggests some of the ideas and materials you might always have available for such situations.

3. Try to avoid the second teacher's experience by deliberately adopting a firm manner during your first lessons with a class and only ease it gradually into the friendly approach you might prefer to present as an English teacher when you are sure that you have established control with a class. It may take months.

COPING WITH THE BUSINESS OF A SCHOOL DAY

The pace of life in a large secondary school can be relentless, and this is exacerbated by the physical demands of a split site. The 'typical' day illustrates how the lack of time to stop and reflect makes effective teaching difficult, however well planned the lessons may have been in the quietness at home. The chief problem posed by lack of time is the loss of opportunities to prepare for each lesson, both in practical terms, to arrange resources and, perhaps more importantly, to prepare the mind to meet each new group of pupils and the particular teaching demands of each new situation. It was only through deciding to miss Assembly that the teacher found time to lay out resources for the mixed-ability class and through luck that the books necessary for the Fourth Year lesson were available. Driving between the two sites provided a brief time for mental preparation of the session on *Romeo and Juliet*, but 'switching on' to Oxbridge and A-level lessons had to be done during the brief walks between blocks. The tenseness at the beginning of the Fourth Year lesson at the end of the day was probably more the result of a tired mind than of Karen's late arrival.

This lack of time is the element of school experience most frequently picked out for comment by young teachers: 'I remember a kind of "swamped" feeling in my first term when there seemed little time for anything and a teaching objective could become surviving until 3.50 p.m.!' They contrast it with the relatively more leisurely programme of teaching practice: 'The obvious difference between training and "real" teaching is time. On TP every lesson was carefully planned and evaluated and there was time to do this.' There is general agreement that the effects of having too little time to rest, reflect and prepare are harmful to teaching:

Society cannot expect the best from us until it gives us more time for preparation, reflection and relaxation. When a new term starts it's as though the starting whistle's blown and the race is on.

Most teachers care about the standard of their teaching and we all have to get used to the feeling that we are being compromised due to the headlong rush of school life.

What to do

1. Beforehand, plan each school day as well as each class's sequence of work. For days when you have no non-teaching periods, balance whole-class lessons with workshop sessions, or noisy lessons with periods of silent, individual reading. The 'typical' day could have been better planned, for example, to finish with a Fourth Year lesson which would have depended less on the teacher's energy and, if it was necessary to hold the Oxbridge class during the lunch hour, to have had it rearranged for a less demanding day.
2. In the course of lessons, try to take short rests once pupils are involved in activity. It is best to stand at the side or back of the room rather than sit at the teacher's desk, which can be fatally comfortable, but it is unrealistic to expect of yourself full concentration on the pupils for 70 minutes.
3. To provide yourself with thinking time after a hurried transition from one lesson to another, it is sometimes valuable to move, after the initial 'settling down' session, straight into pupil-directed activity. Both the GCSE and A-level lessons began in this way, with students reporting back or introducing a topic while the teacher had time to gather her thoughts.

HOW THE REST OF THE SCHOOL'S LIFE MIGHT AFFECT YOU

When one of your lessons fails, it may not be your fault. Part of the previous section considered how the nature of a particular group might account for this, but more frequently the reason for the failure will lie outside your control. English lessons depend on the creation of an atmosphere in which pupils can fully respond to a poem, actively use their imaginations, absorb themselves in discussion or a novel, or explore a line of thought in writing. It is often difficult for teachers to create the atmosphere, and then to sustain it. Their individual classrooms are part of large and complex institutions and the life of the rest of the school will frequently influence what goes on inside them.

During the teacher's day there were several problems over which she had little or no control. The First Year lesson had a late and messy start because their assembly had carried on for too long. The Fifth Year were tired and nervy with the demands of completing course work and preparing for exams. On a warm afternoon in an inadequately ventilated room, the teacher was struggling to repair the damage done to her programme for the Lower Sixth by field trips and career interviews and conventions. In the final lesson her attempts to focus the attention of the whole class were nearly ruined by one pupil's problems with another member of staff. She could equally have found her teaching disrupted by pupils' absenteeism, medicals, window-cleaning, building noise, lawn mowers, faulty equipment, last-minute room changes organized by an administrator, traffic problems in travelling between sites, visiting speakers arriving late or not at all, freak weather conditions. You can probably add many more instances which are particular to your school.

Young teachers are often bewildered by the unpredictability of pupils and situations and, therefore, of their successes and failures:

One week you can be a genius, the next a wreck.

A lesson will work with one class and not with another – so is it the pupils? Some of the time I'm sure it is, at other times it's my fault, or the time of the day, or?

What to do

1. Try like the second of these teachers to evaluate what goes wrong and to be honest with yourself. If the reason for a failure seems to lie outside your control, forgive yourself but learn from the experience about how to react on a future similar occasion, e.g. if you know in advance that pupils will be leaving individually throughout a lesson for eye-tests, plan activities which will not be disrupted.
2. If you were not informed in advance about a school interruption or change of plan, complain about it through the appropriate channels.
3. If an unexpected event occurs such as a violent snowstorm or a child fainting and the atmosphere you needed for a lesson seems irrevocably ruined, don't be afraid to abandon a plan, however cherished, and fall back on one of the kinds of activities suggested at the end of the previous chapter. Alternatively, you could use the occasion itself as the new topic.
4. Recognize from experience that certain times of the day, the week and the term have particular effects on pupils' ability to learn, e.g. Wednesday afternoon is often the 'low point' of the week when pupils are restless; near the end of term pupils get tired too but unlike adults seem to become more nervously energetic as tiredness grows. When

you're aware that pupils may behave in a certain way, be prepared to modify plans to take it into account.

Finally, remember that generalized good advice (including this) is only helpful insofar as you can internalize it – and that depends on the kind of person that you are and the kind of person you are revealing in the classroom. Thinking about likely problems *before* they arrive, and deciding how you will respond to them, is of some help. Living *through* problems, however, and learning from them is a key element in becoming an effective English teacher.

REFERENCES

1. Protherough R 1986 *Teaching Literature for Examinations*. Open University Press
2. Marland M 1975 *The Craft of the Classroom*. Heinemann; Gnagey W J 1981 *Motivating Classroom Discipline*. Macmillan; Wragg E C 1982 *Class Management and Control*. Macmillan; Cohen Lou and Manion Lawrence 1983 *A Guide to Teaching Practice*. Methuen, 2nd edition, section on Management and Control, pp 177–215

The classroom setting

It is very difficult to be enthusiastic over a dog-eared set of battered paperbacks – what do you say to the First Year girl who brings you her copy with obscene remarks scrawled across the page? When all this is happening in an inadequately furnished room which appears to have been used as a picnic area/football pitch during the lunch break your morale is likely to fall.

It is enormously difficult to work in an environment which does not enable you to teach as you wish to. However carefully you plan a lesson, it risks being a failure if the set of books you need has disappeared, if the room is too small for you to supervise group work, if the badly serviced tape recorder fails to work or if a newly mounted display has been splattered with tomato sauce because the room doubles as a canteen.

In schools without specially allocated suites of rooms, English departments often suffer when the timetable is being planned. Administrators and architects have known for a long time that certain subjects, e.g. Physics or Home Economics, need rooms designed and equipped for their specialist needs. They have realized more slowly that English also requires specialist rooms and that allocating spare rooms at random is not satisfactory. This chapter acknowledges that few secondary schools provide perfect physical conditions for effective English teaching. It sets out to show what you and your department might aim to achieve within the limitations of your particular school and what you might look for in moving to a new appointment.

ENGLISH ROOMS

It is usually taken for granted that laboratories and art and craft rooms should be grouped together so that resources, equipment and preparation rooms can be shared. This should be equally true of English rooms. For a department to work as a team it needs enough classrooms to house a timetable block of groups, close together, with as many small areas, rooms and cupboards as possible, for storage, informal tape recording, department work areas and small group activities. For really effective department work there should also be specialist rooms nearby – one large enough and equipped for drama, a sound-proof recording studio and a room with blackout for watching television. To be close to the school library and resources centre is also important.

Pupils will share the department's sense of belonging to the English area if rooms and corridors look attractive and interesting. A teacher in her first year of teaching comments with pleasure on the English suite which is part of a new extension, 'with very unusual and vivid architecture and colour which provides a stimulating environment'. It would be less likely for a new primary school teacher to remark on the way buildings and colour contribute to the 'environment'. For generations teachers of young children have recognized the importance to learning of attractive and stimulating surroundings, but as secondary teachers we have been slow to follow their example. Displays of work, poems, bookshop and theatre posters, book covers and work from the Art Department on notice boards in corridors help to give an English identity. It is often possible to adopt forgotten cupboards and small offices and furnish them with carpet, armchairs or large cushions to make them into rooms where children can read by themselves, rehearse scripts or work individually with a teacher.

It is important that you as an English teacher should have your own classroom. This is not always possible, particularly in split-site schools, but timetabling can at least ensure that a class is always taught in the same room and that each member of the department has one base room on each site. In this room you should be able to store securely your classes' work in progress, folders and exercise books and materials for lessons. It should also be possible to leave out displays and books for reading and browsing through, but many teachers will feel wary of doing this unless the room can be locked when not in use for lessons. They will recognize the teacher's description at the beginning of this chapter of a room which appears to have been used 'as a picnic area/football pitch during the lunch break', and will be able to add stories of popular novels 'disappearing' from the shelves, tape recorders stolen and cherished displays being scrawled on or ripped. English departments have to try to resolve this problem. Ideally there should be open access to rooms so that activity in lessons can 'spill over' into mid-morning and lunch breaks; closing and locking rooms implies that pupils cannot be trusted to respect books, equipment and other people's work. They can help themselves by making it department policy to train pupils to be responsible for themselves in the classroom, to foster enjoyment of but also respect for books and to develop pride in finished work and so, by extension, respect for others' work on display. None of this will be enough, however, without active help from the school's pastoral and administrative staff who, understanding the English Department's policy with regard to their rooms, must support their attempts.

At the same time your secure classroom should not become an island cut off from the rest of the department. As one experienced teacher has realized: 'We have got to break down the barriers of being individuals working alone, and doing our own thing – so that there is this cross-fertilization of ideas and so that you work together.' If classrooms are near to each other, maybe with connecting doors – not folding screens which can be noisy, unwieldy and ineffective – it will be possible for teachers to work together, perhaps in teams, or with a colleague from the Special Needs Department moving between rooms to help individuals.

IN THE CLASSROOM

Activities in English lessons need space. A disillusioned young teacher, when asked what had prevented him from becoming as effective as he had hoped to be, put physical conditions in the classroom high on his list: 'overcrowding – classes working in groups in cramped conditions in a decrepit classroom.' Rooms need to be big enough for pupils to arrange furniture in different ways for different activities; for them to move about to fetch materials, consult about work, or choose books; for the teacher to walk round without jogging writing elbows or stumbling over bags to talk to individuals or join group discussions.

English departments are not used to arguing for specialist furniture and equipment, but the typical all-subject teaching room, containing only thirty single desks in pairs facing a teacher's desk and blackboard, can no longer provide what's necessary. It is possible now to support requests to Heads for funding with reference to the demands made by GCSE English and Literature exams with their emphases on group discussion, continuous assessment and wide reading. This is a list of suggestions for basic furniture and equipment for an English classroom:

1. Double tables and chairs, all light enough to be moved into different arrangements with the minimum of noise and trouble.
2. Pinboard over most of the walls for displays.
3. Lockable cupboard space with shelves wide enough to take GCSE folders, book boxes, storage trays of work in progress, paper, card, glue etc.
4. Display racks and shelves for books.
5. Blackboard or whiteboard.
6. Several electric sockets on two sides of the room with benches to hold tape recorders etc.
7. Screen for OHP and slide projection.

In addition, one or more of the English classrooms should contain:

1. Blackout curtains or blinds for occasions when the whole class watch slides, television or filmstrips.
2. A filing cabinet containing resource sheets for pupils.
3. Speaker(s) fitted on the wall for playing back tapes which need amplification.
4. Sink for washing out glue and paint brushes.
5. In the drama room, blackout, light stackable chairs, light blocks, wall or rostrum mounted spotlights, electric sockets for tape recorder and/or record player.

In your own classroom you will want to think about the way you arrange the available furniture. The advantage of a department having specialist rooms is that any layout you adopt can be retained. If you share a room with a colleague from a department which favours desks facing the front, and this is not the way you wish to organize the furniture, you may have to adopt a compromise layout or be prepared to move everything at the start and finish of each lesson.

When tables or desks are arranged so that pupils can sit round them in groups of four or six, *the chief advantages are*:

1. Group work is easily organized.
2. There is plenty of table-top space for materials.
3. Both teachers and pupils can move around the room and the walls are free.

The possible problems are:

1. The need to rearrange the room for whole-class discussion.
2. When you talk to the class, many pupils will have their backs to you and will need reminding to turn and face you.
3. Some teachers find that pupils concentrate less when the activity is individual writing or reading.

When pupils are seated in pairs at tables or desks facing the blackboard, *the chief advantages are*:

1. With a difficult or restless class you can place yourself at the front as the focus of the room in order, for example, to give a firm start to a lesson.
2. Pair work is easily organized.

The possible problems are:

1. For group work, class discussion or drama the room will have to be rearranged.
2. Large-scale rearrangement of furniture is time-consuming and noisy.

When pupils are seated at tables or desks round three sides of the room, facing the walls, with any extra desks in a block in the centre of the room, *the chief advantages are*:

1. Individual activity, pair work, class discussion and drama can all be easily organized.
2. Small-group talk can go on in huddles of chairs.

The possible problems are:

1. Organizing group work which involves writing and sharing resources.
2. Little free wall space for displays or other furniture.
3. The effects on concentration of being able to look out of windows or study posters on the wall.

It is worth considering where you will place your table in the room. The traditional position, centre front, makes a statement about the teacher's relationship with the class – the teacher is dominant, and in position to transmit knowledge to listening pupils. Moving the desk to the side of the room or to the back suggests that your role is different, you are part of the class, ready to work in the room with pupils. A young teacher discovered this benefit for himself and, rather to his surprise, found that he had influenced other members of the English Department: 'My idea to move the teacher's desk in the room I normally teach in, to the side away from the door, rather than in the middle at the front has been taken up by a couple of other teachers.'

RESOURCES

Books – the stockroom

The stockcupboard offered the complete works of Charles Dickens, *Prester John* and an apparently over-used set of *Kes*. I was pleasantly surprised to find a set of Sillitoe's *Saturday Night and Sunday Morning* in almost perfect condition. 'I'll use those with my Fifth Year CSE group', I thought. Within a week a parent had written to the Headmaster claiming that I was sabotaging her daughter's moral education.

Add to that familiar experience a stockroom which seems miles away from your classroom. The room may also be locked and when you enquire only 'senior members of the department' have keys. Or you may find a convenient and accessible stockroom which only contains 'dog-eared half sets of battered paperbacks', or a room that the stocklist tells you should contain many attractive books but which is empty when you as an innocent arrive on the first day of term. Like gannets the old hands have selected their favourite sets which will probably remain locked in their classroom cupboards for the rest of the term.

For a new English teacher, unsure of department procedures, any one of the above experiences can be devastating. Carefully worked out schemes often rely on a complete set of books being readily available. Although you may be a 'junior' member of the department there are things you can do to improve such a situation:

1. From publishers' catalogues or from book exhibitions, such as the one held annually at NATE's Easter Conference, send for inspection copies and read as much as you can. Give a list of recommendations to your Head of Department who will probably be pleased to have new ideas and should be able to use your pressure to argue for more money in the next allocation of department funds.

2. Discover how the department organizes the administration of books and, if you feel that the system is unfair or inadequate, recommend alternatives. Here are some of the systems commonly used by schools:

   (a) For a small department with a central stockroom, books can be taken out for use as required by individual teachers; the title, number of copies taken, and the date recorded in a central borrowers' book or on an easily visible checklist. Sets are returned as soon as a class has finished with them, staff checking to see that all copies have been brought back and recording their return. Staff know what is available from up-to-date stocklists and single reference copies. The system is checked by a member of the department responsible for stock.

   (b) Books are classified on stocklists as suitable for long (i.e. half or whole term) or short loan (i.e. single lessons or weeks). 'Long loan' sets, usually novels, plays and exam texts, are booked in advance with the teacher in charge, who is able to arbitrate when a set is particularly popular, check that sets are returned in time and, from the extent of the demand, discover what to re-order. 'Short loan' sets are taken out following the record system of (a) above.

   (c) Following departmental discussion and team-planning, most sets of books are linked to agreed units of work, appropriate to different years. The sets are stored in boxes – preferably tough wood or plastic – with envelopes of linked resource material, a contents list and several suggestions for how to plan the unit. The boxes are booked for half-term use. Some sets, e.g. of poetry anthologies and plays, are kept in stock for short-term use.

3. Make sure that as a member of a departmental team you look after stock efficiently. English books disappear in most schools. Sometimes this is almost a cause for celebration – when most of a set of Michael Rosen's poems go because Second Years have enjoyed them – but the majority are lost through pupils and staff being careless. There are no easy solutions to this but departments could adopt some, or all, of these suggested measures:

(a) As a department, make it a policy to demonstrate that teachers value books and expect pupils to do the same.

(b) When books are needed for homework and are therefore most in danger of being left on the bus or under the bed, there should be an effective system of checking on their return to school. All books should be numbered and teachers need to record copy numbers against pupils' names, in mark books specially kept for the purpose. When the book is handed in, the number should be crossed out, and pupils responsible for unreturned books should be checked on until their copies reappear in school. Pupils who lose books should pay towards the cost of replacement.

(c) As many books are lost when pupils leave school, there should be a system for checking that they have been returned. In one school the librarian coordinates a Book Collection Day each July. Before leaving for the external examination revision period, pupils fill in a form with the titles, copy numbers and prices of all the books they have at home, under subject headings. Subject staff check and initial these. When all the exams are over, pupils return their books on a given day and can only collect a 'Leaving certificate' if they can demonstrate that their book form has been checked and all books have been returned.

(d) Once or twice a year the English Department, or the whole school, can organize a 'Book Amnesty Week' when pupils are asked to search through dusty piles in their rooms and bring back long-forgotten books. For this to work it needs to be made into an event – it's worth it when shamefaced Fifth Years smuggle *Danny the Champion of the World* or *Tyke Tiler* back into school.

Choosing a course book

In looking at the best ways to use a department's stock, no mention has been made of the course books which appear in most cupboards. Judging only from publishers' lists, it is clear that these are widely bought and that you may find a range of course books belonging to your department. Whether you decide to make use of them will depend on your long-term plans for a given class and the relevance of material and suggested activities in particular books. Many English teachers feel that course books are limited in their usefulness, often because the underlying rationale does not reflect their own principles for teaching or because the books are not flexible enough to cater for the needs of all the members of a class. You may feel that parts of these books are relevant and worth trying, or you may belong to a department which expects you to employ a course book as part of your programme. If this is so it is important to think carefully about how far any course book can serve your curricular purposes and then to work out what criteria you will refer to in selecting a course book for use. You might ask yourself the question about any book of this kind: 'What sort of signals reveal most clearly the assumptions about the subject, about language, learning and the roles of teachers and pupils?' An effective course book will probably score many pluses and few minuses from this checklist:

1. *Plus*:   reading, writing, talking and listening activities integrated.
   Minus: separate, independent treatment of each of the four (in extreme cases with very limited concern for talking or extended writing).
2. *Plus*:   varied structure (of presentation of material and of emphasis on particular language modes).
   Minus: unvaried format – typically each chapter consisting of:
   Passage to read
   'Comprehension' questions
   Related work on language features
   Exercises
3. *Plus*:   providing materials that teachers can use in their own ways.
   Minus: trying to replace teachers or to force them into author-determined roles ('Now watch carefully while your teacher . . .').
4. *Plus*:   a wide range of language examples in different modes and for different functions, drawn from sources accessible to the students, some of them extended in length.
   Minus: a restricted range of brief extracts, implying what the author thinks English *should* be like rather than what is *is* (in extreme cases drawn almost wholly from out-of-copyright literary sources).

 5. *Plus*:   encouragement for students to draw conclusions about how language works from varied examples of living language.

   Minus: direct attempts to teach grammatical concepts out of context and the setting of artificial exercises (fill in the gaps . . ., pick out examples of . . .).

 6. *Plus*:   emphasis on students formulating their own responses to what they have read or discussed and sharing them with others.

   Minus: emphasis on discovering 'right' answers ('answer the following questions in complete sentences', 'punctuate this passage correctly . . .')

 7. *Plus*:   allowance for a range of interests and activities, with adequate choice.

   Minus: assumption that all members of a class will be working at the same time on the same activities.

 8. *Plus*:   opportunities for students to write and to talk at length, as well as more briefly, in various contexts, and to propose related topics of their own for further work.

   Minus: artificial lists of brief titles as 'topics'; assumption that formal exercises will lead to improved language use in following activities.

 9. *Plus*:   encouragement of pair and small group work by providing specific materials geared to this.

   Minus: assumption that talk will be channelled through the teacher, or sham provision for student talk ('Topics for discussion' followed by nothing more than a list of subjects).

10. *Plus*:   talking and writing activities proposed for different audiences and functions (stories for younger children, rehandling material for different readerships).

   Minus: restricted range of modes for talking and writing, and assumption that all will be performed for the teacher.

11. *Plus*:   encouragement of a degree of self- or peer-assessment.

   Minus: emphasis on formal teacher (or right/wrong) assessment.

12. *Plus*:   encouragement of jotting, rough notes, talking to formulate ideas, drafting and revising.

   Minus: stress on getting it right first time.

13. *Plus*:   material is presented without the author intervening at all, or the author's tone is personal and supportive ('You will probably find it easier to make notes about', 'What do you think . . .?').

   Minus: material is presented impersonally as a series of commands ('Read this passage and then answer the questions . . .', 'Complete the following . . .').

14. *Plus*: the book looks interesting, is 'readable' (in every sense) and does not make undesirable cultural assumptions.

Minus: the book looks a dull school book, contains material that will be uninteresting or inaccessible to many in the group and presents a biased view of some human groups.

Books in the classroom

In addition to the sets of books borrowed from the stockroom for specific purposes, classrooms need the resource of books which stay there for reference, for browsing and reading, or for using in 'dead time' during lessons.

A classroom reference set might include:

1. Dictionaries of various kinds.
2. Thesaurus.
3. Individualized programmes for help with spelling, punctuation or syntax.
4. Reading labs.
5. Booklists and reading lists.
6. Sets of crosswords and word games.
7. Old telephone directories.
8. A simple encyclopaedia.

A class library for pupils' individual reading is essential equipment in any English classroom. Although most schools have well-stocked fiction sections in the library, and many run school bookshops, provision of readily accessible and attractive books in the classroom is the most effective way of encouraging the reading habit. In the Fourth and Fifth Years, when 'wider reading' is part of every GCSE Literature syllabus, class libraries take on even more importance.

Departments have to take policy decisions about how much of the annual budget should be allocated to setting up libraries. It is expensive and, if class libraries are new to a school, departments may need to make out a case for extra funding. Alternatively, they could concentrate on providing for a year or two years at a time. Whatever decision is made, the commitment to providing books for independent reading must be wholehearted. Inadequately stocked class libraries are almost worse than none at all. In some schools, individual English teachers are allocated a specific amount of money so that they can choose books for their own classes. In others, the colleagues responsible for stock choose books for each year, basing their decisions on their own reading, on reviews appearing in publications like *The English*

Magazine and on colleagues' and pupils' recommendations. Once set up, class libraries need adding to from each year's budget, but they can also be supplemented from a variety of sources, e.g. second-hand books bought with petty cash, books brought in by pupils or the teacher's own books on temporary loan.

Judging how many books to order is difficult. As a rough guide, a class of thirty pupils will need as a minimum seventy-five books. This should be just enough to provide sufficient choice. There are other factors to take into account when books are being chosen:

1. If departments wish pupils to share their responses to their reading, there could be a restricted number of different titles with four or five copies of each.
2. If providing as wide a choice as possible is the main purpose, it will be better to buy mainly single copies.
3. If the class covers a wide range of ability, the selection of books will need to provide for very different readers. It will be important to bring colleagues from the Special Needs Department into discussions about what to order.
4. It will be important in choosing books to be guided by the need to provide non-sexist and multi-cultural fiction for each year.
5. Although fiction will make up most of the class library, children will also enjoy the opportunity to read poetry anthologies, biographies and collections of children's writing from other classes or from other schools.

Class libraries need storing in tough boxes – best made of wood or plastic. In rooms where materials can safely be left on display, the books can remain available for browsing and reading at any time on wall-mounted bookshelves, bookcases, a library trolley or a bookshop display unit. If book boxes are used, there needs to be a table or unit top on which the books can be spread about during lessons so that pupils can look at titles and covers and pick copies up for browsing. As most of the books will be paperbacks it is worth spending time and money on covering them with transparent adhesive plastic, which should preserve them and make them more obviously school property.

Paperback fiction is even more likely to disappear than other school books, and departments running class libraries need a simple but effective lending and checking system:

1. Each book needs to have the school stamp in more than one place and a copy number.
2. Each book box should be accompanied by lists, for the teacher and pupils, of the books available. This will only be useful if the lists are kept up-to-date with additions to the library.

3. Individual teachers need to use a simple checking system if books are borrowed to take home, e.g. a notebook in which pupils record titles, copy numbers and date of loan and then the date on which they return them.
4. To follow this up there need to be regular stock checks of libraries, best carried out by pupils themselves to encourage the sense that the class are responsible for their own collection of books.[1]

Equipment

Many teachers come to their first schools enthusiastic to use the full range of resources introduced to them during their training. The reality of what equipment is actually available comes as a shock:

The lack of resources has prevented me from developing the kinds of lessons I would like to have – the lack of video camera, television and video recorder is particularly frustrating.

The lack of electrical apparatus of various kinds has been frustrating.

There were so many things I wanted to try out – I couldn't even get hold of a tape recorder.

If English departments lack 'electrical apparatus' it will probably be as the result of conscious policy decisions. When budgets are tight, Heads of Department and their colleagues may have to choose between ordering, for example, new novels to stock up Third Year book boxes and new video tapes. A decision to choose books, though, only postpones the inevitable department debate about the growing importance to English of work with television, films, photography, sound recording and micros. Many English teachers will probably sympathize with this colleague's wistful acknowledgement of the situation at the moment: 'I'd like to mention the persuasive influence of TV, video etc., which will continue to detract from the important role a school plays in a child's life. This is an inevitable process – at least in English we can often *use* the medium of video to which children are becoming increasingly accustomed. Pity about books, though.' By contrast, staff in schools where the department has been able to buy a full range of equipment talk enthusiastically about (1) the ways in which existing English activities can be enhanced, and (2) the new possibilities opened up.

Enhancing existing English activities

1. Cassette tape recorders:
   (a) for pupils to record material they prepare, e.g. radio programmes, scripted plays, interviews

(b) for pupils to record small-group discussion to play back for their own benefit and sometimes for the teacher to assess

(c) for pupils to gather material, e.g. interviewing for information

(d) for teachers to play back source material for discussion, e.g. recorded performance of poetry and drama; BBC schools' radio programmes; readings of stories and parts of novels, particularly for less experienced readers who could listen in groups with a group listening unit.

2. Slide and film-strip projector: to show slides and filmstrips as stimulus for talking or writing, particularly when combined with sound, e.g. BBC's Radiovision series.

3. Film projector: to show hired films as stimulus to talking or writing, or adaptations of novels and plays (though for reasons of expense and convenience, projectors are increasingly being replaced by video).

4. Video recorder and television: to play back the wealth of valuable material which can be recorded from TV, e.g. TV schools' programmes; performances of plays; controversial documentaries to start or contribute to discussion.

5. OHP: not just as an aid for the teacher but also for pupils, e.g. to create poetry presentations; to display material during a talk to the class.

6. Computer: for pupils to use software, commercially or school-produced, e.g. as an aid to extend thinking; to deepen understanding of literature; as opportunity for group discussion and decision-making; as stimulus for and help with the development of writing; as part of language activities.

7. Word processor: to give pupils confidence with writing; for ease of correction in the drafting stages; for help in developing awareness of the composing process.

8. Reprographics: for producing teaching materials – worksheets, illustrated booklets, handouts – and for circulating student-produced anthologies and magazines.

Introducing new activities

1. Camera, slide projector: for pupils to explore the possibilities of using visual images as an alternative way of presenting information or imaginative creation, e.g. storyboard in pictures; combining with taped sound to produce tape/slide sequences.

2. Video recorder, film projector: to show TV programmes or films as material for exploring the media, considering, for

example, stereotyping in TV commercials; film adaptation of familiar source material; techniques of film direction.

3. Video camera:
   (a) as part of exploring the media, for pupils to discover aspects of film/TV craftmanship through practice
   (b) for pupils to collaborate on making their own programmes.

For all these activities to take place, a department probably needs, as a minimum, the following equipment:

1. A sturdy cassette tape recorder and several blank audio tapes for each teacher in the department.
2. A department store of material on audio tape.
3. Several sets of headphones and group listening units (depending on the size of the school).
4. One good-quality radio-cassette recorder (preferably dual-cassette).
5. Several OHPs.
6. Several typewriters.
7. Several simple cameras.
8. A carousel slide projector and/or filmstrip projector.
9. A store of blank video tapes and recorded material on video tape.
10. A simple spirit duplicator.

Tapes need to be organized with an efficient loan system for the department, and catalogued with the material described in some detail for busy staff who may not have time to play back tapes before they use them with classes.

In many schools the following more expensive equipment is held in a resources centre for use by all departments:

1. Photo-copier (and, in some cases, a printer).
2. Television with a large screen.
3. Video recorder.
4. Video camera.
5. Film projector.
6. Micro-computers and word processors.

If there is a fair and efficient booking system and a good-sized blackout viewing room for television and films, many English departments will feel that there is no need to purchase or hire TV and film equipment exclusively for their own use. The situation with computers is rather different.

In many primary schools, computers are established as part of the classroom equipment. Children, individually or in small groups, accept them and operate them often, easily and naturally and their use is not confined to any particular 'subject area'. In many secondary schools, computers have become the 'property' of Computer Departments, or several have been collected together into a central resource area and systems have been set up for departments to book time so that whole classes can be taken to the Centre to 'work with the computers'. Although time-tabled access to computers is better than nothing, the centraliz-ation of resources is not very helpful to the English Department for these reasons:

1. Pupils need to see computers as part of the equipment and resources which aid learning in English. Visiting a room specially set aside for them with the rest of their class gives computers the wrong kind of emphasis.
2. It is clear that pupils need regular access to computers if they are to make effective use of them, and sharing central-ized resources with other departments in a large school cannot guarantee that.
3. A resource centre rarely provides the right physical environ-ment for the kind of small-group work round a computer that English teachers will want to encourage.
4. Many English activities associated with computers rely on pupils being able to return from the machine to their own places, to apply what they've discovered, continue written work, discuss implications, follow instructions etc. A resource centre cannot provide the necessary flexibility.

Instead the English Department should possess several complete computer systems, i.e. computer, monitor, disc drive and printer, for use in English classrooms. For large schools in particular, this is probably an unrealistic recommendation, but it is an aim they should work towards. In the short term it should be possible for two or three classrooms to share a computer, with teachers working together as a team to plan how and when their pupils will use it. One of the departments will also need to be responsible for the computers, not only as helper to staff who feel unsure, but also in an in-service role to buy and review software and to introduce colleagues to what's available.[2]

Other resources

In time English teachers become like jackdaws. Wherever they go and whatever they read or see they're on the lookout for material that might be 'useful' in a lesson. These are some of the things you might find valuable, either as a resource in the class-room or for one particular topic or lesson: photographs from newspapers and magazines; reproductions of paintings; theatre programmes; articles; maps; free posters, information posters and brochures; *Radio Times* and *TV Times* for analysis of programming; advertisements; different newspapers' reports of the same news story; colour supplements and magazines for pupils to cut up for collages, posters etc.; newspapers for reading and comparing; collections of official forms; crosswords and word puzzles; interesting objects.

It would be impossible to predict the kinds of 'interesting objects' which might prove valuable and to match them up with classroom activities. A quick survey of one English department, for example, produced this list of objects which had been used in lessons during the previous few months (you might like to try reconstructing the lessons they appeared in): vampire mask; platform-soled shoes; gas mask; ration book; photographs of Hull during the Blitz; branch of flowering almond blossom; Oxfam Indian pipe; sea urchin shell; reproduction of a Douanier Rousseau painting; battered sun hat; thirty daffodils; pet rabbit; Sally's baby brother; pet pigeon with a broken wing; several sets of false teeth; Loch Ness monster poster.

You will want to build up your own store of worksheets and workcards, created for different purposes. Some, such as cards giving help and practice in mastering technical aspects of written English, or instruction and reference sheets for use during a block of lessons, need to be stored in the classroom in a form readily available to pupils. Sheets designed for use only in individual lessons quickly build up and you risk losing them if they are stored in the classroom. Many teachers, rather reluctantly, organize storage for materials like this at home or, more sensibly, contribute them to the department's central resource collection. One young teacher expresses her regret about not using such a collection during her first year of teaching: 'When I started teaching I worked very hard – till late at night every night – producing plans, when the school had plentiful books, audio-visual material and sheet resources. My time might have been more usefully spent in getting to know what was available and drawing on the experience of other teachers.' It is true that some worksheets speak with the individual voice of a particular teacher and are not successful in other classrooms, but this isn't a good reason for arguing against the pooling of a department's work. As this new teacher realized too late, reading and using colleagues' materials helps you to draw 'on the experiences of other teachers' as well as saving you time and energy.

As paper materials will be used frequently, it is important to look after them. Keeping sets of sheets in plastic wallets helps to keep them together and uncrumpled. Booklets need to be durably put together with strong stapling or plastic spines. Accompanying visual material is best mounted on card and covered with transparent adhesive plastic. If possible, materials need to be stored in a department office or stockroom close to teaching rooms. So that busy staff know what's available, the materials should be catalogued and a list which is regularly updated given to each member of the department. It's helpful to provide brief details about each sheet/booklet on the list and to keep a folder in the stockroom/office of single copies of everything available for staff to refer to. There are various ways of storing paper resources:

1. In labelled envelope files or plastic wallets in a filing cabinet organized to link in with the department index.
2. In a vertical storage system like Lawco boxes, which act like a stack of trays holding materials and labelled for easy identification.
3. Materials for use in conjunction with sets of books, videos or audio-tapes, e.g. pupils' activity booklets to accompany sets of novels and worksheets as part of a thematic block of work, can be stored in the kinds of boxes described as part of the earlier section on organizing stock loans (page 138).

Paper resources are even more easily mislaid than books and replacing them is a frustrating and expensive use of a department's budget. There needs to be an effective system for recording what has been borrowed, by whom and on what date so that other staff who wish to use a popular set know how to trace the materials and so that the return, or non-return, of the set can be checked. There clearly has to be a member of staff responsible for this, who will also have the job of disseminating information about available materials through the list for staff, of checking for depleted sets and 'topping up' with fresh copies, and of cajoling colleagues into contributing their work instead of keeping it to themselves.[3]

Putting up displays

However unsatisfactory your classroom or equipment, there should be nothing to stop you putting up displays of pupils' work. An old shabby pinboard can be covered with coloured backing paper, while in rooms without pinboard, displays can be stuck to wall surfaces with adhesive material.

Although organizing displays takes time and trouble, there are *many advantages to be gained*:

1. Displays of pupils' writing, drawing, designs etc. help to create the sense of your classroom as a working place – an atmosphere that classes respond to.
2. Pupils' work is seen to be valued.
3. Pupils enjoy seeing their own work being displayed and

read by others, and they like seeing what other classes have done. There is often positive feedback, with requests to read another group's novel or 'do' shape poems.

4. If a display is the end-product of a group's combined work, the deadline for completing and mounting it can act as a spur and discipline. The limitations of the space allocated mean that group decisions have to be made about the best modes of presentation.

5. Displaying work encourages pupils to take pride in what they do and to see the necessity of drafting before the final copy goes up on the wall.

6. For staff in the English Department, classroom displays can be another medium for collaboration. At the simplest level, they provide new ideas and a starting point for discussion of how the lessons went. Colleagues can organize their classes to take up themes from displays in other rooms and to 'answer' them in some way. Sometimes another teacher can be asked to read a class's group displays and to report back to the class on her/his impressions.

7. Visitors to English classrooms, e.g. staff from other departments or parents, can discover a lot about what goes on in English lessons from displays. It is probably worth the teacher or pupils adding an explanatory label to a display to 'educate' visitors and also to avoid misunderstanding.

8. As most pupils show artistic flair and a liking for bright colours, displays help to make the classrooms more attractive to work in.

9. For new First Year pupils used to the variety and quality of primary school displays, well-presented work on the walls is one way of contributing towards successful transfer from one kind of school to another.

10. Displays in A-level teaching rooms rarely have priority, but they can contribute not only to the creation of an attractive working environment but also towards learning. Particularly when parallel groups are working on the same texts, displays can become an ideas exchange, e.g. of 'controversial' extracts from essays; of schematic presentations of the interesting structures of works such as *Catch 22*; of students' own writing arising out of their own reading.

11. When English teachers plan ahead they can aim to use a block of display work as a way of balancing their heavy marking load. In the classroom they will correct and make suggestions about the writing in its drafting stages, but in working for display pupils are writing for a different audi-

ence, their friends and visitors to the classroom. It is important, therefore, to arrange for reactions to the work to be brought back to the pupils.

You'll be mounting or helping pupils to mount a wide variety of displays and it is important for you, and the children, to be aware of *the purposes the displays are fulfilling*. Here are some of them:

1. At the end of a block of work, for individuals to share what they have achieved with an audience. Work may not have been done with display in mind and may need copying out of books and illustrating, e.g. several pieces completed as part of exploring a theme; a range of responses to a class novel.

2. A single piece of work from each individual, composed in response to a shared stimulus and displayed for the class to read and consider each other's work, e.g. experiments with poetic form like haiku; newspaper reports of a trial held in class; pages from a 1914/18 war diary.

3. The end-product of a group's combined work, for the class and other readers to share, make comparisons and comment on, e.g. surveys of different newspapers' handling of sport, front page news, women's pages etc.; a group magazine; notes and designs for the production of a play.

4. Ideas presented in a graphic way to form one stage in a class's exploration and discussion of a topic, for individuals to react to and argue with, e.g. a children's charter as part of considering child/parent relationships; posters for and against animal rights in preparation for a debate; alternative proposals for the use of a piece of spare land, to be decided in a public hearing.

5. As the natural place for large-scale work too big to be presented in exercise books or in folders, e.g. poetry posters; collages to represent themes in books; posters for film or theatre productions of books being read in class.

6. Using a notice board as a 'post bag', for sharing information and views, e.g. book recommendations; reports on films and plays seen; pupils' novels and short stories to be read and reviewed by others.

If good displays can convert dull rooms into lively looking workplaces, poor or out-of-date displays can make them even more depressing. They need changing frequently. Neil's description of 'Room 12 at 2.10 p.m. on September 23rd' shows just that:

The atmosphere of the room is dull and dreary, with people fidgeting and laughing. I'm sitting here writing with the teacher peering over our shoulder looking for mistakes.

The classroom goes quiet for a while until someone starts to fidget on their chair and nearly falls off. The teacher's shoes sound like the boots of a guard in Colditz as they click on the floor. The room is painted in drab colours. There are two torn posters of 'Macbeth' on one wall and near me someone's written Hull K R on the display our group did last term. The uniforms don't help much, black, green and grey, which makes the classroom even more dreary. I just wish that someone would open a window and release the stuffiness of the room.

REFERENCES

1. More about class libraries: Raleigh M (ed) 1982 *The English Department Book*. ILEA English Centre, pp 187–93; Mills R W 1987 *Teaching English to All*. Robert Royce, pp 128–135; Jackson D 1983 *Encounters with Books*. Methuen, pp 41–4
2. More about working with computers in English: Chandler D and Marcus S 1984 *Computers and Literacy*. Open University Press; Chandler D 1984 *Young Learners and the Microcomputer*. Open University Press; Moore P 1985 *Using Computers in English: a practical guide*. Methuen; NATE 1989 *IT's English: Accessing English with Computers*. Knott R 1985 *The English Department in a Changing World*. Open University Press, ch 6; Payne J, in Blatchford Roy 1986 *The English Teacher's Handbook*. Hutchinson, ch 14.
3. More about organizing paper resources: Raleigh M (ed) 1982 *The English Department Book*. ILEA English Centre, pp 169–87 and Beswick Norman 1977 *Resource-Based Learning*. Heinemann

CHAPTER 7

Assessment and evaluation

Consider this cluster of overlapping and slippery words: assessment, evaluation, appraisal, testing, examining, marking and monitoring. The first three originally all had financial associations: they were concerned with fixing prices, values or the amounts of a tax. Now they have distinct educational usages, but not all teachers use them in quite the same way. In general, '*Assessment* is a term used about the familar process of grading and judging personal achievements, abilities and aptitudes. *Evaluation* is a term used about a whole study (lesson, course, project etc.) and is a process of gathering information in order to make decisions about how successful the outcomes have been.'[1] *Appraisal* is increasingly being used for estimating the effectiveness of an individual (a teacher, say) in a given task or role. There seems to be an increasing desire to *measure* all aspects of the education process in these ways.

You may have noticed, when the National Curriculum was first formally announced, that more attention was given to the organization and methods of assessment than to the curriculum itself. The uneasy relationship between these two elements has continued in the frequent changes and revisions of policy under pressure from different bodies: the National Curriculum Council, the School Examinations and Assessment Council, the Task Group on Assessment and Testing, the examination boards and the consortia employed to develop SATs. These shifts reveal, in particular, tension between the traditional emphasis on assessment as an aid to diagnosis and learning and the government's concern for accountability. The latter accounts for the desire to establish criterion-referenced tests in all subjects that will enable the performance of pupils, schools and teachers to be measured and compared. The more fully that this is achieved, the more the curriculum will be assessment-led, rather than the other way round. The result will increasingly be to restrict what goes on in English to those objectives that are to be measured.

The range of assessment

Imagine some of the variety of activities that take place during a typical week in an English classroom. Some actual examples are listed in the left-hand column below. The children are engaged in talking and listening, reading and writing. How would you set about *assessing* them in these activities? What would you chiefly be looking for? (A few proposals are given in the right-hand column, but many others would be possible. What would you add – or delete?)

1. First Years talking to the class about their hobbies or interests. Each pupil to choose a different subject and prepare a talk in advance.

    Limit the talks initially to 3 minutes each plus 60 seconds' question time, enough for two brisk double periods.

    Be prepared to give a talk yourself.

    Sit pupils in a double horseshoe with pencils and notebooks at the ready.

    Do feedback after each talk.

    A quick pace is essential to success.

    You are dealing mainly with *oral* skills, which include clarity, intelligibility, audience contact, interest and pace. The audience might themselves make an assessment. Everyone listening would want to comment on the content and structure of the talk; whether they could hear it; whether it interested them; whether visual aids had been used effectively; what responses there had been to questioning.

2. First Years listening to a Study Skills tape.

    Use the BBC tapes with word games as a common theme:
    Prog. 1 'Alphabet Fantasy Fanfare'
    Prog. 2 'Well-boiled icicle'
    Prog. 3 'My heart was in my mouth'
    Prog. 4 'Appletize'
    Prog. 5 'Collections'
    Stop the tape at fixed points.
    Pupils respond individually, in pairs and in groups.

    You would judge the effectiveness of the audience response by the degree of concentration, their ability to *listen* effectively, their response to suggestions for games and oral drills, their understanding, their readiness to apply what they have heard. Both 1 and 2 are product situations. The oral activity is being presented as a finished article.

3. Third Years staging a mock election.

    You are likely to see group discussion in action and the use

4. Fifth Years preparing a discursive essay: 'Education – what's it for?'
5. Fourth Years adapting *A Taste of Honey* for a radio programme.
   All of the above lend themselves to:
   (a) initial class discussion/preparation
   (b) group work on activity/theme/topic
   (c) group presentations in sequence.
   Your role as a teacher will vary from project initiator to adviser to audience/spectator. This should allow scope for a variety of assessment. Outcomes such as role play, extended essay and radio scripts allow summative evaluation.
6. First Years reading in groups *Balaclava and other stories* by George Layton and as a class *Treasure Island*.
7. Third Years writing up speeches or their views on politics.
8. Second Years responding to a poem 'A Martian Sends a Postcard Home' by Craig Raine and a piece of music 'The Planet Suite' by Holst.
9. Fourth Years writing a review on a book of their choice. You will need to help the pupils structure their responses and both extend and deepen their under-

of talk as process, that is, arguing, airing issues, making proposals and plans, influencing others. Group performances are more difficult to assess than individual.ones but it should be possible to assess how well individuals perform in a group. The shy and reticent pupils might be brought out in other ways. Perhaps they could make notes and report back to the class later.

Different types of *reading* will be involved in 5, 6, 7, 8 and 9. All involve degrees of comprehension without a formal exercise as such.

Reading aloud includes clarity, volume, pace, pitch and intelligibility as well as characterization, humour and emphasis. Projection is more important in a class reading perhaps than in a group reading. Pupils reading out their own work have instant feedback about the effects on an audience of what they have written. Both 5 and 9 particularly require summary skills, selection of key points, rephrasing, synopsis, giving a point of view backed, as in 4 where a formal debate may be involved, by relevant evidence.

standing. You are building up increasing degrees of pupil choice in the selection of material to be used. However, the material is anchored to something given. You will be seeking to create an individual and original response within the pupils' capacity.

10. Second Years thinking about unusual metaphors, doing creative writing. You might take as your starting point images from Raine's poem, printed on separate pieces of card for the pupil to guess at without naming the object, e.g. '—— is when the sky is tired of flight and rests its soft machine on ground'.

The children delight in pursuing unusual images of familiar things to test out on the group.

This task involves pupils considering precise and figurative uses of language. When pupils interpret in writing what they have heard, discussed or read, as in 4, 5, 7, 9 and 10, they are formalizing their language and doing the most difficult thing of all, expressing themselves on paper. Make notes in your head (or on paper if you can) during the lesson, immediately after the lesson or reflectively at home. Build up a profile of activities and achievements for each pupil.

These examples should have raised four key questions:

1. For *whom* do we assess? Primarily to help the teacher and the students to reflect on the learning that has gone on. Secondarily to provide information at intervals to parents (in the form of reports), to colleagues in the department (at times of transfer) or to school administrators (when concerned with subject choice). Assessments on behalf of other agencies – the LEA or the government – have in general to be seen as testing, not as teaching, devices: they do not assist the learning process, although they may influence it.

2. *Why* assess? The rather glib response is that learning in English needs to be coherently planned; education is not a random sequence of diverse experiences. Assessment is both retrospective and prospective: a diagnosis of what chil-

dren can or cannot do and a prognosis about what areas to develop next.

3. *What* do we assess in English? It is very fashionable now to talk of skills. We take it for granted that pupils acquire skills in the way it used to be thought that children catch knowledge, by transfer from one discipline to another (one good example of this is the training Latin was thought to give in the acquisition of English grammar). However, an obsession with measurable behavioural objectives can lead to ignoring less easily measurable conditions of imagination, of sensitivity in response, of awareness of issues or sense of audience.

4. '*How* do we assess?' is inseparably linked with for *whom*, *why*, and *what*. You may find yourself in a school where English teachers use the word *assessment* to describe any (or, indeed, all) of the following activities:

   (a) responding to pupils' talk or writing with interest, discussing its effectiveness and raising questions

   (b) comparing a pupil's work with that done previously, in order to estimate the degree of progress made

   (c) comparing the work of pupils in a group and ranking them by denoting marks or grades

   (d) estimating the degree of success with which pupils achieve certain criteria (as in GCSE coursework)

   (e) pointing out the errors or weaknesses in which the pupils need to improve

   (f) diagnosing the particular needs of pupils before making a prognosis for future work

   (g) considering the effectiveness of the teaching programme that has been undertaken

   (h) administering a ready-made (so-called 'objective') test in order to discover how far a particular level of learning has been successful

   (i) periodically weighing up a pupil's overall work in English (as for an official school report)

   (j) deciding which children in a group need extra help or learning support.

All of these may at times be helpful activities, but they vary in the purposes which they are intended to achieve and in the persons for whom they are primarily carried out. No one form of assessment is wholly accurate and reliable, and schools vary greatly in their practices, as the HMI report *Mixed Ability Work in the Comprehensive Schools* discovered:

A few schools considered that the use of objective tests was necessary in order to discover their pupils' grasp of ideas and acquisition of skills. At the other extreme, a few schools saw any kind of marking based on the assessment of quality as likely to produce in pupils a competitive spirit which they considered undesirable; they limited any assessment communicated to pupils to comments of an encouraging nature, and the records kept by teachers for their own use were vague and unsystematic. However, the majority of schools used some form of grading of pupils' work; some assessed effort as well as attainment; and a few compiled rank orders of pupils.[3]

Progress in English involves development in many different, though overlapping, abilities, and competence is not achieved in a neat, linear fashion. It is unhelpful to imagine that assessment methods practised in other subjects can be automatically applied to English. As the CPVE document states: we allow 'the recognition of experience and qualities which cannot be formally assessed'.[4] In thinking about what to assess, we would want to include areas less quantifiable.

What else are we looking for? The most important criterion of success is the children's enjoyment of what they are doing in the English classroom. As one teacher states:

I believe that the first principle in the teaching of English was, is, and will always be, ENJOYMENT. As long as the system demands it, we must clearly realize the pupils' full potential as regards exams. But, nowadays more than ever, we must try to create a situation in which they will ENJOY taking part in debate and discussion; ENJOY producing a piece of lovely written work; ENJOY discussing a poem; ENJOY having a good read; ENJOY having a spelling battle and, above all, ENJOY words. From this comes my second principle: I must begin each teaching year as if I had never taught before. Therefore all previous materials are put aside because if the pupils are to enjoy the lessons, so must I, and if I am going over the same material in the same way year after year, I shall be bored and boring.

PUPILS AS ASSESSORS

You may be in a school where there is already a tradition of encouraging children to assess their own work and to share in the assessment of one another's. This was uncommon a few years ago, but the shift in methodology from finished product to the writing process has involved a change in the pupil's role.

The self-assessment practices you might encourage could vary from those applied to a single piece of work to those covering a variety of English activities over a considerable period. You may wish to establish a spoken or written dialogue about a piece of writing, to ask for comments on what has happened and why between two drafts, or to suggest some analysis of what kind of writing might next be helpfully attempted. To establish a more systematic form of reflection, you might encourage the keeping of reading journals or learning logs. A number of descriptions of this process are now available, including an account by C. A. E. Marshall.[5] For example, one girl at the end of her fourth year writes in her self-assessment journal:

I found it quite hard to talk 'for' cosmetic experiments as I personally did not think it right to test beauty products on the animals, however I did enjoy expressing an opinion even though it wasn't mine. I get quite nervous before talking in front of the class, especially when giving a speech, but once I've started I actually feel quite confident. I do realize that oral work will be assessed in the new GCSE course and because of that I'm forcing myself to say more in English.

At the end of a block of work or a term you may wish to encourage a summing-up progress in some aspect of English (In what respect do you think your writing has improved during the year? Which pieces have you particularly enjoyed writing, and why?) or a more general self-evaluation that will be helpful for you as teacher. Their comments on the year's work as a whole can be passed on to their next teacher, perhaps in the form of a letter which could be an answer to questions such as:

What parts of English do you think you do best in?
What do you think are your problems?
What have you found most useful?
What would you have missed out of this year's work?
What do you hope to find more of next year?

A similar list of questions is proposed in *The English Department Book*, prefaced by the suggestion:

Please write about yourself and your own work. These are some questions to help you to do this. You do not have to write answers to all the questions and you may add anything which you feel is not covered by them. Please be as honest as you can – and be fair to yourself.[6]

Here is an example of part of a 12-year-old's letter written at the end of the Second Year to the teacher who will be taking him in the following year:

We did many topics, all of which I liked. We did a file of witches and monsters. I like drawing although I am not very good at it. Before that we wrote an imaginary diary of what happened to us on a desert island. Every so often we read a book . . . .
My weaknesses in English are, handwriting and punctuation, well that's what Mrs – said. I am not a very fast writer, I like illustrating my work and writing space and other science fiction stories. My strength is writing topics on my own.
In the future I would like to invent a monster and then write about it and to write poems. Also I would like to write a comic strip.

Alternatively, you can structure a pupil's self-assessment by leaving the first section open-ended and giving headings later:

Things that have interested me were the debates held in class, which not only gives you a chance to air your opinion, but to hear the other side of the argument as well. I also enjoyed the activity where your partner is given a picture and from their description you have to re-draw it, without looking. I also enjoyed reading and creative writing.

I have not enjoyed the oral practice, where we had to give talks to the class.

The subjects covered in English were varied, but I enjoyed Crime and Punishment most, followed by the Future. This subject incorporated reading *Fahrenheit 451*, and discussing whether or not the outlook for the future was good or bad. I also enjoyed the subject of a Teenage View of Life, but I would have liked to have been given the chance to write about the Supernatural.

The subject of Sport didn't interest me at all.

Reading – We have read many books over the last two years that were involved with a certain subject we were covering. We have also read plays, short stories and articles on subjects. I particularly enjoyed this section as all but one of the books we had to read were good, and by discussing and being made to write reviews, you learnt how to criticize the book and note all the details. I enjoyed *Fahrenheit 451, Brave New World, The L-Shaped Room* most of all.

Writing – I have learnt more about writing factual essays, which I never used to like. English has helped me to write in a more logical, structured way. I enjoyed writing descriptive essays the most and we were given the chance to write all different sorts of essays on a range of subjects.

Listening – We have learnt to listen closely and analyse people's talks.

Talking (oral) – We have had to give several talks to the class and also participate in debates and discussions. From this we have had to learn not to be embarrassed to talk in front of the class and how to hold an audience's attention. Also, we have had to listen to the other side of the argument in debates.

(*A Fifth Former*)

You will limit the effectiveness of such pupil assessments if you impose too many prompts. Try to avoid making the activity only an end-of-term, end-of-course exercise. If your pupils review a course in progress, you can use the findings in planning the next phase of the work. You will find that classes used to sharing and small-group work have little difficulty in moving progressively towards more complex forms of peer-group assessment of talking or of writing. In the latter case, some activities to consider are:

1. In pairs, children read each other's work and then, without further reference to the text, tell it back to the author, and then discuss what the author sees as significant omissions or variations.

2. In small groups, pupils listen to each other's stories in turn, and after each the listeners ask questions (no comments or judgements) of the author.

3. Stories are circulated round the group, each with an accompanying sheet of paper on which the readers write

comments and suggestions, so that the story returns to the author with four or five sets of written remarks.

4. Pupils are told that when they read the four or five stories in their group, their chief task is to pick out the best sections in each (and decide why they are effective) and any passage that might be revised. Opinions can be shared, and possibly some group re-drafting attempted.

5. Students are told to concentrate on their responses to the text as they read it, and then to share with the author what they understood, felt or imagined as they progressed through the text.

The whole process of helping students to reflect on their *own* work and to share responsibility for it has led in certain areas, like South Australia, to changes in the public examination system. Students learn how to 'negotiate the curriculum', with the teacher as ally and helper. In this development of the 'contract learning' of 50 years ago, teachers and students progressively define the assessment activities and the standards that will have to be achieved for success at different levels.[7]

MARKING WRITTEN WORK

Sources summarized in the section of Chapter 2 on writing suggest firmly that positive approaches to marking and assessment may yield better results than the merely analytic: pencil in the margin, not red ink in the text; a detailed comment at the bottom, rather than a mark out of 10; encouraging careful preparation before the final draft; and writing for a variety of audiences. You might yourself have been to a school where more traditional approaches to marking were the norm: regular written homeworks, probably in essay form, to be done in exercise books and submitted to the teacher the following day, to be returned next lesson with a mark or grade and a brief comment. Any teacher over 40 will be familiar with this picture!

We were expected to stand in front of the class and teach every lesson for the whole time and then set two forty minute homeworks at least per week and as class average was thirty-five, there was a lot of it about; I personally solved this by doing the marking standing up; it really concentrates the mind!

Although a minor revolution is taking place in our schools in approaches to marking and assessment, you will probably find as an English teacher that you will have a larger amount of marking to cope with than any other subject teacher. There are simple reasons for this: English is a creative subject so essays and stories tend to be long; individual expression encourages developing ideas; written outcomes are stressed; the language the pupils use is important. Young teachers can still complain:

One of the big problems that English teachers have to face is the amount of marking they have to do.

I am envious of those subject teachers who can 'tick and cross' with one hand while they engage in conversation. I find this impossible! I wonder if anyone outside the subject realizes how long it takes to mark thirty 16+ assignments.

I suppose it is the correction of spelling and punctuation that I really detest. Oh to be a Geography teacher and just put ticks!

The comments made above by teachers about their early teaching experience emphasize the special difficulties and unique rewards of the subject. In marking, English teachers are primarily concerned with responding to what has been written, not with information or correcting errors. The relationship between writer and reader is inevitably a personal one.[8] Indeed, the way we assess is bound up with our attitudes to pupils. We must convey the value we attach to our pupils' work and this raises questions about *what* we do in the classroom to preserve the variety and excitement of English for them.

Admittedly, some of what you do will be checking and proof reading, but this should whenever possible be done at the preparatory stage of the work. Grading work is the end of the process and you may share the reservation this young teacher feels:

I've never liked grading work and was rather disgruntled when my first headmaster said that he'd expect to see a sequence of marks for individual pupils at the end of any given term. Nowadays I never grade written work but I make a point of writing as full a comment as possible in response to what I read. Quite apart from my belief that this method is more beneficial to pupils, I enjoy doing it; it is far more personal and it tends to convey the value that I attach to the pupil's work.

Of course there will be requirements by the DES, by examination boards, by schools, by governors, by parents and by pupils themselves for you to grade work. You may be involved in internal examination marking, writing of reports, assessment of folders and scoring tests, all of which produce grades, usually comparing the performance of one pupil with others. However, as an English teacher you must try to be positive, constructive and specific in your comments and reactions to your pupils' work and point out what you have enjoyed and why, and which areas they need to develop further. Your experience will almost certainly confirm the findings of research that the ways in which teachers respond to children's work, both in talk and in writing, significantly affect their students' motivation and ways of working. The traditional view of an English classroom could be caricatured as one where pupils in a relatively homogeneous group seated in serried ranks perform a standard task in exercise books which are checked for errors by the teacher and marked in red ink, possibly with a total out of 10 at the bottom and a terse written comment, before being returned for correction by the pupils. Such a picture involves a set of assumptions:

1. Children should be grouped according to ability.
2. Tasks can be standardized.
3. Checking, marking and correcting by the teacher are paramount.
4. It is possible to deduct marks for mistakes.
5. The key (and possibly sole) audience whom the pupils address is the teacher.
6. For many of the children, the teacher's written mark and comment will be the only regular communication between teacher and taught.

Nowadays, you are more likely to encounter a different picture. Pupils may be encouraged to work on paper in a file. The traditional jotter may re-surface as the rough notebook in which first or second drafts can be written for preliminary discussions with you before a final re-written version is submitted. Children may operate as individuals, or in groups, with a variety of organization from sets to bands to mixed ability. Indeed, all levels of ability – and those with special educational needs include the gifted – may be your responsibility. You may have set a variety of tasks or given your pupils a choice within a common core of assignments. You may also include extension material designed to stretch the able and support material devised to give extra help to the slow learners. In such a situation, talking with pupils about their developing work is likely to be frequent. When written comments are made, they will normally be:

1. Personal ('I enjoyed this, John').
2. Supportive (praise before criticism).
3. Centred on the major purpose of the writing (did it build up excitement, make you laugh, provoke curiosity?).
4. Questioning ('how would she have felt about this?').
5. Practical ('would it be better to start here?').
6. Reinforcing (pointing to effective phrases or sections).

Your English Department may have evolved a positive marking policy as a basis for the assessment of pupils' work. They might conclude that it is important not to record pupils' marks on their work, not to use red ink but pencil, and not to obliterate children's writing by haphazard use of a correction code, as well as stressing the principles tested above. They may expect you to use an agreed correction code like this:

Sp	= spelling	$\odot$	= sentence ends
P	= punctuation	$\wedge$	= word(s) missing
$\sim$	= grammar	$!$	= what on earth . . .!!
NP	= new paragraph	$?$	= what *do* you mean . . .??

Ticks in the margin ($\checkmark$) indicate approval of specific phrases or ideas; double ticks ($\checkmark\checkmark$) of an excellent feature of style. However, enquiries in Hull and elsewhere indicate that children dislike the feeling that work on which they have spent time is 'defaced' by marking: 'I think teachers should not sprawl red ink pen all over your work so as to spoil it and then they go and put it on the wall and it does not look very good at all.'

You will probably find that different teachers in the department have different attitudes to the correction of errors. You will need to work out your own priorities, but in general:

1. Try at least sometimes to read through pupils' work *before* starting to mark errors.
2. Work out what each individual *can* achieve in language use before concentrating on what cannot be correctly written.
3. Be selective and pitch your corrections at the level of the individual (distinguishing those classes of error that are significant at that stage of development, and that might reasonably be expected to be put right).
4. Concentrate on the major shortcomings of the work rather than on the surface details (which may be easier to 'mark').
5. See errors as a necessary feature of learning: cues to the teacher about further strategies.
6. Try to imagine what the effect on the writer will be of the markings that you are making.
7. Make explicit to children (and preferably to their parents) just what your policy is about correcting work, and what you are hoping to achieve.

ASSESSMENT IN THE EXAMINATION YEARS

Some years ago your assessment of students' work in the fourteen and fifteen years age range would have mirrored your expectation of the modes followed by external examiners. With the help of published examiners' reports you would have advised pupils: 'the examiner will want a more organized opening paragraph' or 'you must have a reference or quotation to back up every point you make about Lady Macbeth'. As examining styles changed (from analytic to impression to criterion-based), so teachers learnt to adapt. A terminal examination system exerted a strong pressure not only on syllabus and teaching style but also on the assessments that preceded it.[9] This will remain true of those elements in GCSE syllabuses that are assessed by a final examination.

However, the popularity of Mode III syllabuses in schools has acknowledged for some time that teachers have a part to play in the designing of syllabuses and in the assessment of course work. Revolutionary in its impact on language studies at 'O' level was the Joint Matriculation Board (JMB) (formerly Northern Universities Joint Matriculation Board NUJMB) Alternative D[10] where candidates were totally assessed on the basis of a course-work folder, to include a minimum of twelve pieces but no maximum, and where there was great flexibility in the type of assignments set. Methods of internal assessment were also reflected in the syllabuses offered at 16+ with combined certification at GCE and CSE, e.g. the new NEA Syllabus B and the course-work option in Syllabus A.[11] The GCSE incorporates internally assessed course-work elements in its new syllabuses; in fact, internal assessment will become a compulsory element in all such examinations in English. Already the assessment by teachers of both oral and written work at this level has become a standard feature of many of our secondary schools and this may have repercussions on 'A' level too.

You may find yourself, then, in a school where teachers are already well used to at least some features of continuous assessment of course work. Even if your colleagues still see it as a novelty, however, you will have to establish a coherent policy within the department. Ideally your role as assessor should be a straightforward continuation of what you have done earlier in the school, rather than appearing to be in a conspiracy with your pupils to try to outwit an unknown examiner. What is a new responsibility for many teachers involves coming to terms with the assessment of course-work folders, with oral assessment, and with the arrangements for moderation and awarding. These three aspects are discussed in what follows.

Course work

The setting and assessment of course work is increasingly becoming a feature of A-level work as well as of the GCSE. You may share colleagues' enthusiasm for this form of examining while at the same time discovering its drawbacks and problems. Here are some of those problems, with suggested strategies to cope with them.

1. *For the pupils*
   (a) The pupils can seem always to be on trial if everything they write is seized on for marking and grading.

   Try to show through your attitude and your response to pieces of work that you expect pupils to develop during a two-year course and that each assignment is part of a sequence.

(b) Pupils need to be well organized for course work, particularly as English will be one of several subjects making similar demands.

From the beginning of the course, train pupils to work responsibly; keeping records, organizing homework sensibly, meeting deadlines.

2. *For your teaching*

(a) As assignments should be pupils' own work, how and when is it right for the teacher to intervene when pupils are writing in the classroom?

(b) At what stage is the written assignment to be regarded as finished?

Most syllabuses state that the Boards expect assignments to go through a series of drafting stages. It is right, therefore, for you to help a pupil with prompting questions, discussion, spelling pointers etc. during their early work on assignments. It is expected that pupils will draft their work. The assignment given to you for marking should be the final draft, not a fair copy with mistakes corrected.

3. *Organization*

(a) Boards require a detailed record from teachers at the end of the course of each assignment set.

Unless you are organized throughout the two years of the course, you will find it difficult to provide the required information. Keep careful records of the work you do with classes, according to the specifications laid down in your syllabus.

(b) Source material has to be available for Boards to see.

Most school editions and textbooks are well-known and only require references on the assignment record, but you will need to retain single copies of worksheets etc. during the course for sending at the required time.

(c) It is possible that not only single assignments may go astray, but that whole files might be destroyed or lost.

(d) Pupils sometimes transfer to other schools during the course.

You should have storage space for your groups' files in a lockable cupboard or cabinet. It is advisable to keep the files in school throughout the course; don't let pupils take files home. You need to be able to send the up-to-date file and assignment record to a pupil's new school promptly – another reason for keeping careful records.

4. *Assessment*

(a) Marks, or grades, for individual assignments should be recorded in mark-books/on record sheets, but what should be written on the pupils' work?

For the pupils, your comments should continue to be of greatest importance because they will not only evaluate the success of a particular assignment, but also point forward to what needs doing to make progress in the next. You may also want to put the marks/grades on assignments to give pupils an indication of the progress they are making in the exam course. If you decide to do this, remember that this may be discouraging to weaker pupils in the early months of the course and that all marks/grades have to be removed eventually before moderation takes place.

(b) The degree to which candidates can be influenced in what they write is much greater in coursework examining.

When you read and assess assignments be aware of the possibility that work done at home could be plagiarized. If you suspect a piece of work, because content and style are untypical of the pupil you know, you must check before you mark it. Pupils need to be told at the beginning of the course that copying or adapting other authors' work is cheating.

(c) All aspects of course work take time outside the classroom, but marking, moderation within a department and external trial-marking can become burdensome.

Plan well ahead. (Look back to Chapter 4 for further advice.) In eagerness to fulfil the requirements of the course you may be setting too many assignments. Check with experienced colleagues in the department.

(d) Responsibility for pupils' eventual results can seem unnerving.

Don't work in isolation. If your department only holds moderation meetings near the end of the course, ask if you can exchange assignments with a colleague in the earlier stages so that you can reassure yourself that your assessment is in line with the rest of the department.

Oral work

In working with a GCSE group you will be required to assess their competence in Oral Communication as well as their success as writers and readers. In the earlier CSE and pilot 16+ examinations, oral work was assessed in 'performance'; pupils took part in a variety of rehearsed situations or in interviews. Teachers were often able to call on English colleagues from their own or other schools to moderate these 'tests'. With the advent of GCSE a new stress has been placed on process as well as product evaluation. Thus, the traditional set pattern of solo readings and talks plus group debates and discussions is made more fluid, less discrete, certainly more subtle by constant teacher assessment of all forms of talk, preparatory and otherwise, in the classroom. As in the APU tests, listening and talking are to be assessed as reciprocal activities, not separately. These are some of the problems you might meet in this kind of assessment, with some suggested strategies for coping with them:

1. *Problems for pupils*

    (a) If pupils are aware of 'constant teacher assessment', will they be inhibited in oral work?

    You will need to explain to pupils at the outset of the course how you intend to assess their work. Once this has been said, try to avoid constant reminders; concentrate instead on creating an atmosphere in the classroom which will encourage all pupils to contribute both informally and in more structured situations. Don't hover near groups with a notebook or record card obviously at the ready.

    (b) How can you help pupils to be aware of their progress?

    Decide at the beginning of the course how often you will report back to individual pupils – perhaps once a month, at the end of a unit of work, or each half term. You might evolve a report card with space for pupils to reply to your comments, or arrange for a brief conversation in the course of a lesson. Make constructive comments about all aspects of their oral work with particular reference to particular occasions. Self-assessment journals described earlier can also be

2. *Assessment*
   (a) How can you assess informal or 'process' oral work in the classroom?

used to give pupils opportunity to comment on their own development.

It would be counter-productive to attempt to assess a whole class during one session of group talk. Plan beforehand which individuals you are going to focus on in a given lesson. In order to assess their contribution, you could eavesdrop on their group or establish a routine of audio taping (or video taping) the 'focus' group.

   (b) GCSE syllabuses aim to encourage a wide range of oral activities for assessment. How can you ensure the necessary variety?

In planning units you will need to incorporate both informal talk as part of the total course and specific oral activities such as simulations, talks, debates etc. Remind yourself periodically of the assessment criteria in the syllabus to check whether the activities you plan are giving pupils the relevant opportunities.

   (c) How do you arrive at a final mark?

You will decide on a final mark as the culmination of pupils' work during the course. Unlike pieces of written course work, most individual oral performances cannot be given a mark, so your assessment will be based on your recorded observations of pupils over two years. You will be helped in this by the moderation procedures organized by your Board and, if your department works together, by consulting with colleagues.

3. *Recording assessment*
   (a) What is the best way to record your assessments of pupils' individual 'performances' and of their progress?

Your department may well have evolved a record system which you will be able to use. You may, though, wish to adapt or amplify it. Try these various methods of recording before deciding which suits you best:

(1) a simple grid for each pupil listing the assessment criteria and the oral 'situations' to be filled in with ticks or a simple marking system;

(2) a notebook with a page for each pupil in which you record brief observations after lessons and which you then bring up-to-date at regular intervals with descriptive statements about individuals' progress.

(b) Most syllabuses require teachers to keep a record of 'oral situations'. How should this be done?

You could combine records of course work and oral work as the two are often closely related. It is important to be organized.

TRAINING AND MODERATION

Although it may seem daunting to take on responsibility for setting and assessing a group's assignments in English or English Literature, this is undertaken in partnership, first with your department and then with your Board. The process is essentially one of training in the techniques of assessment and moderation. As a new teacher, you will be invited to attend internal agreement trials, initially as an observer, subsequently as a full participant. By this method the examination boards train their assessors and group moderators. Your Board will issue to schools duplicated samples of course work completed for the previous year's examination. There are then four stages:

1. You give a mark to each candidate without consulting colleagues.
2. The department meets to discuss each of the samples and to come to agreement on a department mark. The teachers' individual marks and the department's are sent to the Board so that the centre's assessment can be checked.
3. Representatives from your department meet colleagues from other schools in the local group and individual teachers are asked to justify the marks they have given, before checking them against the mark awarded by the Board in the examination itself.
4. The department receives a report on the meeting from its representatives, and staff are then in a position to evaluate their own assessments.

Although this process may seem to take up time which could be devoted to preparation and marking for your own classes, it is an important part of your training. Both the departmental and local meetings can be valuable; many useful criteria emerge about content and themes; organization and structure; style, vocabulary, and use of language; creativity and imagination; ability to organize and develop ideas; flair; syntax; accuracy of spelling and punctuation. The aim is to reach a consensus about the overall merit of the candidates' work. Originality and freshness of response are rewarded; dullness and inaccuracy penalized. The process of coming to a consensus will help you to realize how other teachers assess course work, and the final comparison with the Board's marks will give you a standard by which to judge the assessment of your own pupils. It is a good idea to keep the sample course work and to build up a 'bank' of exemplar material for reference.

RECORD-KEEPING IN ENGLISH

When secondary teachers are asked what kinds of record about new entrants they value from primary schools, most of them are dismissive about teacher judgements and test scores. What they really want are lists of books read and samples of work recently written. There is a profound irony, then, that the commonest forms of English record in secondary schools are of the same kind as those rejected from the primary phase: test scores, lists of skills and teachers' verdicts. Valuable records give a picture of the work a child has done rather than an evaluation of it.

For this reason it may be better to begin by considering records kept by pupils themselves, sometimes in consultation with teachers. These may include lists of books read (with comments), accounts of major pieces of writing undertaken, or a check on language features mastered. Periodically, students may be asked to assess what (in writing, or talking and listening, or reading and responding) they think they *can* do or are good at, and what they feel they still need to learn, what their goals are. Making and retaining such records indicate that the process is carried out for the pupils' benefit and not just for the teacher's.

However, it is also certain that you will need to keep records of your own to track progress and to guide your work. The teachers' mark-book is essential. Most schools have a standard hard-backed or soft-backed version, looking like a ledger. Squared pages are often included – sometimes alternating with blank pages appropriate to keeping a record of work. In its absence, you can construct one of your own, using a file with card inserts for easy reference to individual classes. Mark-book or file becomes the handbook for the classes that year, and it is worth considering how most effectively to set it out.

Do not allow the name 'mark-book' to fool you, and tempt you to allocate one page to each class and one line to each name. The book probably will contain a record of numerical marks or grades and of assignments missed, but its chief importance is to build up jotted information about the strengths and weaknesses of individuals, and this demands space.

Many departments have developed their own forms of more permanent record-keeping on cards or folders (see Chapter 8). Any such system has to be judged by questions like these:

1. How much staff time is demanded to complete these records?
2. Who actually uses them and for what purposes?
3. What categories of information are included or given prominence?
4. What impression of teacher–pupil cooperation is given?
5. Is the format flexible enough for all ages and abilities?
6. Would any of the information be better acquired in another way?
7. What assumptions are made about 'progress' in English?

With these questions in mind, you might like to examine one or two approaches and to assess their effectiveness. The first shows the headings only from a four-part system devised by Mike Smith at Howden School.

(1)
> ENGLISH RECORD CARD
>
> PUPIL   TEACHER
> TERM 1   ASSIGNMENT
> Briefly explain what you chose
> to write about and why.

(2)
> ABILITIES & SKILLS
> READING
> LISTENING
> TALKING
> HANDWRITING and PRESENTATION
> SENTENCES and PARAGRAPHING
> PUNCTUATION
> ATTENDANCE, CONDUCT, EFFORT

(3)
> MY WORK IN ENGLISH
>
> My   Teacher's
> comments   comments

(4)

> READING
> *PRIVATE READING*
> Books you have read on your own.
> *TITLE   AUTHOR   VERDICT*
>
> *CLASS & SCHOOL READING*
>
> Teacher's   Pupil's
> remarks   remarks
> on above   on above
>
> Signature   Signature

CLASS........TEACHER.....
....
WEEK BEGINNING TO WEEK ENDING....
(tick and give a brief outline of content where appropriate)

WK 1 WK 2 WK 3 WK 4

LANG.

COMPR.

READING

WRITING

POETRY

HANDWR. & LAYOUT

SPEAKING

DRAMA

LISTENING

Photostat. Give one copy to Head of English and retain original as personal record

---

MY OWN ENGLISH RECORD CARD
CLASS.....NAME...............

WEEK BEGINNING TO WEEK ENDING....
(tick the work you have done and put a few words about it)

WK 1 WK 2 WK 3 WK 4

LANG. WORK

MY OWN WRITING

OTHER TYPES OF WRITING

MY OWN READING

CLASS READING

When you have completed your Record Card, give it to your teacher and ask for a new one.

The following are brief extracts from longer forms:

(i) Tick the most appropriate description under each heading:

Comprehension

Shows little or no understanding ____
Can grasp main parts ____
Understands most of his reading ____
Full comprehension of his own reading level ____

Sentences

Cannot write in sentences ____
Can only use simple sentences correctly ____
Use varied constructions ____
Fluent variation for particular effects ____

(ii) Select best description for each activity:

Listening	Teacher instrs.	Teacher reading	Pair work	Small groups	Class discns.
Generally unwilling and inattentive					
Sometimes listens, but with limited attention span					
Listens passively					
Listens with interest					
Listens and responds to what is heard					

(iii) *Skills list: punctuation*
Initial those pupil has mastered, and add comment if necessary.

full stop
comma
exclamation mark
question mark
apostrophe for possession
apostrophe for omission
semi-colon
parenthesis
colon

(iv) *Writing*
Comment briefly on each mode attempted during the year.

fictional story
story based on personal experience
story in response to one heard or read
personal letter
formal letter
descriptive response to stimulus
response to story or poem
factual account or description other

TEACHER'S SELF-EVALUATION

Assessing pupils and what they have learned means inevitably drawing conclusions about the relative success of your own teaching (sometimes assisted by the students' spoken or written comments on how *they* perceive the process). As one teacher remarked: 'Teachers need constantly to evaluate what they do. You should look at ways of trying to improve things. English teaching is a developmental process. As a teacher you are constantly searching for ideas to make your teaching more effective and interesting.'

This kind of reflection is not an artificial exercise to be undertaken only on teaching practice. Deciding 'what counts as success' for you in particular situations is an essential professional skill, and can be guided by published self-appraisal frameworks.[12] How do you react to the following accounts by three teachers, distinguishing between their good and bad lessons, and how far do you identify with their feelings?

A bad lesson may occur particularly at the end of the day when I'm tired. I am then less patient and react more to provocation from silly children and create an unpleasant atmosphere with my threats. I hate doing this and go home feeling miserable and angry with individual pupils. If I am thwarted in presenting something I know *should* go well, I blame the pupils, whose fault it often is, but it could also be my own lack of fizz, enthusiasm, or sufficiently detailed explanation.

Good lessons occur usually in the morning! One lesson with First Years recently was delightful. We were to begin reading *The Hobbit*, which some had already read with great enthusiasm, as a class reader and became immediately side-tracked by pupils discussing *how* to settle down and read for maximum enjoyment. It was 'a learning experience' and also revealed who read what. When we did begin reading, I selected some able readers to create the best effects and draw other less confident readers into the story. We ran out of time before I could sign out the individual copies, but several pupils asked when they could take the books home. Wonderful!

Often, one can leave a classroom feeling quite euphoric and the resultant work is poor, showing that the elation was rather one-sided, and vice versa. One utterly disastrous lesson was when I was trying to talk about rhythm and metre to a literature group; I was challenged about stress, so I first went round the class asking for the stressed syllables of a variety of words which I spelled to them (incidentally, only three of the nineteen got it right); the original challenger was still dissatisfied, so I handed her a dictionary and asked her to spell any words she chose, having shown her first how the stresses were marked. She asked me about ten after which I smiled, having, as I thought, proved my point. Imagine my dismay when she handed me the dictionary, round-eyed with wonder, and said, 'Madam, it must have taken you years to learn all those!' I had forgotten one of the most important principles of teaching: never take anything for granted with pupils (not even a GCSE Literature group).

A new term with a new theme: 'The Modern World.' Class and I were new to each other. Started to discuss the theme in a clinical fashion relating it to labour-saving devices. Class unresponsive/suspicious. They did volunteer ideas for a blackboard list. Their silence disturbed me and I felt very much 'on show' and doing a performance for them. My mistake lay in not having them discuss their ideas for the theme – even though I well knew that this would have made it theirs, resulting in a caring approach.

I showed no irritation at their lack of interest – they were all behaving well and politely – but towards the end of the first double lesson I introduced the idea of working either alone or with a friend to devise a machine of their own which would do a job they hated doing. (This was a copy lesson after I'd overheard a staff-room conversation!) As I later saw, it was largely very badly done, with no heart – not surprising!

A lesson that went well (how do I know? – the feedback was red-hot!). This lesson followed closely on the one described above. At the start I began with informal discussion and the honest admission that I felt we had neither of us performed well over the last couple of weeks. Why? Useful things said and class really opened up on their likes and dislikes. Asked for suggestions as to what we might work on connected with the term's theme. As soon as 'fashion' was suggested, a definite excitement from all. Me: 'Tell me what you mean by fashion' – contributions from just about everyone. I confessed genuine ignorance as to the latest trends – and asked what 'trendy' meant – for their age group.

Pupils had a hand in making a blackboard list of vocabulary, volunteers coming out to help compile this. Me: 'How could we use this idea in our work in English, bearing in mind we have to etc., etc., . . . ?

A fashion magazine suggested.

I made an instant decision to let them form groups which would make a magazine, trying to be innovative – collecting pictures if they wished but doing much of the writing/drawing themselves.

At the time of writing this is still going on, with some very good results – both on paper and audibly with rarely a thing being said in lessons which is not about the work in hand. Boys and girls are equally 'taken' with the subject.

I must find poetry and prose to do with this and find a vehicle for having the magazine work shared – possibly some drama about the magazine world? – time will run out and we will probably want to do lots more. A lot of incidental learning has taken place ('Is there an apostrophe in Levi's?' etc.). The magazine idea is old but their enthusiasm is new. What made the difference – the pupils having responsibility for the work – an agreement from the class that this would be of interest – the honesty between the parties – the element of fun in the work (this time not the teacher's idea of what would be fun, but theirs).

I feel that all teachers have to think on their feet and this is not easy. In my bad lesson I had planned an idea and wanted to carry it through, regardless of the class's feelings. When I remember to have what is a human approach and a caring attitude I know the resulting work is better – the clinical approach usually fails – I fail as an imparter of knowledge.

REFERENCES

1. Chubb Brian S 'Some initial thoughts on evaluation'. Unpublished paper. Also see Cohen Lou and Manion Lawrence 1983 *A Guide to Teaching Practice*, 2nd ed. Methuen pp 245–67
2. *The National Curriculum 5–16* 1987 a consultation document. DES
3. HMI 1978 *Mixed Ability Work in the Comprehensive Schools*. HMSO
4. *The Certificate of Pre-Vocational Education* 1984 Consultative document. Joint Board for Pre-Vocational Education
5. Marshall CAE 1984 *Mixed Ability Teaching: Reading journals, learning logs, assessment*. Duplicated paper by author
6. ILEA English Centre 1982 *The English Department Book*
7. Brian Johnston S 1983, 1987 *Assessing English. Helping Students to Reflect on Their Work*, revised edn. Open University and St Clair Press
8. For further suggestions on marking policy, see Protherough Robert 1983 *Encouraging Writing*. Methuen, Ch. 7; Allen David in Chapter 12 of Blatchford Roy 1986 *The English Teacher's Handbook*. Hutchinson; Dunsbee Tony and Ford Terry 1980 *Mark My Words*. Ward Lock
9. See Protherough Robert 1986 *Teaching Literature for Examinations*. Open University Press, Chs 1–3
10. Joint Matriculation Board: Examinations Council GCE Regulations and Syllabuses. Manchester
11. NEA Joint GCE/CSE English Syllabus A and B 1987
12. A useful guide is Peacock Colin 1990 *Classroom Skills in English Teaching: a self-appraisal framework*. Routledge. Also see Wragg E C 1984 *Classroom Teaching Skills*. Croom Helm.

Beyond the classroom

CHAPTER 8

Belonging to a department

What can you reasonably expect of the department that you enter as a new teacher? This chapter will develop the following points in more detail, but briefly you have a right to:

1. Extend your expertise by working in a greater variety of ways with a wider range of pupils.
2. Be consulted about department policy and to take a share in making decisions.
3. Be given specific responsibilities that are within your capabilities.
4. Be kept informed about wider developments that are likely to affect you and your work.
5. Discuss your own professional development with your Head of Department.
6. Be provided with adequate resources to support the work for which you are timetabled.
7. Share ideas and opinions regularly with other members of the department.
8. Be supported in maintaining an effective learning environment in the classroom.
9. Expect help in dealing with such problems as disruptive pupils.
10. Receive advice on how to liaise with parents about their children's progress.

The extent to which these expectations are met and the general attitude of your colleagues will determine how quickly you feel you *belong* to the department. Some comments of probationary teachers are significant. One writes:

There is much to be done in our department and I was surprised at how much I was left on my own to develop my own teaching style. Perhaps this is an isolated case but with no departmental meetings, little coordination between staff and personality clashes within the department very little progress seems to be made.

Very different experiences seem to underline comments like these:

1. People don't all rush off at the end of the day – even on Friday. They hang around – just chatting or talking shop.

2. It is not so much guidance that is needed but a forum for ideas.
3. Good colleagues can mean the difference between being tired at the end of term, and being suicidal.
4. Teaching is a very solitary job but it is nice to know of others in a similar position to yourself.

English teaching is especially tiring ('emotionally it's very wearing, and physically, and mentally') and the sheer fatigue of the job is best relieved by 'just chatting or talking shop'.

Practical help may involve finding the right poem in the stockroom, making the video-recorder work or dealing with problem pupils. The department should also be 'a forum for ideas'. How these ideas circulate is discussed later.

Essential are 'good colleagues', without the intrusive personality clashes which can ruin professional working relationships. It is not uncommon to find disputes in an English department over methodology (see pp 29–30) but these issues should not polarize the people who have to work together. Unfortunately, there may sometimes be a philistine unwillingness to talk shop or discuss lessons: 'I received virtually no help at all in the actual practice of teaching and learnt through a process of trial and error. Talk on teaching theory was limited and generally in the staff room there was not much discussion about teaching methods or principles.' Put another way: 'More mention of down-to-earth practicalities would have been helpful, e.g. what to do when everyone else in the department teaches from *The Art of English*; techniques of good class control, e.g. seating, starts and finishes of lessons etc.; being a form tutor and so on.' Good colleagues can give that necessary support.

One of the findings of a recent research report into the views of effective English teachers was that the dominant influence on their development had been the support of other classroom teachers.[1] It is very important that teachers should be able to discuss lesson failures and discipline problems without losing face, and should develop the ability to share ideas and materials. The same report usefully summarises the ways in which a good English department can become a major training agency.[2]

The key figure for a young English teacher will be the Head of Department. Repeated comments testify to the importance of a person that can strike the right balance between professional tutor and critical friend, giving support without undue interference:

I have been helped considerably by a Head of Department who provides a super balance of being there in times of trouble and yet not interfering; leaving me to tackle my classes on my own.

Undoubtedly, my Head of Department has been my biggest source of help and advice. Not only has he given periodic help with initial problems, he has encouraged me in my pursuit of my own interests. I have also found that he has been most fair in allocating examination classes.

The H of D is very supportive and honest in his dealings with myself and other departmental colleagues without being at all obtrusive or tyrannous.

Most of the help that I have received has come from my Head of Department, although perhaps the most helpful aspect of his approach has been to leave me to get on by myself. However, he is always approachable and open to suggestions and ideas.

My Head of Department has been invaluable in many areas, including marking and planning.

A good head of English will attempt to promote your personal development in a number of ways:

1. Allocate appropriate programme of work. You will need to be given a proper balance of classes on a reduced timetable. Clearly, it is desirable for you to have a range of ages and abilities. You should not initially be given lower sets and notoriously difficult classes. You might expect your fair share of examination groups.

2. Outline policy. You will need clear guidelines on departmental philosophy, discipline, what is taught and how it should be assessed. However, you should feel able to develop your own ideas and approaches within that broad framework.

3. Show resources. You will need to know not only the location of books and other materials but also the range. You need to understand the issue and retrieval systems and who in the department is responsible for what.

4. Check files. It is the responsibility of your Head of Department to ensure that you, as a new teacher, are preparing work appropriate to your pupils and that you keep proper records.

5. Inspect books. Every so often you will need to collect in exercise books or folders from your pupils as a basis for a discussion with your Head of Department about written work and standards of marking.

6. Discuss pupils. As well as talking about their development, you may have concern about the problems or the disruptive behaviour of individuals (see Chapter 5). In most schools, the first step with difficult children is to refer them to the Head of Department.

7. Report your progress. After consultation with colleagues and senior staff, the Head of Department will evaluate your

strengths and weaknesses before writing the comments to be officially reported to the advisory service of the LEA. This obligatory report is discussed in more detail later in the chapter.

DEPARTMENTAL IDENTITY

Cohesion within a department is affected not only by the personalities within it, but also by its size, by the extent to which it consists of specialists, by the length of time staff have been in the school, and by the physical base for the department. These three comments give some indication of the possible range:

There are two English teachers in the school and we split the timetable down the middle from First to Sixth Form.

The English department comprises eight full-time English teachers.

We are a department of sixteen.

Lucky English departments are located in a suite of classrooms with an office or a place where people can meet (see pp 133–5). They may have control over a library or resources area. This meeting place allows the department to become 'a forum for ideas'. Not all English departments are so fortunate. However, everyone should be able to manage a noticeboard for current circulars, timetables, syllabuses and class lists. A copier or duplicator is desirable as a means of getting information round teachers quickly. Links with the outside world are helped by a telephone; internal relations are more harmonious if there is a kettle to hand!

When you enter a new department, you may at first not be aware of some of the problems of personnel that make it difficult to work as an effective team. Quite apart from involving you as a new colleague, the Head of Department may be having to cope with any of the following (which you should also come to recognize):

1. The one-sex staff. It is not unusual for a male Head of English to have an all-female department. This may be as true in a co-educational as a single-sex school. Although this need not be a problem, there will be issues of sex stereotyping to be resolved and the common identification of English, especially Literature, by the pupils as 'a girls' subject'.
2. The older staff. The innovative Head of Department may have difficulty with senior colleagues who are rather set in their ways and resist both new methods of working and curricular change and you may find their scepticism disheartening.

3. The Head/Deputy Head. Members of a senior management team are seldom able to give the time, energy and commitment to a department that full-time teachers can offer. Inevitably, they are pulled out of the classroom, often at short notice; cannot attend all departmental meetings or training days, or even prepare lessons in as much detail as they themselves would like.
4. The unpromoted but experienced teacher. It is difficult constantly to re-enthuse a well-established teacher with a responsibility allowance who is unlikely to move. Job rotation can help. All too often, however, such a teacher is a block to progress for a junior member of the department.
5. The non-specialist. Most English departments will use staff from other subject areas, especially Drama, Special Education Needs and PE. Despite their enthusiasm and commitment, their first loyalty will be to another department and their teaching style may be inappropriate to English. They also require subject-specific training.

The way in which the human balance can influence a young teacher's view of departmental identity can be exemplified by this probationer's comments:

I am one of four new teachers in our department. Two are Scale 2 with three or more years' experience. There is also a Scale 1 with a couple of years behind her. The Head of Lower School English is new to the job and this fact as well as the new membership means that the department is entering a new phase. There is no rigid mould into which I have to fit. (We also have a new English block – this is a contributory factor.)
Thus I feel that I can contribute to establishing the new 'look' of the department with no fear of breaking unwritten codes or conventions.

MEETINGS

Departmental meetings are the formal structure within which the 'forum for ideas' can become a reality. Ideas will circulate informally outside the framework, but only in meetings can proper discussion and decision-making take place. For this reason, time should not be wasted on routine administration.

Schools vary in the frequency of meetings but once a month is probably average. They need not be long – an hour is ample – and can sometimes be organized within a double period when teachers are free or, less conveniently, in lunchtimes or after school.

In an effectively run department, you will probably find that:
1. The dates of meetings are announced well in advance.
2. Agendas and papers for discussion are supplied in time for you to read them before the meeting.

3. Somebody is responsible for taking minutes, to avoid subsequent arguments about what was decided.
4. There are arrangements for you and others to raise matters that concern you.
5. Much of the detailed work is referred to individuals or small groups that report back to subsequent meetings.
6. On occasions a deputy or member of another department is invited to attend for discussion of matters that have implications beyond the department itself.
7. A finishing time is agreed, so the meetings do not drag on unproductively!

An analysis of the minutes over four years of one English department showed the following to be the most commonly discussed topics, in order of frequency. Would you have expected this order?

(a) examinations and testing
(b) grouping and setting
(c) books
(d) reporting and assessment
(e) libraries
(f) literature
(g) money
(h) audio-visual provision
(i) stock rooms and cupboards
(j) creative writing
(k) withdrawal of pupils
(l) timetable
(m) oral work
(n) curriculum
(o) resources
(p) equipment
(q) discipline
(r) departmental responsibilities
(s) rooms
(t) prizes
(u) students
(v) school magazine

English departmental meetings are usually of two kinds: about ideas and about issues. Although as a new teacher you may initially feel reticent about making a contribution to the latter, you have much to offer to the former. More recently trained, you may have fresh insights and approaches which will benefit your more jaded colleagues. Valuable sharing and brainstorming sessions may discuss successful ideas for lessons, samples of pupils' work, recent books for class use, new modes of assessment, materials for thematic writing and so on. They are particularly valuable if someone records the ideas and duplicates them as a shared resource.

Meetings about issues are also necessary to resolve differences of viewpoint among individual members of a department into an agreed and workable policy. As policies must be available to the wider communities of school and parents, they need to be thoroughly talked through and properly documented. Since departmental meetings are essentially public, it is possible for private stances to harden when adopted in front of other people and for views to become polarized. Even small niggles can seem critical of the whole way the department is being run. In such circumstances new teachers and probationers can be inhibited from speaking at all. Yet, here again, you may have a lot to offer because you have the fresh outsider's view of any weaknesses and inconsistencies of approach. You should not be afraid to air those views, because they can be most valuable.

FRAMING POLICY

Some suggestions about how you might read and use formal policy statements were offered on pp 58–61. Although a single person may write such a document, it should embody departmental agreement on key issues discussed elsewhere in this volume:

1. How to group pupils.
2. Marking and assessment.
3. Examinations.
4. The teaching of literature.
5. Learning support.
6. How to receive the new intake.
7. Libraries.
8. Audio-visual equipment and resources.
9. Homework.

Because of changes in personnel, as well as in principles and practice, such papers need to be in a state of almost perpetual revision.

Statements are of two types: first, summaries of an agreed consensus or strategy within a department and therefore *retrospective* (they crystallize existing practice and consolidate future action) and, secondly, declarations of intent which are *prospective* (they identify key issues for debate and delineate forward planning). The first extract that follows is an example of a retrospective statement while the second is prospective.

The English Department operates as one of a number of broadly autonomous departments within the school. It is not integrated with other subjects and Drama is taught separately. Nor is it conceived merely as a service department. We have operated for a number of years a mixed-ability system. Our thinking, influenced by Jackson, Marland, Kelly *et al*, is that early selection according to ability prejudices a child's chances and that the subject lends itself to whole-class, small group and individual learning. With that in mind we teach theme-based English and are committed to the development of resource-based learning. Our English teaching is literature orientated. We also have a language syllabus in Years 1–3.

In our reading policy, we would try to develop reading skills per se and also reading for enjoyment/satisfaction. A few items in our approach:

(i) preliminary testing of intake year in September – CLOZE procedures, plus Sentence Evaluation tests as screening process;
(ii) use of GAPADOL tests in 13+ age group; GAP test in First Year plus spelling test, handwriting, extended piece of writing;
(iii) use as part of policy for:
  • learning support
  • alerting teachers to possibility of reading extension.
(iv) INTENSIVE reading – to be based as much as possible on current texts – either course work or reading books – to develop lower order and higher skills, e.g. inference, empathy, where appropriate.
(v) EXTENSIVE reading – through broad library provision during lesson times and lunchtimes; class libraries; talking about books; alternatives to, as well as, reviews etc.

Policy statements embrace both the ethos of a department's approach and the classroom practicalities. No policy is any good if it is ignored in practice or if the nuts and bolts of its implementation have not been worked out.

Particularly if you are working in a large department, you may find that much of the work in formulating or revising policy is delegated to working parties. These are small groups, sometimes consisting of only a pair of teachers, who undertake to investigate a problem, examine the evidence, come up with solutions and make recommendations for action. You may well find that serving on such a group is another helpful way of feeling involved in the department.

Such working parties, feeding back their findings for discussion at department meetings, have been established in schools to examine such issues as:

1. Reports and assessments.
2. Ways of improving spelling.
3. Storage, issue and retrieval of books.
4. Study skills in the Sixth Form.
5. Liaison with feeder schools.
6. Effective comprehension work.
7. English as a second/foreign language.

Working parties are particularly useful because they diversify the talents of a department and put creative energies and imaginative solutions to best effect. They operate usually by taking a brief – e.g. what are the most effective strategies for teaching spelling? – and by examining current practice, desirable aims and available resources come up with a practical solution for the problem.

DEPARTMENTAL ACTIVITIES AND RESPONSIBILITIES

Job-sharing within the department has become increasingly important as administrative pressures on the Head of Department have grown. You may find yourself in a department where specific responsibilities are allocated to individuals over a long period of time, to build up expertise, or in one where the tasks are rotated, to widen experience. Although it might be unwise to undertake extra responsibilities during the probationary year, young teachers will find that it is a valuable extension of professional training, to learn how to run a year, construct an exam, be responsible for a book cupboard, conduct meetings, liaise with other staff inside and outside the department, and compile resources.

Not all posts now attract allowances. Certainly paid posts of responsibility should have a clear job description, but it is short-sighted to link responsibility only with pay. Teachers should, within limits, be prepared to undertake extra departmental duties, if only because they are often a good training ground for future paid responsibility.

Areas of need usually involve administering learning materials, overseeing a particular year, handling equipment, keeping records, being responsible for an area of the curriculum, initiating or developing an extra-curricular activity.

One departmental head identified these areas of need:

- audio-visual aids
- bookshop
- class cover
- contacts with NATE, local colleges, university
- creative English
- departmental minutes
- discipline
- displays
- drama
- English requisition
- external examination entries
- film and media studies
- language across the curriculum
- liaison with feeder schools/other departments
- libraries

- non-book requisition
- oral work
- outside speakers
- probationers

- resources, storage, cataloguing
- reviewing new children's books
- Sixth Form English
- slow readers
- stationery supplies
- stock cupboards
- students
- theatre visits
- timetable

- visits

- year leader

A formal job description might read:

Year Leader
With specific responsibility in one of Years 1–5 for:

1. Allocation of pupils to groups.
2. Internal examinations and assessment.
3. Maintenance of records.

4. Minor problems of discipline.
5. Stock, maintenance and extension.
6. Syllabus development.
7. Visits, films etc.

What might each of these responsibility sub-headings involve?

1. *Allocation of pupils to groups*:
   (a) keeping productive friendship groups, splitting up difficult pupils
   (b) maintaining a proper balance within groups by ability,
   sex, number
   (c) offering a variety of teachers and teaching styles with
   stability in exam years
   (d) trying to meet pupils' individual wishes, preferences,
   and special education needs.
2. *Internal examinations and assessment*:
   (a) setting and duplicating examination/test papers
   (b) devising model answers and mark schemes; liaising with
   school's exam office
   (c) collating results, marks, grades, lists, statistics
   (d) submitting marks/grades to pastoral head of year.
3. *Maintenance of records*:
   (a) distributing class lists to teachers, administrative and
   senior staff
   (b) dealing with reports: collecting, checking, collating
   (c) maintaining pupil records and keeping up-to-date;
   filing, issuing
   (d) bringing departmental stock lists up-to-date once a
   term.
4. *Minor problems of discipline*:
   (a) seeking to avoid teacher–pupil confrontation by
   sensible group allocation
   (b) transferring pupils to other groups where necessary to
   minimize disruption
   (c) providing temporary withdrawal facilities to problem
   pupils
   (d) giving Head of Department assistance in dealing with
   offenders.
5. *Stock maintenance and extension*:
   (a) duplicating class sets of materials: worksheets, booklets,
   instructions
   (b) ensuring that teachers have a variety of books; keeping
   a rota
   (c) sending off for inspection copies and ordering new
   books or materials
   (d) integrating new materials into departmental stock
   cupboards.

6. *Syllabus development*:
    (a) developing materials about particular topics/themes: booklets, worksheets, audio-visuals
    (b) coordinating a team of teachers in the preparation of such materials
    (c) seeing that the proper balance of English activities is maintained
    (d) paying special attention to an appropriate literature input.
7. *Visits, films etc.*:
    (a) organizing outside visits to places of interest: correspondence, transport, insurance
    (b) arranging visiting speakers to the school: reception, vote of thanks
    (c) ordering films, videos etc. of relevance to a particular theme
    (d) ensuring adequate feedback from these activities: reports, questionnaires.

Some duties are proper to the department as a whole, rather than to individuals. One example is keeping up-to-date with new books (a topic that has been considered in Chapter 6). It may be sensible for one person to receive and distribute catalogues, look after publishers' representatives and make out official orders. However, the major tasks can be shared between you and others:

1. Dividing up selected new books to read and review.
2. Browsing through reviews in *The NATE Newsletter, The Use of English, The English Magazine* and other sources to identify books for consideration.
3. Asking your pupils to read and comment on some new readers.
4. Developing a 'specialism' for a particular genre or age-group.

In addition, members of a department can sometimes work together on a specific task that can be completed quickly. As a newcomer, you may be particularly aware of what needs doing most:

1. Comparing the state of the classrooms and the provision of storage.
2. Tidying or reorganizing the stock of resources.
3. Creating new displays.
4. Preparing examples of work and materials for parents' evenings.
5. Organizing an 'options fair' to inform pupils about the choices open to them.

GROUP AND TEAM TEACHING

As one English teacher remarked, 'The job is done as a team and not in isolation.' Increasingly, this has come to be true. With the advent of GCSE, where groups move about more between teachers, and with the growth of modular courses, where teachers present units of work to different populations in turn, teaching styles are changing. Group teaching is also well suited to integrated courses, which involve planning by teachers, who may be drawn from several departments, of all aspects of a course of study. This approach is well established in primary and middle schools where a unified curriculum is more easily fitted into a timetable with fewer constraints.

More usual perhaps – though still not common – is team teaching in which teachers in twos, threes or fours do a joint presentation with single or combined groups. The great advantage is the pooling of ideas and the sharing of responsibility. As one teacher commented: 'Team teaching with someone you feel comfortable with can be a very rewarding experience.' It allows one teacher to focus on individual pupils while another conducts a session with a larger group. This method is ideally suited to work with literature, either with joint presentation on books or using a modular scheme. Class groups in Years 4 and 5 are often blocked on the timetable which makes organization easier.

Suppose two of you, both teachers in the Third Year, decided to tackle the theme of Old Age. How might it be done? Here is a brief record of one such attempt.

Ideas

First we met in one of our classrooms during a free period. We brainstormed ideas about old age, we put down words and ideas, like pensions, retirement, loss of dignity, wisdom, grandparents, etc. Then we tried to match our ideas with what resources we could think of – a videotape called *Life on the Pension*, Ray Jenkins' play *Five Green Bottles*, with the character Gramp, short stories like *Old Ma Porter* by Katharine Mansfield and *Uncle Ernest* by Alan Sillitoe, and such poems as *The Old Fools* by Philip Larkin; in addition, a tray of picture resources, pamphlets from the DHSS, and library topic books about treatment of the elderly in bygone days.

Structure

Four double periods could be structured, opening with a session which outlines the work and invites vocabulary associated with Old Age which is written up on the blackboard for brief discussion. A television programme will involve note-taking and discussion of attitudes among the young towards the old, followed by a factual report on treatment of the elderly, past and present. In a second session groups could subdivide and opt for a play reading or listening to a story on tape, with questions to guide discussion. In a third session pictures might provoke creative writing; a reading of a poem, a piece of practical criticism and a personal response. Finally, threads could be drawn together in a fourth session at which some of the work might be presented in display form and fascinating interviews with grandparents played on tape.

Outcome

Lesson 1

The pupils arrived late from registration and both groups crammed into one classroom. Chairs were in short supply; some pupils sat in pairs on one seat; others on a windowsill. My colleague led the first lesson. She explained about the topic and asked for words about old people which I scribbled on the blackboard. Predictably they started off with the depressing ones but by the end were more positive. We over-ran by five minutes; I made a copy of the vocabulary list at the end.

We got the kids into the library where the TV was; there was some agitation but no pandemonium. They settled quite quickly. After a short introduction from me, they watched the videotape. Most of the combined classes took notes: some cursorily, some in great detail. We had time for feedback about the historical background and the interviews with old people. Much oral contribution. Consolidated ideas for a factual report to be done as an assignment.

Vocabulary list

old-fashioned	cataracts	wisdom
grey, wrinkled	arthritis	give presents
tired	war	jolly
need help	hats	small
pensions	rheumatism	Darby and Joan
grumpy	walking stick	mugging
retired	cheap fares	nostalgia

First assignment

1. Using your notes on the programme *Life on the Pension*, and any other information you have gathered, describe *Old Age – Past, Present and Future*.

Lessons 2 and 3

We congregated at the beginning to get sorted. We had brought with us: two sets of short stories, one set of a play and photocopies of the poem. I led – my colleague helped distribute the resources, which included audiotapes of the stories and two cassette players. Stories and plays were popular – those who couldn't make up their minds got the poem! We had reserved two extra classrooms and groups went into these. Play-readers sat in huddles in corridors. Poetry-readers stayed in the room where we were. The next session we changed over until everybody had done story, play and poem. There was hubbub but not excessive noise. Groups functioned quite well unsupervised. We circulated and talked.

Second assignment (choose one)

2. After reading *Five Green Bottles*, write a play about a family (at home? on holiday?) which includes children, parents and grandparents. (Remember to write characters' names on the left and dialogue on the right.) Give your play a *title* and a *cast list*.
3. Write a review of one or both the short stories you have read (*Uncle Ernest* by Alan Sillitoe; *Old Ma Porter* by Katherine Mansfield). Remember to write about plot, characters, ideas, humour, pathos, and say in detail what you thought of the story or stories.
4. Take a copy of *The Old Fools* by Philip Larkin. Read the poem carefully again. Then, by quoting from the poem, describe what picture of old people the poet gives.

Lesson 4

We had run out of time. We did not use the pictures in the tray except cursorily for pupils who had finished early. Some kids brought in materials they had got from post offices and magazines. A few enterprising pupils made taped interviews with their grandparents or ageing neighbours which they played back to us. The majority finished the first assignment, about half the second. The vocabulary had been useful and appeared in the work. The themes listed below emerged quite strongly. This was a final feedback and discussion lesson in which we asked what they thought of the work they'd done. We both led as appropriate. Responses were mixed: some pupils bored; some interested in parts; a small minority quite enthusiastic. All felt they had learnt something about old age and knew better how it felt. One girl wrote in response to Larkin, 'This poem is about old age and the coming of old age. It mocks nostalgia and incontinence and senility but later softens and wonders what it is really like for the person', and another concluded, 'the poet insults old people all the time. I think his attitude is wrong because one day he will be old and will be like them. The poem scares me because it makes me think about when I'll be old (if I live that long)!' Later we put up a display of work.

Themes

grandparents   loneliness   old people's homes
relations with teenagers   reminiscence

THE DEPARTMENT AS TRAINING AGENCY

An English Department has a statutory role in the training of students and probationers, but it has a wider responsibility for the development of all its members. There are strong arguments for extending the existing links between training institutions and schools to provide continuous school-based training for all English teachers. The Bullock Report concluded:

> The appropriate unit for in-service education in the secondary school will more frequently be the English department, and clearly the head of English has a particular responsibility for helping in the continuing professional education of his colleagues within the department . . . Thus, the head of department should keep his colleagues up to date with information on new developments, maintain a continuing dialogue on policy, and encourage shared decisions on where the English teaching can be strengthened by help from outside the school. (24.6)

One example of this process in a local school occurred when some teachers were influenced by a DES/Regional course on *English 11–16*, and particularly by sessions on indicators of development in language and writing, conducted by W. S. Harpin and Leslie Stratta. Also drawing on NATE workshops and publications from Bretton Hall, a departmental working party formulated an experiment employing the notion of 'staging points' to assess the writing of pupils over a half-term period. Their findings were reported to departmental meetings, and this led to an assessment policy for the First Year of the secondary school. A collection of pupils' work was built up with accompanying notes and commentary to illustrate in detail the criteria employed for making a diagnosis (analysis of achievements and constraints) and prognosis for future work.

As a young teacher, you will have a particular contribution to make to the department's work with students. Because you are closer to the training year than more experienced colleagues, you may be more aware of the likely anxieties and worries that students will be facing. They will feel closer to you and will be aware that you are unlikely to be formally involved in assessing them. The chief problems identified by probationers are virtually identical with those experienced by students. They mention in particular the need for guidance in five respects.

Ideas

I am constantly looking for ideas.

Perhaps I haven't had enough time to share ideas with as big a group of teachers as I would like.

Three other probationers started out with me and it was very helpful to discuss work, ideas and problems with people who were also starting out as English teachers.

Balance

I wanted to know how ideas had been planned and organized in the classroom. A look at the worksheets that had been used by other members of staff would have proved very helpful, or to be told how a short story had been used as the stimulus for a piece of work, and how the lesson had been organized after the initial reading; what the follow-up had been.

Observation

I haven't seen enough good teachers in action.

Teachers have to break down the barriers of being an individual, of working alone, and doing your own thing. You have got to bring other people into your environment so that there is this cross-fertilization of ideas and that you work together.

Reflection

Time for reflection is missing.

I feel irritation with administration at the expense of preparing work.

Evaluation

Teachers need constantly to evaluate what they do. You should look at ways of trying to improve things. English teaching is a developmental process. As a teacher you are constantly searching for ideas to make your teaching more effective and interesting.

Formally or informally, an effective department will ensure that students and young teachers have adequate opportunity to:

1. Share experiences of successful and unsuccessful lessons and analyse the differences between them.
2. Translate a general syllabus or list of aims into specific lessons for particular groups.
3. Discuss possible approaches for dealing with common errors.
4. Think of ways to avoid teacher overload, to provide moments of calm in a busy week, and to lessen the marking burden.
5. Continue to observe different kinds of lessons.
6. Compare their self-assessment with the views of others.

During any period of probation, when you are being formally assessed (by Head of Department, adviser or professional tutor), their observations should be fully discussed with you and the criteria for assessment made plain. In most cases this will involve:

1. *Content and organization*: suitability of material; adequacy of knowledge; sequence of presentation; range and appropriateness of resources; variety of activities; appropriateness of assignments.
2. *Relationships with pupils*: management of learning environment; relationships with class as a whole; reactions to individuals and their needs; class control; ability to anticipate or react to problems; encouragement of pupil interaction; differentiation for range of ability.
3. *Personality and communication*: classroom manner; use of voice; ability to receive and respond to pupil contributions; ability to arouse and maintain interest; questioning technique.

However, a more long-lasting concern for staff development (whether or not connected with 'appraisal') is rapidly replacing the notion that after formal 'probation' teachers may be left alone to work out their own salvation. It is increasingly likely that as a young teacher you will be called upon regularly to discuss with your Head of Department such aspects of your work as:

1. Your lesson planning, evaluation and keeping of pupil records.
2. Your assessment policies and practice.
3. Your carrying out of routine administrative tasks.
4. Your wider contribution to the life of the department and of the school.

There should also be provision for you to evaluate the level of support and guidance you are being given and to suggest in what additional ways your development may be aided.

One of the dangers in the past was that you could become isolated in the classroom. During a time of widespread educational change, this is far less likely. The school is likely to involve you in staff or regional discussions and training days on new modes of assessment, on education for personal and social development, on provision of work experience and CPVE courses. The department, in addition to the activities already outlined in this chapter, should act as a channel for information that will assist your further development:

1. The activities of the National Association for the Teaching of English, locally and nationally.
2. Conferences and courses organized by local colleges and universities.
3. The work of the Schools' Poetry Association, the Schools

Libraries Association, the United Kingdom Reading Association, the education work of the British Film Institute.
4. Relevant theatre productions and films in your area.
5. The Writers in Schools scheme and the work of the Arvon Foundation.
6. Appropriate publications from the APU, Schools Curriculum Development Committee (SCDC), SEC and NFER.

The proliferation of helpful materials and courses is itself a potential problem. You may be tempted to feel that the situation is so complex that there is no hope of keeping up-to-date. However, that is where departmental sharing and discussion are particularly helpful. Effective English teaching increasingly depends on the support that others can give you.

REFERENCES

1. Protherough Robert and Atkinson Judith 1991 *The Making of English Teachers*. Open University Press. See the section "Formative influences" in chapter 2.
2. Ibid, the final section of chapter 9.

Wider perspectives 1: beyond the class

Teachers do not operate in isolation, although it may sometimes seem like it when you look at the rows of closed classroom doors. Much of this book has dealt with ways of surviving the pressures on a young English teacher. However, as was said at the end of the last chapter, effectiveness means more than just coping with the successive demands of a number of classes and classrooms. Somehow you have to find time for reflection and investigation, to be a thinking teacher and not just a busy one. These final two chapters consider two major topics. First, how does the work you are doing in English fit into the total pattern of children's development in school and beyond? Second, on the frontiers of your subject, how do *you* fit into the complex life of the wider school community?

A SENSE OF DEVELOPMENT

You have to learn to see your individual teaching in perspective. The pupils who are all-important to you in one particular year are only in your care at one stage in an unending and complex process of development as language users. Your teaching matters to them, but so did the previous phases of their progress in English and so does their continuing development through formal education and beyond. That development is not smooth and even: there are many linked abilities, and spurts and occasional regressions take place in all of them. However, there are a number of particularly significant changes in situation (beginning school, learning to read, shifting from spoken to written language) which can bring about profound changes in individuals. Some of those which will affect you as a secondary school teacher are considered in what follows.

MOVING FROM PRIMARY TO SECONDARY

The problems of adjustment for pupils when they move between primary, middle and secondary schools are well documented. These are the changes in English that seem to affect pupils most:

1. In primary school, children are accustomed to several hours of language activity each week. When particular projects are under way, like writing workshops or preparations for a play, time can be extended and the day's programme reorganized. By contrast, secondary timetables are rigid, less space is given to English and it is rarely that time is salvaged from other subjects so that larger periods of the day can be spent on activities. 'What I notice is that I just seem to get started on something and the bell goes.'

2. It is likely that in their last year at primary school, children will have been taught for most of the time by one person. The style and expectations of their class teacher will have become familiar to them. Bewilderingly, at secondary school each subject has a different teacher, a cause for concern for many children about to change schools: 'I am very worried about all the teachers at the school.'[1] The teachers are 'specialists' and this is reflected in their style and set of expectations – the point this 11-year-old is making to her English teacher: 'You treat us like 18-year-old intellectuals. The only problem is, we aren't. I wish you would explain things more clearly, then we could understand.'[2]

3. The fragmented curriculum of the secondary school has a significant effect on pupils' writing, perhaps most markedly on the amount they do. Research in local schools as part of the SCDC Writing Project team's work in Sheffield discovered that in the top classes of primary schools 60 per cent of the writing done was for English, compared with 32 per cent in the First Year of secondary schools.[3]

4. Pupils' experience of reading will also be different. At secondary school most of them will no longer be learning the mechanics of reading. If a reading scheme was employed at their primary school, it will no longer be in evidence when they move on – a change in emphasis which can have the kind of powerful effect remembered by a 15-year-old quoted by David Jackson:[4]

> The first ever book I read was the first book from a Ladybird series of thirty-six books. I began where everyone else began, on book 1a, and at the moment, it seems that it was such a stupid way to start off. On one page there were large printed words like 'John caught the ball' and on the page opposite there would be a picture which explained the phrase you read. My teacher always helped me on and once I had finished the first book there was no stopping me. I went on and on until I reached the final few books, 12a, 12b and 12c. By then the words had shrunk and grown in quantity. There were still pictures though and the wording of the phrases had become more complicated.
>
> I was one of the first people to get into 12c and this encouraged

me to read more sophisticated books after school time. But once I left primary school I ceased to be interested in books, probably because I was more interested in sport.

5. Experience of fiction reading at primary school is usually through individual reading or in shared listening to stories and novels read by the teacher. Although individual reading continues into the secondary school, literature becomes part of lessons – as stimulus for talk and writing or for 'study': 'At my last school we just had stories, now we have to do books.'

6. Several studies, but particularly that described in *Moving from the Primary Classroom*,[5] analysed the effects on pupils' progress of moving to secondary school. The most worrying discovery is that after one year in their new schools a large proportion of children have either made no progress in English, or have fallen behind in their work. Galton and Willcocks discovered that in a sample of eighty-one children, 63 per cent had made some progress, 7 per cent had made none and 30 per cent had fallen back.

7. After the security of a smaller primary school, life in secondary school can be stimulating, bewildering or terrifying. Children are understandably concerned with aspects of life which could seem trivial to teachers: myths, 'while you're in the shower they put razor blades in your underpants which is pretty painful when you put your clothes on'; dinner arrangements, 'we get squashed and pushed about in the dinner queue'; bullying, 'if you ever get bullied, where do you run to?'; punishment, 'I heard the Head of First Year had a great long cane in his cupboard'; being the youngest again after being 'top of the school', 'when I was at junior school I was the eldest and I was allowed to boss everybody about'; getting lost, 'this place is so big I never stopped getting lost'. Pupils bring these preoccupations with them into their lessons during the early stages of the First Year, and English is one of the subjects in which they can be explored. It is important not to underestimate the difficulties of transition. Although most children make the change successfully, many might echo this pupil's feelings: 'I still don't understand it. I was enjoying myself in the juniors and then I went to senior school and everything stopped. I suddenly didn't want to go to school!'[6]

MOVING FROM THIRD YEAR TO FOURTH YEAR

This change marks the transition from 'Lower School' English to GCSE courses, a stage often emphasized in split-site schools by the physical move from one building to another, and in some cases from one set of teachers to another. Although most GCSE syllabuses give teachers the opportunity to build courses which lead on naturally from Third Year work, pupils perceive Fourth Year English as a definite change of gear.

1. The fact that what pupils do is eventually to be externally assessed appears to change the tone of both lessons and work:

    English wasn't considered very important.

    After Lower School, English for GCSE seems much more serious.

    English in the 3rd form was more kind of relaxing. The lessons were more leisurely.

2. The continuous assessment element of GCSE seems to be largely welcomed by pupils, although there are some dissenters:

    I think that we should have an exam because if you aren't very good at assignments there should be an alternative.

    Pupils see a variety of advantages to the system:

    When you do the assignments it is just like doing a normal piece of work.

    The idea of building up a folder of assignments is far fairer and more realistic of the sort of person you *really* are.

    I like the idea of being able to select a few best assignments from the ones you've written.

    Marking is good in Fourth Year as you know how you're doing.

    At the same time some pupils are fully or half-conscious of the different kind of pressure entailed in course work:

    There are a lot of assignments and I feel that everything I do is going to be assessed.

    You have to worry about doing good work for the whole year, instead of just during an exam.

    Sometimes when you have other weekend homework and have to do a 3-hour assignment too, it tends to get on top of you.

3. Pupils see changes in the writing they do: in the greater range of kinds of writing, 'it used to be mainly stories', 'we never wrote essays or work similar to that'; in the choice of topic, 'we wrote about more or less what we wanted, for GCSE we don't have so much choice', 'pupils should be able to choose or help choose the English assignments that they would like to do'; in the demands made of their writing, 'we used to write but not in as much detail or

depth', 'I feel as if I know better what I'm supposed to do when I write'.

4. The fact that oral work is also assessed seems to heighten their awareness of its importance in lessons:

> It involves far more class participation than before and it helps if you contribute to the lessons rather than leaving it to louder individuals.

Group work is promoted.

> It appears also to act as a spur to pupils who have formerly drawn back from talking:

> Before I hardly spoke in English, now it's forcing me to say things more often.

> For shy people like me the oral exam is not so nerve-wracking at the end because you are assessed in class too which is easier to cope with.

5. For pupils who are also taking a GCSE Literature course, changes in reading and work with books seem to bulk large. The inclusion of 'wider reading' as part of the exam is generally welcomed: 'You don't have to read the books the examiner chooses, but you can follow your own ideas.' At the same time, some pupils find this too demanding if the reading is to be done at home:

> In the Third Year we used to have lessons where you could choose books and read them for whole lessons which was great because I love reading when it's a good book and I have chosen to read it. But at home I don't have much time for reading and now it has to be at home and it's a book that I haven't chosen completely by myself.

There is a general awareness that some of the books chosen for class sharing by the teacher are markedly different from those read in the previous year:

> It seems that now we are given best-sellers and Oscar winners and I wish sometime that we could work on an ordinary book.

> We started off by *One Day in the Life of Ivan Denisovich*. I advise to start off the year with something light-hearted and work up to more serious literature. Whereas we did it the other way round completely.

After a year of a GCSE Literature course, pupils are divided in their views of the new emphasis they see in their work:

> We now do a lot more work on books.

> We do plays and think about the things behind it like the charac-

ters and the relationships between things in the story or the play. I find this a much more enjoyable and adult way of doing English.

I don't like writing about the 'attitudes' of certain characters we have studied.

MOVING FROM FIFTH YEAR TO SIXTH FORM

A-level students are understandably aware of an enormous change in their experience of English. At the simplest level they will be working in much smaller groups, following a course they have chosen and, in most cases, concentrating on the study of Literature rather than following the 'unitary English' course which will have characterized their previous years. There seems, though, to be a general feeling that the change is too great and that work at 16+ does not prepare them for the demands of A-level work.

1. Many students are conscious of a sudden shift to more demanding reading and an expectation from teachers that reading should also be more extensive:

   We spent the majority of the two-year course in the Fourth and Fifth Years concentrating on just the three set books.

   Earlier, the books were chosen with our tastes in mind. Now the books are meant to broaden our horizons.[7]

2. The approach to books is seen as strikingly different and not always welcome:

   It is not the study of a book which puts me off, but the *way* in which the book is studied.

   At 16+ you are not taught how to criticize books, you were just expected to like and enjoy them.

   Now you go deeper into the book and the author's ideas.[8]

3. Students recognize that they are expected to develop their own responses to reading, articulate their own views and be responsible for their own progress. Many feel that work lower down the school had not prepared them for this. In the Fifth Year, 'You didn't express your own opinions', 'you relied on the teacher more', 'we had a definite answer to the questions then', whereas in the Sixth Year, 'Nobody says you've got the wrong idea' and 'it's your responsibility now, not the teacher's'. 'You are now free to use your own mind.'[9]

4. At the same time, some students are half, or fully, conscious that the exam situation constrains both them and their teachers. Some students are able to say confidently:

'I feel at liberty to say whatever I like as long as I am able to back up my argument.' Others are not so sure that their own responses will be valid enough for an A-level examiner: 'You feel confident in your own judgements if the teacher agrees', but without that agreement, 'you don't believe in them enough to write them down in the A-level exam'.

5. A-level students have firm views about the teaching methods employed at A-level. A recent survey[10] shows that whole-class discussion is seen by them as the most important method of study, followed by writing essays, small-group discussion and students making their own notes. They consider that seeing productions, films and TV adaptations makes a significant contribution. Least favoured of the methods was the dictation of notes.

Another interesting feature of the survey is that *teachers* give importance to reading outside the syllabus, imaginative writing related to the text, and acting and improvising. By comparison, students give all three a low order of priority.

6. Although some students are disappointed, frustrated or bored by A-level English, most have consciously chosen it and see a variety of benefits:

It has helped me mature and given me a certain amount of self-knowledge.

It has made me more receptive to ideas and opinions that differ from my own.

I no longer dare read Enid Blyton and *Beano*.

MOVING ON FROM SCHOOL

For students who choose to pursue further English studies at undergraduate level, there are marked changes between A-level and degree course work. In Robert Protherough's survey already quoted, 'nearly three-quarters of the undergraduates believed that although they had mostly enjoyed their course work there were ways in which their A-level work had failed as a preparation for literary studies at university'. The undergraduates comment on the narrowness of A-level reading and their lack of training for the 'self-reliant attitude' later required. They feel that 'you were not encouraged to think for yourself', and at its most extreme one student considers A-level 'was a waste of time, boring and excruciating'. Although allowing for the trend in young people to feel and express dissatisfaction with the previous stage of education, the picture of students' A-level experience is a worrying one.

Those who go on to vocational courses in further education colleges have greatly enjoyed some aspects of work in school but many feel it fails to provide them with essential skills. According to one survey:

The majority of students were critical of the English they were taught at secondary school, and saw little purpose in much of what they had done . . . ten or eleven years of being taught English had left them with a strong sense of failure, a feeling of their own inadequacies and, above all, the conviction that 'poor' English prevented academic success, restricted job opportunities, and caused them to be seen as 'uneducated'.[11]

When those students who wished to continue the study of English at college were asked their reasons, their replies stressed utilitarian purposes. The most frequently cited reasons were: to learn to spell, to learn correct grammar, to learn to speak 'properly', to choose and use correct words, and to lose an accent. Those who rejected any further study of English said that they had already 'done it' at school, that it was not necessary for their proposed job or task, or that it was irrelevant to their college courses.

WHAT TO DO

Once you are aware in a general way of the different transitions in pupils' progress in learning English, it is possible then to take steps to discover more about the particular children you teach – to 'track' their progress.

These are some of the activities which will help you to relate the work you do with your classes to what went before and what will follow:

1. *Inform yourself about individual pupils' previous progress.* Some teachers are reluctant to do this before meeting a new class, feeling that there is a danger of taking a prejudiced view of individuals and wishing instead to make a fresh start. Although this is an understandable reaction, it is short-sighted. It works against educational continuity, risks a teacher overlooking information which is crucial to the understanding of a particular pupil's needs, by implication undervalues the pupils' previous experience in English, and in the end wastes rather than saves time when teachers have to discover for themselves helpful information which could have been taken from pupil records. Sources of information:
   (a) Many departments have a system of record cards which are centrally stored or passed on to the next teacher at

the end of each year. Alternatively, teachers may pass on mark-books and written comments supported by discussion between staff.

(b) Pupils' exercise books, folders of work and journals may be passed on from year to year, sometimes with the pupils' own written assessments of their year's work and progress.

(c) Year or House Heads may keep in a central store general files and copies of past reports for individual pupils so that you can relate their progress in English to their development in other subjects.

(d) Many departments have well-established liaison arrangements with feeder schools. If you are to teach a First Year group, take advantage of links between the schools, to study and take note of records, read previous written work and meet children.

If you find yourself in a situation in which none of these sources is open to you, don't be afraid to ask for information from colleagues or to suggest systems for record-keeping or liaison.

2. *Inform yourself about your pupils' previous and future experiences of English.* There are two aspects to this: (a) finding out about the content and teaching methods of courses, and (b) finding out how pupils see different stages in their experience of English. In investigating both, you will be helping to ensure that there is continuity in pupils' language development, instead of a series of fresh starts which can both bewilder children and harm their progress.

(a) (i) Take advantage of existing liaison arrangements with feeder schools – or, failing this, ask for them to be set up. It should be possible to discover the books, topics and kinds of writing, talking and acting your pupils have encountered in their final year at the feeder schools. Visits, teacher swaps, or jointly planned projects will give you the opportunity to observe lessons or work alongside primary or middle-school colleagues. This should help you to discover what similarities and differences there are between your own teaching methods and those your First Year class will have experienced.

(ii) If you teach in a department in which individual staff plan their own programmes of work according to agreed guidelines, make sure at the end of a year that you have received for each of your new groups an outline of their previous year's course. This, combined with individual pupils' records and folders of written work, should put you in a position to plan a year's programme which will both build on what has already been achieved and make links with pupils' previous experience.

(iii) During your first year or two of teaching you will be unlikely to take groups through the whole age range of an 11–18 school. Although you may not be teaching GCSE, one-year Sixth and A-level groups at first, you can only see your work with younger pupils in perspective if you are informed about the kinds of courses they will later follow. Equally, if you teach only examination classes, it is essential to be informed about the nature of your pupils' previous experience of English. Syllabuses – for the department, for GCSE, for CPVE, for A-level – should be readily available for you to study but, perhaps more importantly, try to spend time observing colleagues working with the kinds of groups you have not yet met.

(iv) In teaching 16 or 18-year-olds there is a temptation to feel that responsibility ends here. Pupils will leave school and most will not be seen or heard about again. School-based education, however, is only part of a process, and English teachers' responsibility extends outside the classroom, in the basic sense that they will be concerned about the nature of the young adults they have helped to direct, but also more narrowly in their need to be aware of the demands their pupils will meet. Find out, and evaluate for yourself, the expectations local employers have of school-leavers' achievements in English and the language demands they might make on young employees or trainees on youth schemes. In the light of your discoveries you may wish to modify aspects of your work with 15 and 16-year-olds. With A-level students who will be going on to higher education courses, particularly in English, it is important to look beyond the 'watershed' of the final exams and to bear in mind that through Sixth Form work you are helping school pupils to become students of English. Try not to lose touch with developments in university and polytechnic English departments – in thinking, teaching and methods of assessment – and be prepared to modify your methods. It is important to know, for instance, that the survey already quoted[12] has shown that 95 per cent of the university English teachers questioned felt that there were ways in which A-level work had failed as a preparation for literary study at university.

(b) The best way to discover how pupils view their experience of English is to ask them! When a situation is set up which assures children that anything they say or write will be taken seriously and, where possible, acted upon, they will respond honestly, thoughtfully and, often, shrewdly. It has already been suggested in Chapters 4 and 7 that there is value for both pupils and teacher in the regular use of self-assessment journals or self-consideration entries in profiles or record cards. Both pupils and teachers can be helped to prepare for the next stage in English by question-and-answer sessions with pupils who have already moved on. For example, First Years can exchange ideas with top-class juniors, GCSE pupils can talk with Third Years, and A-level students with Fifth Years.

3. *Build up your own picture of how children develop as language users.* After two or three years of teaching you will be in a position to stand back and look at the children you've worked with; to draw comparisons, to consider what they have been capable of or have found difficult, to begin to describe for yourself how pupils develop. If you teach the whole ability range, you will be aware of the vastly different rates of development represented in any one of your classes – you will have seen, for example, how the work of a mature writer in the Third Year is comparable with that of an able Fifth Year, or how an inarticulate Fourth Year may not be able to tell a story to the class as effectively as a fluent First Year. In considering this you might like to compare your findings with the picture of development suggested by the list of precise objectives for each age group which appears in HMI's *English 5 to 16*.[13] Then, by contrast, try to look at the material from Bretton Hall Language Unit.[14] Through the use of 'staging points in writing', it suggests a way of viewing development which acknowledges the differences between individuals, and helps teachers to recognize achievement, diagnose problems and then work with pupils towards the next 'staging point', irrespective of their chronological 'stage'.

Although it's clear that individual pupils develop at very different rates, it is possible to make some links between children's development in language and their chronological age. You might have observed, for example, how, from about Easter of the Second Year, it becomes increasingly difficult to find novels which will 'work' with a whole class; how, from the beginning of the Fourth Year, pupils begin to be able to present and argue a case; or how, in the Fifth Year, pupils begin to give reasoned evaluations of their reading. Rather, though, than considering each separate year stage, you will find it helpful to look at wider spans of time. David Jackson in *Continuity in Secondary English* divides development in English into four phases:

(a) The first phase (11–12)	First Year to the middle of the Second Year
(b) The second phase (12/13–14)	Upper Second Year–Third Year
(c) The third phase (14–16)	Fourth and Fifth Years
(d) The fourth phase (16–18)	Sixth and Seventh Years[15]

He goes on to describe the characteristics or 'markers' of pupils at each phase, in the different 'areas' of English, as he has observed them over years of teaching. You would find it valuable to attempt the same activity from your own observation; for example, what do you think are the markers of children as talkers during the First Phase and during the Second Phase?

As comparison, here are David Jackson's observations:

First Phase
Markers
1. Spontaneous wit, a revelling in word play for its own sake.
2. Directness and frankness of utterance.
3. Often have unique wavelengths of jaunty irreverence, free-wheeling inventiveness and a sense of wonder.
4. They think through spoken anecdote.

Second Phase
1. More capable of standing back from immediate here-and-now involvement – comparing, contrasting and synthesizing.
2. More concerned with social relationships and the outside world – more critical of school and accepted values.
3. Often more moody and temperamental in group exchange.
4. A challenging often abrasive style often presents difficulties for teacher's class control.
5. Occasional uncertainty about their own social position is reflected in their wavering between mature insights and silly behaviour.

When you have been able to build up a picture of pupils' development in English, it can then inform your planning and your work with individual children. Look again, for example, at the department's allocation of class novels to year groups and your own choice of when to use them. If you have agreed with David Jackson's perception of a stage in development midway through the Second Year, how will this affect your choice of a class novel for the summer term of that year? If the Bretton 'staging points' project has made you aware of the potential of able young writers, how will this affect the ways you frame and present writing assignments to a mixed-ability class in the Third Year?[16]

REFERENCES

1. Findlay F (ed) 1987 *Moving On*. NATE, p 24
2. Ibid. p 56
3. Ibid. p 61
4. Jackson D 1983 *Continuity in Secondary English*. Methuen, p 29
5. Galton M and Willcocks J 1982 *Moving from the Primary Classroom*. Routledge and Kegan Paul
6. Findlay, *Moving On*, p 20
7. Protherough R 1986 *Teaching Literature for Examinations*. Open University Press, p 18
8. Ibid. p 18
9. Ibid. p 19
10. Protherough R 1987 'Who become students of English?', *English in Education*, vol XXI no 2, summer, pp 67–75
11. Austin-Ward B 1986 'English, English teaching and English teachers: the perceptions of 16 year olds', *Educational Research*, vol XXVIII no 1, February, p 32
12. Protherough, 'Who become students of English?', p 71
13. HMI 1984 *English from 5 to 16. Curriculum Matters 1*. DES
14. Dixon J and Farmer I 1981 *A Policy for Writers 9–12: staging points in personal narrative*. Bretton Hall Language Development Unit
15. Jackson, *Continuity in Secondary English*, p 8
16. More reading on development in writing: Wilkinson A 1986 *The Quality of Writing*. Open University Press; Dixon J and Stratta L 1981 *Achievements in Writing at 16+*. Schools Council and 1987 *Writing Narrative – and Beyond*. NATE. Development in response to reading: Protherough R 1983 *Developing Response to Fiction*. Open University Press; Atkinson J 1985 'How children read poems at different ages', *English in Education*, vol XIX no 1, Spring, pp 24–34; Thomson J 1987 *Understanding Teenagers Reading*. Croom Helm

Wider perspectives 2: beyond the department

Chapter 3 considered some of the reasons why it is so difficult to say where your responsibilities as an English teacher stop. In subject terms, you are almost certain to be encouraging improvisation and work on plays, to be looking at the ways in which language is used in newspapers and on television, and to be concerned with the language difficulties of children with special needs. How does the situation change if your school has separate departments of Drama, of Media Studies or of Learning Support, with teachers designated to be responsible for them? Alternatively, how does it change if you as an English teacher find yourself in part of a wider integrated grouping? English may be placed with Languages in a faculty of communication, with Art and Drama in a faculty of expressive or creative arts, with History, Geography and RE in a faculty of humanities. It may be an essential ingredient in Modern World Studies or Man: A Course for Study. It may – especially as a Literature component – be part of a team-teaching enterprise in middle schools or the junior years of the secondary school.

Beyond the departmental boundaries there are whole-school programmes of activities that are likely to make demands on your particular abilities and training. Of these, language across the curriculum and the increasing concern for study skills are likely to be most significant. Quite apart from teaching responsibilities, you are almost certain to be given a role in the pastoral structures of the school as a house or year tutor. These may involve further training in what is rather clumsily becoming known as Personal and Social Development. And beyond all these formal demands on you will be the daily informal shaping of your place in the community: getting to know teachers of all subjects, engagement in out-of-school activities, contacts with parents and establishing links beyond the school. Balancing these different demands and avoiding conflict between different roles have posed difficult professional problems for most of the young teachers quoted earlier in this book. The following sections briefly consider some of the English teacher's wider responsibilities.

DRAMA IN ENGLISH

Drama, like English, is a significant method of learning *across* the curriculum as well as being a subject in its own right. The situation is confused because some teachers in English departments have been trained as drama specialists, some have followed courses in educational drama as a support to English, and some have had no training or experience in the subject. This brief section does not pretend to deal with the methodology of drama teaching, which is well described in a number of recent books,[1] or with the relationship between English and Drama departments where they exist separately. It argues simply that drama is an essential element of English, and that students are impoverished if they are denied the experience.

Quite apart from social or personal benefits to be gained from drama work, students in English classes can be helped, for example:

1. In the development of their oral abilities: pairwork for social development: giving directions, asking advice, making complaints, telephone situations; group stories, serials, who am I? True or False? Simple role-playing in conflict situations.
2. In relation to their writing: drama workshops around a theme to serve as the basis for a story or description; short cut-off plays: now what happens? What will you do? As a means to assist the writing of dialogue.
3. In understanding stories and poems: improvisation to establish mood or theme before reacting; adapting section of story for play, film or radio; interviewing key characters for their views.
4. In their approach to the texts of plays: enacting sections in different ways: with texts, from memory, in mime, as tableaux; speaking as characters in sub-text exercises or characters observing *other* characters; playing for different theatrical effects; making director's notes for a scene.

A few illustrations from actual English lessons indicate some of the possibilities: creating an imaginary island as a preparation for reading *Lord of the Flies* or setting up the trial scene to bring to life Tom Robinson's predicament in *To Kill a Mockingbird*. The ability to project is particularly useful in enhancing a historical situation and authenticating the past (fifteenth-century Verona, life in the trenches, occupied Europe during the war). In addition, improvisation can be used to create the right atmosphere for a poem or a story (reacting to ghostly sounds in de la Mare's 'The Listeners', imagining swimming under water in Lessing's 'Through the Tunnel'). A Western story based on the improvisation 'The Way West' gains immeasurably in descriptive realism, a simple role-playing exploring a 'Friday Night at the Bus Station' can bring to life the dialogue in a narrative or the theme of vandalism; a class who have travelled in a time machine or re-enacted Ray Bradbury's 'A Sound of Thunder' will write better science-fiction stories.

As well as using literary antecedents, improvisations often develop successfully using societal frameworks: explorers living with a remote tribe; space travellers arriving on a newly discovered planet; migrants on a journey to some distant territory; guests isolated in a hotel; prisoners kept under surveillance in a confined room. The pupils are asked to project themselves into a situation and to develop a character in role.

If you are going to use drama methods, then you obviously have to consider certain fundamental problems:

1. How to keep noise at a reasonable level – work in an outside classroom, warn the teacher next door first and encourage pupils to move furniture and to conduct themselves in a disciplined way.
2. How to get enough time – a double period a fortnight is better than one period a week.
3. How to negotiate with a class – being in role can help a teacher to move pupils into unfamiliar territory.
4. When to intervene – stock responses and stereotyping, yes; exaggerated characterization, perhaps – and when to leave well alone.
5. Whether to script the drama – that will depend on the intended outcome, it can inhibit.
6. When to stop an improvisation – trust to instinct here and sense boredom, sterility or the need for a new impetus. This is particularly true of an improvisation sustained over a number of weeks.
7. When to 'perform' – single groups to other groups in preparing a whole-class drama in stages, or occasionally simply to please the pupils.
8. When to teach theatrical devices, e.g. make-up, costume, lighting, sound-effects – clearly, when drama develops into a piece of theatre before an audience.
9. What to do with reluctant pupils – they may be cajoled with the help of the group if the classroom atmosphere is secure, but the refuser may have to be excluded from the group temporarily and kept with the teacher.
10. Where to use for drama work – the hall is rarely suitable, even if available, because of its daunting size and most English classrooms are too cramped. Only one school in five is likely to have a drama studio and, even if you are

lucky enough to have one, your problem may not be over, as this young English teacher discovered!

I got my Scale 2 for Drama and then the headmaster proceeded to frustrate all attempts I made at doing my job – having told me to go ahead and 'sort out the lights' that the Drama Studio needed, he then prevented me from bringing in an outside agency to give advice and an estimate; he told me to clear the Drama Studio out (it was something of a repository for broken furniture etc.), then told the caretaker to put the stuff back! Having given me permission to timetable Drama, he then informed me that we could only have the Drama Studio if it wasn't being used for (a) exams, (b) visiting speakers to the Sixth Form.

MEDIA STUDIES

You can think of the media in three ways: as a potent influence on the lives of children outside school (almost all of them will spend much longer watching television than reading), as a medium of instruction in different subjects, or as a separate subject to be studied in its own right. They cannot be ignored. As John Dixon wrote ten years ago: 'This complex interweaving of verbal, visual, kinetic and musical communication . . . makes the "audiovisual" media so powerful in impact, dangerous in use and difficult to perfect.'[2] English teachers have been quick to 'teach the media' ever since the end of the war, but in the 1950s most of them were teaching 'discrimination' of an essentially literary kind but using advertisements, newspapers, comics and radio programmes as raw material for analysis. It was on their interest, however, that later work has come to build. In some schools, Media Studies are still the concerns of the English teacher, or they are left to any interested staff in any subjects: media across the curriculum. However, other schools have well-established Media Studies courses, which may have evolved from a Film Studies course or may be part of an Integrated Studies or Communications course. Media Studies usually appears on the timetable as:
1. Part of a Third Year English course.
2. An option in the Fourth and Fifth Years.
3. A subject in its own right in Core English in Years 4 and 5.
4. A modular course in the Fourth and Fifth Years.
5. Part of a pre-vocational course at 17+.

The GCSE examination offers syllabuses which match both modular and integrated courses. Certainly the aims and activities of Media Studies, as identified by specialists, will be close if not identical to yours as an English teacher. For example, Masterman identified the three key features as 'discussion, participation in and critical judgment of' media issues.[3]

Murdoch and Phelps[4] suggested three aims for Media Studies. Compare them with aims (g) to (i) in the NEA Media Studies Syllabuses A and B (1988):

Murdoch and Phelps
Aims of Media Studies should be:

NEA Media Studies
To provide pupils with opportunities to:

(1) to encourage pupils to be discriminating in their role as consumers

(g) develop an understanding of the significance of the media for different groups in society

(2) to give pupils some insight into the development and workings of the contemporary mass media

(h) develop an awareness of the processes involved in the present day work of the media including the financial and institutional organization which constitute the media

(3) to give pupils the opportunity to originate and produce their own mass media materials.

(i) put their skills and understanding of media processes into practice with the production of appropriate media texts.*

* The term 'media texts' refers to any written or audio-visual material. The 'media text' may be an item as simple as television graphics, a photograph or the front page of a newspaper.

One Media Studies teacher explains why giving pupils the opportunity to originate and produce their own media materials is important: 'Pupils who make their own learning materials teach themselves more in a few weeks than their teachers do in a few months using conventional methods . . . What is produced is often useful in other departments and is used by teachers as learning resources.'

If you are asked – or if you wish – to take part in Media Studies courses, it is well to be aware of some of the practical problems that are inseparable from the advantages of such work:

1. Managing (as well as having the technical ability to use and instruct the use of) the range of technical equipment now available: not only film projectors and audio recorders, but video cameras, sound mixing and editing, interactive video, micro facilities like *Fleet Street Editor*.
2. Acquiring an adequate bank of materials for work on advertising, newspapers, popular films and records (or, if

the school has such a stock, familiarizing yourself with it and analysing where it needs supplementing).[5]

3. Finding time, both for yourself in the demanding tasks of preparation, setting up and clearing away, and for the students (short periods are very difficult for practical projects; a whole afternoon is much easier).

4. Realizing when making a television programme, tape-slide presentation or magazine that the process is more important than the final product. As an English teacher, you are likely to be familiar with organizing activity-based group work, but in Media Studies it may involve more time out of the classroom and less under your direct control.

5. Finding a balance in time and in activities, between your 'English' and your 'Media' work, and between the three aspects of media study that Masterman distinguishes.

6. Possibly overcoming the views of some colleagues that your groups spend their time 'just watching the telly' or 'messing about taking pictures'. If there is such prejudice, then it may be helpful in the early stages to give the work a local bias with end-products that can be seen as practical and helpful:

   (a) producing a booklet about the school
   (b) preparing an advertising campaign for the school bookshop
   (c) making a radio programme for the school broadcasting service
   (d) shooting a video of the school play
   (e) printing a class newspaper
   (f) publishing a school magazine
   (g) creating a 15-minute promotion video for the school rock group or some other school activity.

RELATIONSHIPS WITH OTHER SUBJECTS

It has been suggested throughout this volume that English combines a concern for some unique 'subject-specific' areas with a much wider concern for all the teaching and learning activities that go on through language. That responsibility may give you some headaches. Few of your colleagues will have strong opinions about the teaching of Physics or German, but almost all of them will have firm convictions about the kinds of language teaching that they think appropriate. One young teacher reports three particular kinds of problem:

1. The sneer that language work in English is not 'real' work, because it is perceived as being enjoyable and often concerned with children's out-of-school experience.

2. The tendency to blame all pupils' shortcomings in talking and listening on the English Department, which is perceived as a 'service' for the rest of the school. ('It's my job to teach them history/science/geography; you're here to teach them how to write.')
3. The complaint that emphases in English are unhelpful for other subjects: that we fail to teach terms like indicative and subjunctive (as some modern linguists would wish) or formal impersonal passive styles of report-writing (to help the scientists).

It also has to be said that such resentment can be intensified by the intolerance (even contempt) that some English teachers show for such attitudes, though sometimes the complaints have to be tackled head-on: 'When other teachers ask "what do you lot do during your lessons? A.N. Other can't spell, he can't punctuate", my reply is "What are you doing about it?".'

You will have to discover what policy is being practised in your new school. In broad terms, most English departments attempt one of the following:

1. To work within an agreed school Language Across the Curriculum policy. It has to be said that despite the early interest shown, very few schools have actually managed to achieve such cooperation across subject boundaries. It is a time-consuming process and one that demands constant attention. One of the pioneers, Mike Torbe, wrote that a language policy 'is a series of strategies in the classroom and in the whole school, and a *process* of discussion, of asking questions, finding answers to those questions. Once begun, the process continues permanently.'[6] He then suggests the following starting points:

   (a) teachers from different departments visit each other's lessons or teach together
   (b) teachers tape, take slides of, videotape their own lessons
   (c) teachers follow one pupil for a day to experience his/her view of the school
   (d) teachers analyse the writing, reading, talking and listening a pupil engages in during one day or longer
   (e) teachers ask pupils for their comments on their language experiences in schools by means of question-naires, diaries, tape transcripts
   (f) teachers in all departments are asked to write about their approaches to various areas of language work.

   Here are twenty ideas for a classroom enquiry into language and learning. Why not try some of them out?

S1	*Sample worksheets* (a) by subject (b) by class (c) by year	P1	*Pupil evaluation* *sheets* What do you think you have learnt today? (one week)
S2	*Sample pupil's* *writing* in all subjects (one pupil, one week)	P2	*Pupil questionnaires* What have you (1) talked about, (2) read, (3) written, (4) listened to . . .? (one day, one week)
S3	*Sample range of* *writing* in one class (mixed ability/setted)	P3	*Pupil diaries* Keep a record of your lessons – good, bad, average, with a comment on each (one day, one week)
S4	*Sample variety of* *writing tasks* in one subject (one week)	P4	*Pupil reports* Keep a record of (a) reading work aloud, (b) hearing others (one week)
S5	*Sample marking/* *assessment* in all subjects (one pupil, one day or week)	P5	*Pupil reviews* Keep a record of (a) reading from textbooks/worksheets, (b) reading for pleasure. (one week)
Q1	*What did I plan?* What actually happened!	R1	*Tape recording* (*a*) One lesson. Do a transcript. (15–20 minutes only)
Q2	*What kinds of* *talking?* Itemize oral activities (one week)	R2	*Tape recording* (*b*) Small group discussion (pupils only)
Q3	*What kinds of* *listening?* Itemize aural activities (one week)	R3	*Record an interview* (a) with a pupil, (b) with a teacher (one subject)

Q4	*What kinds of reading?* (a) by pupils, (b) by teachers (one week)	R4	*Triangulations* Report on same lesson by (a) pupils, (b) observer, (c) teacher.
Q5	*What kinds of writing?* From a sample (one week)	R5	*Video recording* Play back later for your own/group analysis. (one lesson)

Key.
S = Sampling   P   = Pupil centred
Q = Questioning   R   = Recording

2. To cooperate with a particular department that is concerned about and sympathetic to the demands of language in learning. Some young science teachers influenced by the Science Teachers' Education Project have been increasingly concerned with the problems of writing about experiments and have discussed this with English specialists. Mathematicians are similarly becoming anxious to discuss different language systems. 'Communicative' Modern Language teaching has led to increased discussions of the similarities and differences between mother-tongue and second-language learning. Some student teachers expressed the distinctions and the overlaps in this way:

They are both getting away from the grammar approach, using real situations.

English is, I think, more personal; teaching a language is still within rules but English is more child-centred, getting a response from them, *their* ideas, whereas it's *your* ideas and *them* participating in French.

One of the differences in Languages is that you expect pupils to sit down and listen. In English it is not altogether expected that *you* are the focus.

English has to do with feelings. In French you want them to talk.

In English I taught them how language is used, in French, how to react.

A 'language awareness' programme of the kind discussed in Chapter 3 has, in some schools, been organized jointly by French and English departments.
3. To concentrate on the 'special' uses of language that occur primarily in English. This implies that all subjects must be

responsible for the language used within them, and that English should be concerned with personal, imaginative and literary modes. In some schools, of course, this may include a responsibility for teaching English as a *second* language. In one school a teacher encountered:

(a) two traveller pupils who also spoke Romany
(b) three Dutch siblings brought up in Israel
(c) a mixed-race American–Vietnamese girl
(d) two South Korean brothers
(e) the son of an African diplomat
(f) visiting students from Italy and Spain.

All had different needs. How do you meet those needs? Your approach will be – like any other language teacher's – multisensory. You would probably try:

(a) to organize one-to-one communication
(b) to develop vocabulary through themes and situations
(c) to stimulate an oral response using pictures, maps, diagrams
(d) to encourage concentration and listening skills
(e) to reinforce language structure through drills and patterns;
(f) to promote conversation about what interests the pupil.

4. To concentrate on providing what is not offered elsewhere. To do this means diagnosing what language uses and study skills are *not* being effectively covered in other areas of the curriculum and ensuring that they are given systematic attention. The diagnostic stage will be very much as in framing a Language Across the Curriculum policy, but the difference lies in accepting that English teachers will accept the responsibility for specific skills teaching (which some are unhappy about accepting).

SPECIAL NEEDS

You will find that since the Warnock Report of 1978 and the ensuing Education Act of 1981 raised general awareness of children with special education needs, considerable attention has been given to how best to provide for those needs. Terminology has changed with the altered emphasis and there is less talk in schools of 'remedial pupils' and 'withdrawal' and more of pupils with *special education needs* and of *integration*. Alongside this change of emphasis has developed the concept of *learning support*. It is increasingly recognized that in comprehensive schools these needs are the concern of all the staff and that they are best met wherever possible by and within the mainstream curriculum. If you are new to a school, then you will need to begin by assessing what kinds of help are available to pupils in your care and what your own responsibilities are.

First, find out how the Special Needs Department operates. Provision may vary from a total withdrawal system to total support with no withdrawal. In ideal circumstances, a Special Needs Department can provide either or both, as circumstances demand.

You need to be able to tell the special needs person what *you* need. What are the problems you cannot solve yourself? Are they primarily difficulties of *access* (Is the curriculum appropriate to the needs of all my pupils? Can they read the material I provide? Are there special problems for hearing-impaired, or visually-impaired pupils, or others?) or difficulties of *response* (Can they communicate what they think and feel? Can they write coherently or in sentences?).

Remember that success is not the same for everybody. Try to look at the success or inability to meet the demands of the task from the point of view of the *individual* child. Ask the Special Needs teacher: 'Is it reasonable for me to expect such-and-such of this pupil?'

Have a clear grouping policy – not always by friendship or teacher-directed. Pupils could draw numbers from a hat, so that everybody gets to work with everybody else in the course of a year.

Use a Specific Learning Difficulties Checklist of the kind proposed in the list of references at the end of this chapter.[7]

Keep a book in which you write down the features from such a list, and enter opposite the names of pupils in your class who are *outstanding examples* of these. Be objective. You will end up with a list of names with specific difficulties.

When you need to ask for advice, you then have a list of *needs* as part of a class profile. Have some idea(s) about what you can do to attack the problem(s) positively. Ask 'What can I do?' rather than state 'The child has a problem'. Make suggestions and offer strategies to the Special Needs teacher.

Perhaps a teacher in the English Department has a special brief for overseeing special education needs. Liaise with that teacher and with the parents and other outside agencies where appropriate.

Staff attitudes are crucial. Try to say to yourself: 'There's a problem. How do we solve it?' This is an objective, not a blame-apportioning approach. Accept that there may be a gap in the curricula provision but that it is not a personal slight against you or the pupil.

Pupil self-esteem is very important. There is a fine line between making inappropriate demands on pupils and patron-izing them by making assumptions about what they might reasonably aspire to. Don't assume because a pupil can't read or write properly that (s)he can't think.

You may find that learning support within the classroom is offered in different ways, which imply different roles for you:

1. Team teaching: support staff and subject staff prepare and present together.
2. General support teaching: responsibility for curriculum rests with subject staff.
3. Specific support teaching: support staff go into subject lessons.
4. Collaborative teaching: support staff work with subject staff on materials.

A support team of counsellors, teachers, parents, Sixth Formers and peer groups can also be built up.

Finally, remember the truism that in a sense *all* children have special needs. You may have an individual in your group who is:

- a reluctant talker
- foreign
- emotionally unstable
- gifted
- physically handicapped
- a victim of assault
- hearing or visually impaired
- a slow learner
- a non-reader, writer, speller
- newcomer
- absentee
- dyslexic

A special need is not a weakness in you or in the pupil but a need to be met.

CONTACTS WITH PARENTS

Meeting parents has been of great help. Talking to them about their children's problems has enabled me to see what is needed in certain areas as well as to direct work to certain children's needs. It also gives an insight into the children's lives away from school and to build upon their interests.

Contacts with parents are important in theory, but in practice you never see the ones you really need to meet: only the proud mummy with successful kids or the dads who want to complain.

These important relationships between two groups of people primarily concerned for the development and well-being of children can be viewed in different ways from both sides. You will find that parents are increasingly being offered a larger part in determining the policy and curriculum of schools, in assessing the success of the schools, and in assisting in the educational process itself. As a young teacher you will probably be most aware of parents in these different contexts, to be discussed in this section: at regular parent–teacher meetings, or on occasions when they complain about your teaching or your treatment of individuals, or when arrangements are made to involve them in the work of the school or in the learning of their own children.

Parent–teacher meetings

Although these can be daunting for all teachers, they can appear particularly threatening if you are young and inexperienced, and uncertain of what to expect. Until you get to know them as individuals, parents can easily seem to fit into a few conventional stereotypes:

1. The expert in unfavourable comparisons: 'She used to enjoy English until this year. . . .'. She always got good marks with Miss X.'
2. The expert in educational organization and principles: 'I fail to see how you can go in for this mixed-ability teaching. It stands to reason, the bright ones will always suffer.'
3. The expert in control of disruptives: 'If you take my advice, you'll make them toe the line. You may discipline my son in any way you see fit.'
4. The expert in buttering-up teachers: 'I just wanted to tell you how much she has enjoyed doing literature with you this year. . . . She's always talking about you.'
5. The expert in blame-shifting: 'I know he's doing badly but . . . it's because he was put in the wrong group . . . the work is so much more difficult this year . . . the staff ought to make him work harder . . .' etc.

You have to remember that parents also find these regular meetings artificial (or frightening in some cases), and that they may exaggerate in order to enlist your support. Some can be easily reassured, but there are a number of issues about which their concern is understandable:

1. The changing pattern of examinations, the new emphasis on course work, questions of assessment or moderation, the value of qualifications.
2. The meaning of marks or grades, their comparative and their positive significance.
3. Homework: whether it is inappropriate, too much or too little.
4. The standard of discipline (usually with comments on the unsatisfactory behaviour of *other* children).

Understanding discussion of these issues can lead to greater cooperation between home and school. It is all too easy to alienate parents by unintended brusqueness or by retreating into the role of the expert who knows best. When you go to a meeting, have the pupils' work with you, marked up-to-date and a detailed mark-book or file for reference. Try to see the positive and avoid negative criticism unless it is justified. Know when to use your professional judgement in being quite firm. Try to enlist parental support in such matters as reading, writing and spelling. Many children suffer from over-protective parents and you must be their guardian. Some, however, have neglectful parents whom you will not see, unless the school has developed a strategy for ensuring this.

Complaints about your English teaching

These may be brought up at a meeting, or raised specifically (by visiting the school, or by letter or telephone). In the latter case it is professionally unwise to deal with these matters yourself. Inform your Head of Department and, where appropriate, the Headmaster. You may need to enlist the support of your union representative if charges of professional incompetence or negligence are laid against you. (Likewise, in cases of alleged assault, you may need legal advice.) However, most complaints are more restricted (and probably trivial from *your* point of view, though not from the parent's). A few of these are common, and you should be aware of the department's policy (to ensure solidarity) before responding to them. Some schools have, in fact, produced standard letters to counter the most common criticisms. There is information in this book to provide at least *some* answers to the following complaints, but reply in terms appropriate to the individual who is complaining:

1. You don't correct all the mistakes in the written work.
2. Why hasn't my son started Shakespeare yet?
3. The book my daughter brought home is full of obscene language and swearing.
4. I object to the way you keep ramming your ideas on sexism (or politics, or hunting, or disarmament, or racial discrimination) into the heads of these children.
5. My daughter and her friends are embarrassed by the way you keep on pointing out these so-called sexual allusions in the literature they are studying.

Enlisting parents' help

Some English departments sensibly pre-empt complaints by writing to parents to explain their policies over setting written work, over marking and over choice of books. There is a strong case for informing parents about syllabuses and course-work requirements so that you enlist their cooperation in planning ahead. This will be especially valuable with GCSE. The one danger is that you may increase the pressure on the pupil at home as well as in school. Letters home should be passed through the Head of Department. There may be standard pro-formas for certain occasions so remember to check:

1. Detentions: notifying parents by giving 24 hours' notice.
2. Theatre trips: simply fill in date(s) and details.
3. Lost books: ask for return or replacement.
4. Withdrawal: explain why children have special needs.
5. Homework: point out children are not giving in work at all or on time.

Increasingly, parents are able to offer support in the classroom. Though help with reading is common in primary and junior schools, it has been relatively rare at secondary level. Areas with a high immigrant population or ethnic minorities have benefited directly and culturally from schemes encouraging active parental involvement. Links between home and school have been fostered by village schools and community colleges. Parents can participate in many ways, most notably as:

1. *Speakers* – they are a rich resource of expertise and knowledge in a variety of jobs, skills and experience.
2. *Listeners* – they will welcome being invited to participate not only in formal occasions but informal ones too, like talks and plays.
3. *Readers* – they can be used as voluntary teachers' aides by reading to groups of children and hearing them read.

What other ways can you think of?

PASTORAL–ACADEMIC TENSIONS

In many schools there is occasional tension between the role of teacher and the role of tutor, between academic and pastoral duties. You may find yourself accountable to both a Head of Department and a Head of Year. You may meet parents in two quite separate roles, as subject teacher or as form tutor. Not only is academic work time-consuming with its preparation, marking and report-writing, but so too is the wider responsibility of registration, assemblies and pupil welfare.

One teacher expressed it vividly:

The theories of Piaget, Bruner, A. S. Neill, Rousseau and Bryant didn't help me with 16+ marking, explaining *Paradise Lost* or even with something as practical as writing on a blackboard.

I was left to guess how to discipline a boy who happened to be reading *Playboy* and I had no idea of how to administer a tutor group or how to counsel a teenager whose parents had split up.

The diversity of responsibilities is something for which neither training institution nor school gives adequate preparation. Indeed, the responsibilities increase year by year as more emphasis is placed on the teacher's wider brief to develop the *whole* child academically, socially and morally.

Within school, what specific duties both as form tutor and members of staff must teachers carry out as well as their subject duties?

Form tutor	*Member of staff*
marking the register	checking attendance
collecting money	collecting books and materials
attending tutor meetings	attending departmental meetings
going to assemblies	going to staff meetings
home contacts	parents' meetings
litter and other duties	break and other duties
liaising with Head of Year	liaising with Head of Department
discipline of individuals within group	discipline of individuals within group
checking pupils' homework	marking pupils' homework
enforcing homework policy	enforcing homework policy
supporting school dress policy	supporting school dress policy
writing tutor reports	writing subject reports
interviewing pupils who are on report	putting pupils on report
assisting with option choices	giving subject-specific careers information
counselling	academic support
intercession with staff	intercession with staff

This by no means exhaustive list shows two things: first, the twin duties of subject teacher and form teacher originally evolved by the independent public school system are entrenched in the notions of 'form' (or 'class') and 'house' (or 'year'); secondly, the duties of a teacher, although parallel and complementary, impose the necessity for making choices and establishing priorities. Sometimes your English work may be affected by what goes on in 'pastoral' sessions. For example, it is not uncommon in school to have a silent reading policy in registration time or to 'teach' active tutorial work that includes a good deal of group talk and improvisation. Conversely, and not unusually, subject teachers may well encounter factors outside the classroom which affect pupil responses to work. In addition, teachers may be involved with pupils in extra-curricular activities. How are such tensions to be resolved? First, by differentiation of role; second, by allocation of time.

Those duties above the dotted line in the table are capable of differentiation. This is because they are performed at different times during the school week and, though not mutually exclusive, involve teachers in one role or the other. Those below the dotted line have considerable areas of overlap and it is to these that a school must address itself and establish its priorities. What do English teachers have to offer here?

1. *Careers/option choices* – English teachers will want to stress particularly the need for clear communication and self-expression in such areas as journalism, the theatre, teaching, librarianship, advertising and the media.
2. *Counselling and support* – it is likely that English teachers have a good knowledge of the pupil by the nature of the subject. Personal writing and self-expression are at the heart of English. Issues are more likely to emerge in class discussion in English than anywhere else.
3. *Discipline* – is perhaps less likely to be a problem for English teachers than others because we put emphasis on creativity and individual choice; we often debate personal values and stress the importance of reasoned argument in communication. Literature should also emphasize a liberal and humane moral code. Methods of grouping and modes of assessment are likely to favour the growth of the individual.

THE WIDER COMMUNITY

English teachers frequently attract more attention – favourable or unfavourable – for what they do in the school beyond their actual teaching. According to our respondents, they may be expected to:

1. Participate in drama productions.
2. Provide reading for assembly.
3. Organize public speaking competitions.
4. Run debating societies.
5. Produce the school magazine.
6. Sponsor creative writing competitions.
7. Run the school libraries.
8. Lay on a school bookshop.
9. Be represented on all staff working parties.
10. 'Sell' literature to parents.
11. Come up with the impossible quotation in *The Times* Educational Crossword!

When it comes to framing school policy, English teachers (who are usually articulate and committed to particular educational principles) can sometimes find themselves in disagreement with colleagues or with senior management. For example, nationally, English teachers seem to have pressed more strongly for mixed-ability groupings than teachers of other subjects. You should perhaps be aware of some of the topics which have been reported as potential causes of conflict:

1. Homework. Some English departments object in principle to setting homework. Others blur distinctions by allowing work to be done in the classroom or at home, at the pupils' choice. There is an increasing tendency to allow written work to be done and revised over a lengthy period. Disputes are possible with those who wish pupils to be tied to a rigid homework timetable with fixed time allowances.

2. Marking of reports. A refusal to give 'meaningless' marks out of ten, or to estimate progress by adding up columns of such marks, can bring about contention. At public examination level there can be disputes about the appropriate criteria for course-work assessment, or the extent to which teachers may legitimately intervene in the writing process. The stock language of school reports often alarms English teachers more than others.

3. The expression of views. Because English lessons are a forum for the expression of ideas, discussions of school policy (about permissible dress or school rules) or of wider issues (sexual behaviour or the politics of education) can lead to accusations that English teachers are 'subversives' stirring up 'radical' views.

4. The administrative burden. Because English teachers have a heavy load of preparation and marking and frequently major responsibilities outside the classroom, they are sometimes impatient with routine administrative work, which can be seen as getting in the way of 'real' work. They say, for example:

I feel impeded by administrative duties.

These outside influences dictate that school work can't be done properly.

Half the paper work is just to keep the machine going.

Especially when demands for reports and reviews coincide with times when teachers are tired and under pressure, this can lead to recriminations and quarrels.

Little helpful advice can be given about such 'conflict areas' except to say:

1. Anticipate that there may be disagreement, and try to understand *why* (some English teachers seem unable to

realize that others may have different opinions from their own).

2. Discover what the past history of the particular debate has been and what line the English Department has taken.
3. If you are going to speak about this, ensure that your views are clearly expressed and supported by evidence.
4. Remember that it is frequently more effective to put your argument in writing, which gives it a more lasting impact.

In times of major social and educational change, you will have to be aware how school policies interlock with those determined nationally or regionally. For example:

1. *National policy:*
   - the general effects of Local Management of Schools, pressures to opt-out, the curriculum, records of achievement
   - the pressures on English exerted by the National Curriculum, standard assessment tasks, changing GCSE criteria, new syllabuses at A-level.

2. *LEA policy* – with such initiatives as Health Education, Personal and Social Development, Active Tutorial Work, Multi-cultural Education, Special Education Needs, Anti-Sexism and others, pressure will mount on all subjects, including English, to accommodate them.

Future developments about which you, as an English teacher, should keep informed include:

1. *Graded testing* – already in use in some language departments – is likely to spread, with such initiatives as Certificates of Educational Attainment into more English departments.
2. *Word processing* – with examination boards debating the acceptability or otherwise of work produced by word processors, with inbuilt spelling corrections, you will need to know how they work and what their potential is.
3. *Pupil profiling* – will be a natural adjunct to the process of continuous assessment at GCSE. Formative evaluation will complement summative evaluation.
4. *Learning logs, pupil diaries* – there is increasing interest in their use as a means of deepening pupil responses, especially to literature; they will surely catch on and be a useful adjunct to first and second drafting.
5. *Developments at A/S and A-level* – in the wake of GCSE are coming initiatives which will change the nature of examining at 18+. The demands of course work on wider reading have implications too.

If 'keeping informed' is not to be a bad joke for busy teachers, then there must be allocated *time* (perhaps one use for those 'Baker days'), and a better channelling of in-service provision (not just for those curricular areas that are the government's flavour of the month). One teacher suggested:

We need more teachers seconded to university and college departments to talk to students, not in lectures and endless seminars but in personal tutorials and private sessions of just what I like to call brain-picking. Incidentally they shouldn't just be high-flying heads of departments but all types and scales of teachers. We also need far more in-service training for those who have recently joined the profession and we also need more propaganda circulated about the teaching of English. By this I mean that it's too easy for scientists and mathematicians to say 'What are you doing in English?' We should have good answers for them in year one of teaching not by year five or six.

INSET is normally organized at three levels:

1. *Out of school*:
    (a) secondment to college or universities
    (b) part-time degree, further degree and other award-bearing courses
    (c) work for examination boards
    (d) subject association activity including working parties
    (e) involvement in projects such as the National Writing and Oracy Projects.
2. *Between schools*:
    (a) moderation meetings of examination boards
    (b) consortium meetings to set up and run new exam courses
    (c) weekend and day conferences drawing on staff expertise locally
    (d) meetings organized for GCSE and other examinations
    (e) subject-specific meetings organized by local teachers.
3. *Within schools*:
    (a) departmental meetings
    (b) year team meetings about development of English
    (c) informal contacts during break times
    (d) marking and assessment procedures, including orals
    (e) discussion of syllabus, choosing of books, shared writing of reports.

A recent study found that English teachers were particularly frustrated by poor provision for curricular development and by the lack of incentive to equip themselves better for their work. They felt that there was a serious mis-match between their views of what they needed and the policies of the "providers" (the DES, local authorities and – in some cases – school management).[8] In recent years, in-service provision for English teachers has been particularly unfavourable. Heads of English in many areas are therefore now coming together to formulate their in-service needs and to explore ways of meeting these. If you do not feel that your in-service needs are being met, then raise the matter forcibly within the Department, with the school's INSET organiser and with your LEA adviser.

REFERENCES

1. For further reading about drama in English, see: Parry Christopher 1972 *English through Drama*. Cambridge; England Alan 1981 *Scripted Drama, A Practical Guide*. Cambridge; Evans Tricia 1984 *Drama in English Teaching*. Croom Helm; Seely John 1976 *In Context*. Oxford; O'Neill Cecily and Lambert Alan 1982 *Drama Structures*. Hutchinson; Burgess R and Gaudry P 1986 *Time for Drama*. Open University Press
2. Dixon John 1979 *Education 16–19*. Macmillan, p 19
3. Masterman Len 1985 *Teaching the Media*. Comedia
4. Murdoch G and Phelps G 1966 *Mass Media in the Secondary School*. Cambridge
5. Also see: Knight Roy 1973 *Film in English Teaching*. Hutchinson; Masterman Len 1980 *Teaching about Television*. Macmillan; and other books suggested in the excellent annotated bibliography to Masterman's *Teaching the Media* (see above). Useful materials for class use are produced by the English Centre (e.g. *Choosing the News*), the British Film Institute (e.g. *Selling Pictures*), the Clwyd Media Studies Unit (e.g. *The Press, Coronation Street*), by Bethell A 1981 *Eye Openers*. Cambridge; and Jones K 1985 *Graded Simulations*. Blackwell
6. Torbe Mike 1976 *Language Across the Curriculum*. Ward Lock. Also see Marland Michael 1977 *Language Across the Curriculum*. Heinemann.
7. Hinson Mike and Kelly Thomas A 1986 'Specific learning difficulties: one LEA's approach in practice', *Support for Learning*, vol 1 no 2, Longman. Also see Wade B and Moore M 1987 *Special Children — Special Needs*. Robert Royce; and Walsh Bernadette 1989 *Shut Up!* Cassell
8. Protherough Robert and Atkinson Judith 1991 *The Making of English Teachers*, chapter 9. Open University Press

INDEX